THE
SHIFTING
POINT

by Peter Brook

THE
SHIFTING
POINT
. . .
1946–1987

A CORNELIA & MICHAEL BESSIE BOOK

HARPER & ROW, PUBLISHERS, New York
Cambridge, Philadelphia, San Francisco, Washington
London, Mexico City, São Paulo, Singapore, Sydney

MR

The author wishes to thank Nina Soufy, Georges Banu and Marie-Hélène Estienne for their help in assembling the material in this book.

Copyright acknowledgments and photo credits follow the index.

FIRST EDITION

Copy editor: Ann Adelman
Designer: Kathleen Westray
Indexer: Brian Hotchkiss

Library of Congress Cataloging-in-Publication Data
Brook, Peter.   The shifting point.
"A Cornelia & Michael Bessie book."
1. Brook, Peter.   2. Theater—Production and direction.
3. Moving-pictures—Production and direction.   I. Title.
PN2598.B69A3   1987   792′.0233′0924   87-45026
ISBN 0-06-039073-5

87 88 89 90 91 MPC 10 9 8 7 6 5 4 3 2 1

8-32-89

FOR MICHELINE ROZAN
who is the vibrant point
from which so much in this book
found its life

contents

illustrations

preface

I have never believed in a single truth. Neither my own, nor those of others. I believe all schools, all theories can be useful in some place, at some time. But I have discovered that one can only live by a passionate, and absolute, identification with a point of view.

However, as time goes by, as we change, as the world changes, targets alter and the viewpoint shifts. Looking back over many years of essays written, ideas spoken in many places on so many varied occasions, one thing strikes me as being consistent. For a point of view to be of any use at all, one must commit oneself totally to it, one must defend it to the very death. Yet, at the same time, there is an inner voice that murmurs: "Don't take it too seriously. Hold on tightly, let go lightly."

THE
SHIFTING
POINT

part I

A SENSE
OF DIRECTION
. . .

THE FORMLESS HUNCH

. . .

When I begin to work on a play, I start with a deep, formless hunch which is like a smell, a color, a shadow. That's the basis of my job, my role—that's my preparation for rehearsals with any play I do. There's a formless hunch that is my relationship with the play. It's my conviction that this play must be done today, and without that conviction I can't do it. I have no technique. If I had to go in for a competition where I'd be given a scene and told to stage it, I'd have nowhere to start. I could produce a sort of synthetic technique and a few ideas built from my experience of doing plays, but it wouldn't be much good. I have no structure for doing a play, because I work from that amorphous non-formed feeling, and from that I start preparing.

Now, preparing means going toward that idea. I start making a set, destroying it, making it, destroying it, working it out. What kind of costumes? What kind of colors? All of those are a language for making that hunch a little more concrete. Until gradually, out of this comes the form, a form that must be modified and put to the test, but nevertheless it's a form that's emerging. Not a closed form, because it's only the set, and I say "only the set" because the set is only the basis, the platform. Then work starts with the actors.

The rehearsal work should create a climate in which the actors feel free to produce everything they can bring to the play. That's why in the early stages of rehearsal everything is open and I impose nothing at all. In a sense this is diametrically opposed to the technique in which, the first day, the director gives a speech on what the play's about and the way he's going to approach it. I used to do that years ago and I eventually found out that that's a rotten way of starting.

So, now we start with exercises, with a party, with anything, but not ideas. In some plays, for instance with the *Marat/Sade,* for three quarters of the rehearsal period I encouraged the actors, and encouraged myself—it's a two-way thing—to produce excess. Simply because it was a very dynamic subject. There was such an outrageously baroque excess of ideas that, if you'd seen us three quarters of the way into the rehearsal period, you'd have thought the play was being submerged and destroyed by a surplus of what's called directorial invention. I encouraged other people to produce everything, good and bad. I censored nothing and no one, not even myself. I'd say, "Why don't you do this?" and there'd be gags, there'd be silly things. It didn't matter. All of it was for the purpose of having, out of that, such a lot of material that then, gradually, things could be shaped. To what criteria? Well, shaped to their relation to this formless hunch.

The formless hunch begins to take form by meeting that mass of material and emerging as the dominant factor from which some notions fall away. The director is continually provoking the actor, stimulating him, asking questions and creating an atmosphere in which the actor can dig, probe and investigate And, in doing that, he turns over, both singly and together with the others, the whole fabric of the play. As he does so, you see forms emerging that you begin to recognize, and in the last stages of rehearsal, the actor's work takes on a dark area which is the subterranean life of the play, and illuminates it; and as the subterranean area of the play is illuminated by the actor, the director is placed in a position to see the difference between the actor's ideas and the play itself.

In these last stages, the director cuts away all that's extraneous, all that belongs just to the actor and not to the actor's intuitive connection with the play. The director, because of his prior work, and because it is his role, and also because of his hunch, is in a better position to say then what belongs to the play and what belongs to that superstructure of rubbish that everybody brings with him.

The final stages of rehearsal are very important, because at that moment you push and encourage the actor to discard all that is superfluous, to edit and tighten. And you do it ruthlessly, even with yourself, because for every invention of the actor, there's something of your own. You've suggested, you've invented a bit of business, something to illustrate something. Those go, and what remains is an organic form. Because the form is not ideas imposed on a play, it is the play illuminated, and the play illuminated is the form. Therefore, when the results seem organic and unified, it's not because a unified conception has been found and has been put on the play from the outset, not at all.

When I did *Titus Andronicus,* there was a lot of praise for this production being better than the play. People said that here was a production that made something of this ridiculous and impossible play. That's very flattering, but it wasn't true, because I knew perfectly well that I couldn't have done that production with another play. That's where people so often misunderstand what the work of directing is. They think, in a way, that it's like being an interior decorator who can make something of any room, given enough money and enough things to put into it. It's not so. In *Titus Andronicus,* the whole work was to take the hints and the hidden strands of the play and wring the most from them, take what was embryonic perhaps, and bring it out. But if it isn't there to begin with it can't be done. You can give me a police thriller and say, "Do it like *Titus Andronicus,*" and of course I can't, because what's not there, what isn't latent, can't be found.

STEREOSCOPIC VISION

• • •

A director can treat a play like a film and use all the elements of theatre, actors, designers, musicians, etc., as his servants, to communicate to the rest of the world what he has to say. In France and Germany, this approach is much admired, and it is called his "reading" of the play. I have come to realize that this is a sad and clumsy use of directing: it is more honorable if one wants to dominate totally one's means of expression to use a pen as a servant, or a brush. The unsatisfactory alternative to this is the director who makes himself the servant, becoming the coordinator of a group of actors, limiting himself to suggestions, criticisms and encouragement. Such directors are good men, but like all well-meaning and tolerant liberals, their work can never go beyond a certain point.

I think one must split the word "direct" down the middle. Half of directing is, of course, being a director, which means taking charge, making decisions, saying "yes" and saying "no," having the final say. The other half of directing is maintaining the right direction. Here, the director becomes guide, he's at the helm, he has to have studied the maps and he has to know whether he's heading north or south. He searches all the time, but not haphazardly. He doesn't search for the sake of searching, but for a purpose; a man looking for gold may ask a thousand questions, but they all lead back to gold; a doctor looking for a vaccine may make endless and varied experiments, but always toward curing one disease and not another. If this sense of direction is there, everyone can play the part as fully and creatively as he is able. The director can listen to the others, yield to their suggestions, learn from them, radically modify and transform his own ideas, he can constantly change course, he can unexpectedly veer one way and another, yet the collective energies still serve a single aim. This enables the director to say "yes" and "no" and the others willingly to assent.

Where does this "sense of direction" come from and how in fact does it differ from an imposed "directorial conception"? A "directorial conception" is an image which precedes the first day's work, while a "sense of direction" crystallizes into an image at the very end of the process. The director needs only one conception—which he must find in life, not in art—which comes from asking himself what an act of theatre is doing in the world, why it is there. Obviously, this cannot stem from an intellectual blueprint; too much committed theatre has sunk in the whirlpool of theory. The director may have to spend his life searching for the answer, his work feeding his life, his life feeding his work. But the fact is that acting is an act, that this act has action, that the place of this action is the performance, that the performance is in the world, and that everyone present is under the influence of what is performed.

The question is not so much "What's the event about?" It is always about something and this is what pinpoints the director's responsibility. This leads him to choose one sort of material rather than another —not just for what it is, but because of its potential. It's the sense of the potential that then guides him to finding the space, the actors, the forms of expression, a potential that is there and yet unknown, latent, only capable of being discovered, rediscovered and deepened by the active work of the team. Within this team, everyone has only one tool, his own subjectivity. Director or actor alike, however much he opens himself, he can't jump out of his skin. What he can do, however, is to recognize that theatre work demands of actor and of director that he face several directions at the same time.

One must be faithful to oneself, almost believing in what one does, yet faithful to the knowledge that the truth is always somewhere else. Because of this, one values the possibility of being with oneself and beyond oneself, and one sees how this in-and-out movement grows through interchange with others and is the basis of the stereoscopic vision of life that the theatre can bring.

THERE IS ONLY ONE STAGE
• • •

A great misunderstanding exists in theatre nowadays—this is the tendency to think that the theatrical process falls into two stages, as in other fields. First stage: making. Second stage: selling. For centuries, except in certain forms of popular theatre and some particular forms of traditional theatre, this has been the process. The period of rehearsing is used to prepare the object and in due course the object is put on sale. Just as a potter molds his pot, the author writes his book, the director makes his film and then sends it out into the world. This misunderstanding relates to the playwright's work as much as to the designer's and the director's. Although most actors understand instinctively that preparation is not construction, yet, even in the title of Stanislavsky's great work *Building a Character,* this misunderstanding persists, implying that a character can be built up like a wall, until one day the last brick is laid and the character is complete. To my mind, it is just the opposite. I would say that the process consists not of two *stages* but of two *phases.* First: preparation. Second: birth. This is very different.

If we think along these lines, many things change. The work of preparation may last only five minutes, as it does in an improvisation; or it may last for several years, as in other forms of theatre. It is not important. Preparation involves a conscious, rigorous study of any obstacles and the manner in which to avoid or surmount them. The paths must be swept, quickly or slowly depending on their state. I would like to replace the image of a potter here by that of a rocket leaving for the moon: months and months are spent on the great task of preparing for takeoff, and then, one fine day ... POW! The preparation is checking, testing, cleaning; flying is of a quite different nature. In the same way, preparing a character is the opposite of building—it is demolishing, removing brick by brick everything in the actor's muscles, ideas and inhibitions that stands between him and the part, until one day with a great rush of air the character invades his every pore.

This process is well understood in sport, where no one would mistake training before a race with planning the course of the race; and to my mind sport gives the most precise images and best metaphors for a theatrical performance. On the one hand in a race, or in a football match, there is no freedom at all. There are rules, the game is calculated on the most rigorous lines, just as in theatre, where each performer learns his role and respects it down to the last word. But this all-guiding scenario does not prevent him from improvising when the event occurs. When the race starts, the runner calls up all the means at his disposal. As soon as a performance begins, the actor steps into the structure of the mise-en-scène: he too becomes completely involved, he improvises within the established guidelines and, like the runner, he enters the unpredictable. In this way, everything stays open, and for the audience the event occurs at this precise moment: neither before nor after. Seen from heaven, every football match looks the same; but no match could ever be repeated, detail by detail.

So the strict preparation does not rule out the unexpected unfolding of the living texture which is the match itself. Without the preparation the event would be weak, messy, meaningless. However, the preparation is not to establish form. The exact shape comes with being at the hottest moment, when the act itself takes place. Once we accept this, we see that all our thinking must work outwards from this one moment, which is the only moment of creation. If we then proceed logically, all our methods and conclusions are turned on their head.

MISUNDERSTANDINGS
• • •

I first began working in the theatre not with any particular love for it. It seemed to me a dreary and dying predecessor of the cinema. One day I went to see a man who was a big producer in those days. I had directed an amateur film, *A Sentimental Journey,* in Oxford. I said to this man: "I want to direct films." It was unthinkable at that time for a young man of twenty to direct a film. But the request sounded reasonable enough to me. It must have seemed quite ridiculous to the pro-

Peter Brook at nineteen, filming *A Sentimental Journey*

ducer, and he replied: "You can come and work here if you like. I'll give you a job as an assistant. If you take it you can learn the trade, and at the end of seven years I promise to give you your own film to direct." That meant I would become a director at twenty-seven years old. I think he spoke generously and in earnest, but to me so long a wait was inconceivable.

It was because no one would give me a film to direct that I turned with appalling condescension to the task of producing a play in the only tiny theatre that would have me. In the weeks before the first rehearsal, I carefully prepared my script as for a movie. The play began with a dialogue between two soldiers: I decided that one of them should be discovered tying his boots and that the fifth line would be enhanced if in the middle of it the shoelace snapped.

The first morning, I wasn't at all sure how a professional rehearsal starts, but the actors clearly indicated that we should sit down and begin with a reading. I at once told the actor playing the first soldier to take off his shoes and put them on again as he read. Somewhat surprised, he complied, leaning forward, his script awkwardly balanced on his knee. In the middle of the fifth line, I told him the lace should now come apart. He nodded and went on reading. "No," I stopped him. "Do it." "What? Now?" He was amazed, but I was amazed at his amazement. "Of course. Now."

"But this is a first reading . . ." All my latent fears of not being obeyed came to the surface, this smelled of sabotage, of authority disputed. I insisted, he angrily complied. At lunchtime, the lady who ran the theatre gently took me aside. "That's not the way to work with the actors . . ."

It was a revelation. I had imagined that actors, as in a film, were hired to do at once what the director wanted. After my first reaction of injured pride had subsided, I began to see that the theatre was a quite different affair.

I remember a trip to Dublin at about this time, where I had heard of an Irish philosopher who was very fashionable in university circles. I had not read the book he had written, and I hadn't even met the man, but I remember a phrase of his, quoted by someone in a bar, which struck me at once: it was the theory of the "shifting viewpoint." It didn't mean a fickle point of view, but the exploration as made in certain types of X-rays, where changing perspectives give an illusion of density. I still remember today the impression it made on me.

At first, the theatre was neither a this nor a that. It was experience. I found it interesting, touching, exciting, all from a purely sensory point of view. I was like someone who begins to play a musical instrument because he is fascinated by the world of sounds, or who begins painting because he likes the feel of brushes and paint. With the cinema, it was the same thing: I liked the reels of film, the camera, the different types of lens. I enjoyed them as objects and I believe many other people must be attracted to film for the same reason. In theatre, I wanted to create a world of sounds and images; I was interested in relationships with actors in a direct, almost sexual way, a joy that came from the energy of rehearsal, the activity itself. I did not try to judge or restrain this attraction. I was quite simply convinced that I had to plunge into the stream, it was not ideas but movement that could lead to discoveries. This was why I found it quite impossible to take any theoretical pretensions to heart.

During those first years, I worked a good deal but I travelled a lot as well, probably as much. For the first five or ten years, I considered my theatrical activity to be the lesser part of life. If I had any principle at all, it was to develop a certain understanding, based on the idea of rotation: the idea of alternating one field of activity with another. When I had worked for a while in a "cultural" environment, in opera or the classics (Shakespeare, etc.), I switched to boulevard farce, low comedy, a musical, television, a film—or else a journey. Each time I returned again to one of these fields, I found that unconsciously I had learned something new. Still it was no accident that the theatre and the cinema both excited me, for the same reasons, but I was not yet overly concerned with actors. I was most interested in creating images, in creating a world. The stage really was a world apart from the world surrounding it, one of illusion into which the audience entered.

So naturally at that time my work was very much concerned with the visual aspects in the theatre; I liked to play with models and make sets. I was fascinated by lighting and sound, colors and costumes. When I directed Shakespeare's *Measure for Measure* in 1956, I thought the director's job was to create an image which would allow the audience to enter into the play, and so I reconstructed the worlds of Bosch and Brueghel, just as I had followed Watteau in directing *Love's Labor's Lost* in 1950. It seemed to me then that I should try to produce a striking set of fluid pictures to serve as a bridge, between the play and the audience.

When I studied the text of *Love's Labor's Lost,* I was struck by something that seemed to me to be self-evident, but which at the time seemed to be unheard of: that when, at the very end of the last scene, a new, unexpected character called Mercade came on, the whole play changed its tone entirely. He came into an artificial world to announce a piece of news that was real. He came on bringing death. And as I felt intuitively that the image of the Watteau world was very close to this, I began to see that the reason that the Watteau *Age of Gold* is so particularly moving is that although it's a picture of springtime, it's an autumn springtime, because every one of Watteau's pictures has an incredible melancholy. And if one looks, one sees that there is somewhere in it the presence of death, until one even sees that in Watteau (unlike the imitations of the period, where it's all sweetness and prettiness) there is usually a dark figure somewhere, standing with his back to you, and some people say that he is Watteau himself. But there's no doubt that the dark touch gives the dimension to the whole piece.

And it was through this that I brought Mercade over a rise at the back of the stage—it was evening, the lights were going down, and suddenly there appeared a man in black. The man in black came onto a very pretty summery stage, with everybody in pale pastel Watteau and Lancret costumes, and golden lights dying. It was very disturbing, and at once the whole audience felt that the world had been transformed.

I think for me everything shifted around the time of *King Lear*. Just before rehearsals were due to begin, I destroyed the set. I had designed one in rusty iron which was very interesting and very complicated, with bridges that came up and down. I was very fond of it. One night, I realized that this wonderful toy was absolutely useless. I took almost all of it out of the model and what remained looked much better. This was a very important moment for me, especially since I was often asked to work with amphitheatres at this time and I could never understand how I could function without a proscenium and an imaginary world.

Suddenly, something clicked. I began to see why theatre was an event. Why it did not depend on an image or a particular context—the event, for instance, was the fact of an actor simply crossing the stage. All the work we did during our first experimental season at the LAMDA Theatre in 1965 was the result; and perhaps the most significant exercise we performed in public was having someone just do nothing, nothing at all.

It was a new and important experiment for the period: A man sits on stage with his back to the audience, and for four or five minutes he does nothing. Every evening we would try out various experiments in actor's concentration to see whether this situation could be heightened, whether a way existed to make a seeming nothingness more intense. We watched carefully the point at which the audience grew bored and began to complain. Bob Wilson's theatrical experiments in the seventies showed how very slow, almost nonexistent movement, how lack of motion that is inhabited in a particular way, can become irresistibly interesting, without the spectator understanding why.

From that moment on—for the experiment had gone to an extreme point—I became increasingly interested in whatever is a direct element in performance. When you set off on that path, everything

Peter Brook in the middle of controversy created by *Romeo and Juliet*

THE TATLER
AND BYSTANDER
JULY 23, 1947
103

Juliet a lost child, not a glamour girl, says actress

he Stratford
estival

meo and Juliet

..TFORD, NOT alas in flower but palpitating
the mud, reopened last Saturday. Excite-
ran almost as high as the Avon and we
had swans as well as geese in the foyer. We
d assurance that Sir Barry Jackson's hus-
of last season was bearing seed and it
likely we should get it. Peter Brook,
production of *Love's Labour's Lost* exercised
g a spell last year, was mounting *Romeo*
with fresh notions and a youthful cast.
…y, excitement ebbed a little before
…–Jol… The villain of the …
who stoo… …a good …
…little scene …–why?…
up as a darkie—why?… …couching
ing in the evening. But despite all …
…il, it is an oddly remote and …ring people
Romeo. However, one well sees why people
nowadays find it worth while fighting their way to
Stratford, and I want to emphasize that if this
kind of performance were to be given in Prague or
Moscow, we should never hear the last of it.

—PHILIP HOPE-WALLACE

The touch
of genius

THIS did not deter Mr.
Guinness, nor did it
terrify young Peter
Brook, who, at 21 years of age,
has become a significant figure in
the theatre.

Two years ago I saw his production of Cocteau's 'The
Infernal Machine' at the Chanticleer, and ventured the opinion
that here was a boy with a touch
of genius. Since then he has
won laurels at Stratford-on-
Avon, and now adds to their

The Brothe
live agai

in the glory with this remarkable presentation of 'The Brothers
Karamazov.'

At the Play

"LOVE'S LABOUR'S LOST"
(STRATFORD)

THE originality of Mr. PETER
BROOK's production is immediately
evident in a brief dumbshow prologue
showing the tearful women of Navarre
confronted by their royal master's
ungallant proclamation, and it is sustained with a boldness and judgment
made more remarkable by the fact
that he is not yet twenty-one. The
brittle charm of this most
artificial of courts, its airy
…of mock chivalry
…rody of

Stratford Festival's
Production

There are five plays yet to come at Stratford Festival
but it is safe to say on last night's showing that "Love's
Labour's Lost" will be one of the outstanding …
the season. It is a truly …

A
Young
…
fancy

PLAY—"Romeo and Juliet."
Memorial Theatre, Stratford-on-
Avon.

Nineteen-year-old Daphne Slater's
…conception of Juliet will infuriate
…eryone over 35 who has seen the
…reat—and much older—actresse
…as the part.
Miss Slater gave a livelier, mor…
…actical interpretation. Sh… …e
…the languid speaker of the …
…ds, but much more a passio…
…who knew not what …
…ted.
…at was the stress point…
…uction. In every scene …
…sacrificed to acting …
…a fast, sometime…
…tion by a young …
…elders in the audie…
But they also …
Slater, though …
…ideal Juliet, w…
In th… …comely …
esque …Laurence Pay…
comedy …Romeo.—L. M…
Shakes… …in the fes…'s cap and
for Mr. Peter Brook…
yet come of age. His…
as a masque of yout…
remarkably complic…
elusive values, and …
sistent with itself. …
on the stage a pub…
shifting chiaroscu…
experness, and of …
fading out a scen…
significance.
Mr. Brook has ai…
youthful company to …
of the humour, …
verbal antics of …
the backg…

STRATFORD-ON-AVON, Monday.

CRITICISM aroused by the new approach to "Romeo and
Juliet," with youth at the helm, was welcomed here today by the entire Festival company. Mr. Peter Brook, the
21-year-old producer, and the players read notices, letters
and telegrams, and in dressing-room discussions justified
their innovations.

Mr. Brook has been … …ocited, violently breaking
with tradition a… …Daphne Slater, playing

Date … April 15, 194…

…TFORD FESTIVAL

…E'S LABOUR'S
…OST".

…DON-ON-AVON,
…Monday Night
…ere to part …
…resent at …
…if that …
…ook's …
…have …
…oduca…
…oakes…
…fantasy
…tumes,
…s of the
…kespeare
…approved
…craftsman.

…ry of the allusions
…fashions long since …
…the Arcadian simplicity of
…king of Navarre's court has
…ven a golden age? The wit-
…den phrases," and the light
…in the Elizabethan
…ring with the note
…sweet and musical
…llo's lute, strung
…'s production sets
…ing in faithful echo,
…ting setting, the opulent
…dramatic lighting, and
…f that from time to time
…characters in a frieze of
…these things conspire to …
…is the war is unprovided for,
…lare, of necessity, been
…in the cast. Laurence Payne
…medy to flavour a wooing
…gotogrous fight to escape
…s yet he deals feelingly with
…etry, and Donald Stephenson, John
…e academic retreat from
…Paul Scofield repeats his
…ketch of Armado, the fan-
…Spaniard, whose creaky
…eters good humouredly on
…rsons; and John Ruddock
…leasantly as Boyet, Leigh
…and John Blatchley, as
…and Holofernes respec-
…ake fritters of rhetoric, and
…Jones puts up a pert clown
…Veronica Turleigh, as
…cess is a little on the light
…t makes her levity pleasing,
…Lloyd is fluent as Moth and
…points with an assurance
…highly commendable in so
…an actor.   T.C.K.

Miss Daphne Slater, 18-year-old Juliet, with Mr. Peter B…
21-year-old producer. "I believe we have put on the stag…
play Shakespeare wrote," said Mr. Brook yesterday…

Sweet
Juliet
By HUBERT
GRIFFITH

For the opening of t…
year's Stratford sea…
season had engage…
Jackson had engaged …
young Romeo (Laur…
Payne), Romeo (Laur…
(Paul Scofield), a …
Count Paris (Donald …
den), a young …
(Peter Brook, aged 2…
young Juliet (Daph…
Slater, aged 18)…
18)…

…hing the underwor…

…ness of the thing is genera…
…enery achieves some lov…
…little bits of isolated reali…
…light, as it might be in a …
…yet here too was some fr…
…which went counter to th…
…te play: the tomb, for example…
…of bomb-damage, gives none
…gestion. There was some bad
…d with some ill-advised cuts clar…
…r suffered a little. And then, one
…r, hallowed lines seemed constantly
…spoken out into the wings, or he…
…s, as if the producer set more store b…
…agined picture of what it ought to look…
…y the sound of the play, which is of
…only reality. Yet often it is a wonderful
…llet of a Verona we see—the brawls are
…t and what with the general lack of
…e on our stage today, that is no small
…e were vivid and memorable sc…
…hot Italian sky. Yet som…
…seemed to ove…
…much; the …
…t…

£250 film is Surprise
for Wardour-st.
By Mary Hunt

…he …NE tiny Chanticleer
…which is now embe…
…season … to Ibsen.
…sented Jean Cocteau
…Chicken, based on the
…fter theme, and …
…seemed unfit for t…
…ublic. I believe that …
…d Peter Brook w…
…ducer who may …
…something first rate.

I WATCHED a film this week
at the Torch Theatre pro-
duced by England's tiniest film
Arms (President of the Oxford
University Film Society), is 18
the rest of the cast are all …

…k, spoiled a …
…fixedly (I doubt if
…much); a strong, dark voice
…ran to monotony and
…ing, the ecstasy on one hand
…the other. In another
…n more than an appealing
…oung and has a genuine

He is a young man
having been a profe…
writer at 14, …
Faustus at Oxford …
graduate and direct…
writing and direct…
Sterne's 'A Sentim…
the O.U.F.S. …
t production …

else falls away. I now realize that I haven't touched a spotlight for at least ten years, whereas before I was forever climbing up and down ladders to adjust them, etc. These days I simply say to the lighting technician: "Very bright!" I want everything to be seen, everything to stand out clearly, without the slightest shadow. The same idea has often led us to use a simple carpet as our stage and set. I have not come to this conclusion through puritanism, nor do I want to condemn elaborate costumes or ban colored lights. Only I've found that the true interest lies elsewhere, in the event itself as it happens at each moment, inseparable from the public's response.

I TRY TO ANSWER A LETTER . . .
. . .

Dear Mr. Howe,

Your letter comes out of the blue and puts me on the spot.

You ask how to become a director.

Directors in the theatre are self-appointed. An unemployed director is a contradiction in terms, like an unemployed painter—unlike an unemployed actor, who is a victim of circumstances. You become a director by calling yourself a director and you then persuade other people that this is true. So, in a way getting work is a problem that has to be solved with the same skills and resources that you need in rehearsal. I don't know any other way apart from convincing people to work with you and getting some work under way—even unpaid—and presenting it to any public—in a cellar, in the back room of a pub, in a hospital ward, in a prison. The energy produced by working is more important than anything else.

So don't let anything stop you from being active, even in the most primitive conditions, rather than wasting time looking for something in better conditions that might not come off. In the end, work attracts work.

Yours sincerely,

A WORLD IN RELIEF

• • •

We talk of "directing." The notion is vague and includes too much. For example, although film making is a collective activity, the director's authority is absolute and the other partners are not on an equal footing. They are merely instruments through which the director's vision can take form. Most people questioned on the subject would reply that things are the same in the theatre. The director assimilates the world, including the playwright's, and produces it afresh.

Unfortunately that idea ignores the true riches that are latent in the theatre form. According to the accepted idea, the director is there to take the various means at his disposal—lighting, colors, set, costumes, makeup, as well as the text and performance—and play on them all together as if on a keyboard. By combining these forms of expression he creates a special director's language in which the actor is only a noun, an important noun, but dependent on all the other grammatical elements to give it meaning. This is the conception of "total theatre," taken to mean theatre in its most evolved condition.

But, in fact, theatre has the potential—unknown in other art forms—of replacing a single viewpoint by a multitude of different visions. Theatre can present a world in several dimensions at once, whereas the cinema, although it tirelessly seeks to be stereoscopic, is still confined to a single plane. Theatre recovers its strength and intensity as soon as it devotes itself to creating that wonder—a world in relief.

In theatre there occurs a phenomenon akin to holography (the photographic process that gives relief to objects by the interplay of laser beams). If we receive the convincing impression that a moment of life has been fully and completely caught on stage, it is because various forces emanating from the audience and the actor have converged on a given point at the same time.

When a group of people meet for the first time, one is struck initially by the barriers created by their various viewpoints. If we welcome this difference in a positive way, we allow contradictory views to sharpen themselves, one against the other.

The basic element of a play is dialogue. It implies a tension and presumes that two people are not in agreement. This means conflict; whether it is subtle or overt is not important. When two points of view clash, the playwright is obliged to give each one an equal share of credibility. If he is unable to do so, the result will be weak. He must explore two contradictory opinions with the same degree of understanding. If the playwright is blessed with infinite generosity, if he is not obsessed with his own ideas, he will give the impression that he is in total empathy with everyone. Chekhov, for example.

Beyond that, if there are twenty characters and the playwright manages to invest each one with the same power of conviction, we come to the miracle of Shakespeare. A computer would have difficulty in programming all the points of view his plays contain.

Faced with such an abundant scale of values, with such dense material, we can better understand the task facing the director. We can appreciate that one who is content to express a single point of view, strong though it be, impoverishes the whole.

On the contrary, the director should encourage the apparition of all the cross-currents that underlie the text. Actors are easily tempted to impose their own fantasies, their personal theories or obsessions, and the director must know what to encourage and what to oppose. He must help the actor both to be himself and to go beyond himself so that an understanding can emerge which exceeds each person's limited notion of reality.

There is a golden rule. The actor must never forget that the play is greater than himself. If he thinks he can grasp the play, he will cut it down to his own size. If, however, he respects its mystery—and consequently that of the character he is playing—as being always just beyond his grasp, he will recognize that his "feelings" are a very treacherous guide. He will see that a sympathetic but rigorous director can help him to distinguish between intuitions that lead to truth and feelings that are self-indulgent. More important for actors than Hamlet's famous Advice to the Players is the scene when he furiously denounces the notion that a man's mystery can be sounded by putting "fingers on his stops," as though he were a wind instrument.

There is a very strange relation between what is in the words of a text and what lies between the words. Any idiot can declaim the written words. However, to reveal what happens between one word and the next is so subtle that in most cases it is hard to discover with certainty what comes from the actor and what comes from the author. In the nineteenth century, great acting very often sprang from mediocre writing; there are page-long descriptions of the rich series of conflicting emotions that Sarah Bernhardt was able to convey in the moment between seeing her lover enter her sickroom and her cry, "Armand!"

This filling-in by highly charged facial expressions and gestures of human detail seems to have been the characteristic of nineteenth-century playing, and the thinner the text the better the opportunity for the artist to give it flesh and blood. I remember working with Paul Scofield on an adaptation that Denis Cannan had made of Graham Greene's *The Power and the Glory*. At the beginning of rehearsal there was a short, vital scene that was underwritten. Paul and I were very dissatisfied, for it was sketchy, like a first draft. However, it took several weeks for the author to get round to rewriting it.

When eventually Scofield was presented with a vastly improved version, he turned it down. I was very surprised, because Scofield is in no way capricious. Then I understood his actor's logic. During the period in which we had rehearsed the first version he had discovered many secret impulses that enabled him to complement the inadequacies of the text with a rich inner life. This structure was now so intertwined with the words and the rhythms that he could not cut it out and stick it into the new pattern. In fact, the new text in saying more expressed less. So he stayed with the old scene, and in performance it was remarkably powerful. Often, when an actor or a director finds a striking way of playing a scene, it is impossible to tell whether the vital ingredient comes from his creativity or whether it was there all the time, waiting to be discovered.

Sets, costumes, lighting, and so on find their place naturally as soon as something real has come into existence in rehearsal. Only then can we tell what music, form and color need to enhance. If these elements are conceived too soon, if composer and designer have crystallized their ideas before the first rehearsal, then these forms impose themselves heavily on the actors and can easily smother their ever-so-fragile intuitions, as they feel for deeper patterns.

A few weeks into rehearsal, the director is no longer the same person. He has been enriched and broadened by his work with other people. In fact, whatever understanding he had reached before rehearsals began, he has now been helped to see the text in a new way. So the essential step of fixing the shape of the play should take place as late as possible—in fact, not until the first performance. Every director has experienced this: during the last rehearsal the show seems coherent, but in the presence of an audience the coherence explodes. Or, inversely, during its first public performance a good piece of work may find its coherence. But once the play has passed its test of fire in front of an audience, it will nonetheless be in danger—for a performance has to find its shape each time anew.

The process is circular. In the beginning, we have a reality without form. At the end, when the circle is completed, this same reality may suddenly reappear—grasped, channelled and digested—within the circle of participants who are in communion, summarily divided into actors and spectators. Only at that moment will reality become a living, concrete thing, and the true meaning of the play emerge.

part II

PEOPLE ON
THE WAY
—A FLASHBACK
. . .

• • •

I believe we are here to receive influences. We are constantly being influenced and in turn we influence other people. That is why, in my opinion, there can be nothing worse than giving oneself a trademark, acquiring a particular signature, getting known for certain characteristics. A painter comes to be recognized for his particular style, and it becomes his prison. He cannot assimilate anyone else's work without losing face. This does not make sense in the theatre. We work in a field that must be one of free exchange.

GORDON CRAIG
A Meeting in 1956
• • •

"*K...K...K...Katie* ... in the c...c...c... cowshed... " he will be singing. Then he will pause, think for a moment. "Cracky!" he will say. "It's all cracky!" With this, his favorite word, he will express both his perpetual surprise at the oddities of the world and his enjoyment of them.

He is a mischievous figure of eighty-four, with a child's skin, flowing white hair, the head slightly cocked to one side in the way of the very deaf, and a courtly stock round his neck. He has a cramped bedroom in a tiny *pension de famille* in the South of France. Here it is barely possible to move: close to the bed is a table, screwed to its side a rack for the rubber bands of every size that he hoards like a squirrel; below them, a row of engraver's tools; on the table, a magnifying glass, an odd Victorian farce—*Two in the Morning,* or *My Awful Dad*—a spoon and a sack of tonic mustard seeds. On the ground piles of books and magazines; in the cupboard, neat paper packets of letters labelled "to Duse," "to Stanislavsky," "to Isadora Duncan"; on the walls, from the bedhead, from the mirror, from every screw or nail, wads of newspaper cuttings covered with trenchant remarks in bold red pencil: "Nonsense!" "Fiddlesticks!" and, just occasionally, "At last!"

Gordon Craig is two men. One is the actor—you can see this in his broad-rimmed hats and in his Arab burnous which he flings around him like a cloak. He is deeply rooted in the theatre—his mother was Ellen Terry, his cousin is John Gielgud—as a young man he played with Henry Irving. This is an experience he has never forgotten. His eyes light up, he springs to his feet with excitement and describes in vivid pantomime how Irving tied up his boots in *The Bells* or how Irving kicked his legs in the air as he watched his enemy taken to the guillotine in *The Lyons Mail.*

In complete contradiction to this is the other Gordon Craig, the man who wrote that actors should be abolished and marionettes put in their place, the man who said there should be no more scenery, only folding screens. Craig loved Irving's theatre—its painted forests, its thunder sheets, its naive melodrama—but at the same time he dreamed of another theatre where all the elements would be harmonious and whose art would be a religion. This notion of art for art's sake has vanished from the world: today, a good artist is so often a successful and wealthy figure that it is hard to remember that only a short time ago artists were still considered special beings and their art something remote from life.

About half a century ago, Craig gave up acting in order to design and direct a tiny number of productions, whose aim was quite simply to create beauty on the stage. These productions were only seen by a handful of people, but, underlined by the theories and drawings that he published at the same time, their influence reached across the world, into every theatre with any pretensions to serious work. Today, in many places, his name is already forgotten, but producers and designers are only just catching up with his ideas. At the Moscow Arts Theatre, of course, where he designed *Hamlet,* they still remember him. Old stagehands speak of him with awe and his models are hallowed in the theatre museum.

Before the First World War, Craig had already staged his last production. He retired to Italy, edited a magazine, *The Masque,* firing broadsides at all that he considered shoddy and false, built himself a model and began experimenting with a system of scenery based on screens and lights. The purity of the screens, the formal beauty of the equations from which they were derived, fascinated him completely; despite many offers he never worked in the living theatre again.

It was said maliciously that he did not want to see his unpractical ideas put to the test; this is not true. Craig never returned to the theatre because he refused to compromise with practice. He wanted nothing less than perfection, and seeing no way of achieving this in the commercial theatre, he looked for it in himself.

Now in his little room, as in other such rooms over the years, in Florence, in Rapallo, in Paris, his life is self-contained. He studies, he writes, he draws; he devours booksellers' catalogues, he collects obscure Victorian farces, binding them in strange and beautiful covers of his own design. He is writing a play, *Drama for Fools,* 365 scenes for marionettes, for which he has designed the sets and the clothes, enchanting drawings in bright primary colors, as well as immaculate working drawings, showing how to build the scenery, and how to get the puppets' strings in and out of the doors. Continually he revises, taking a scene from one of the boxes on the floor, changing a word here, a semicolon there, until it is as near perfect as can be. It may never be read, it may never be staged, but it is complete.

For a very long time Craig has been ignored by his own country. But he has no bitterness at all. Admittedly, some days he feels sad, tired and old—and he is always desperately poor. Then he swallows a spoonful of his mustard seed and suddenly his great zest returns: it may be a new visitor, the color of the light, the whiff of battle, the taste of wine, and he is on top of the world again. "It's cracky, the theatre," he says. "Anyway, it's better than the Church." The next moment he is dreaming of a new production of *The Tempest* or *Macbeth,* and will begin to make a few notes, perhaps a drawing or two.

It is said that the gold hidden away in banks is the basis of a nation's prosperity, it is said that it is the priest tending the hidden flame that keeps a religion alive. The theatre has few wise men and few who jealously defend its ideals; we must honor and cherish Gordon Craig.

THE BECK CONNECTION

• • •

Julian Beck and Judith Malina's production of Jack Gelber's play *The Connection* in New York is fascinating because it represents one of the few clear ways opening up for our theatre. I think we agree that all forms of theatre are going through a deep crisis: where's the culprit? Is it the apathy of the audiences or is that in turn caused by the wrong shapes of the playhouses—or is it the commercializing influence of the impresarios—or is it the lack of daring of the authors—or is there suddenly no talent and no poetry around—or is this age of managers and technicians essentially untheatrical? Is the answer really to be found in song-and-dance; is it really to be found in a new form of naturalism? All we know is that the time-honored forms have shrivelled and died in front of us.

We know that the first artistic wave after the war was a tired attempt to reassert pre-1940 cultural values—and this was followed by a "putting into question," as the French call it. The English theatre revolution, like the similar movement in French films, has been a send-up of story, construction, technique, tempo, good curtains, effective moments, big scenes, climaxes—all of which simultaneously became as suspect as the Royal Family, heroics, politics, morality, and so on. Technically speaking, the revulsion has been away from "lying."

What is lying? Well, all those grand-sounding, meaningless platitudes we learned at school were lies—in one form or another. But also all that those older actors told us when we came into the theatre were lies of another sort. Why, after all, should the curtain come down at a "strong" moment, why should a good line be "pointed," why should a laugh be "got," why should we speak "up"? Against ordinary everyday standards of common sense and truth, all rhetoric is a "lie." What once passed for language is now seen to be lifeless and in no way expressive of what really goes on in human beings, what once passed for plot is now seen not to be plot at all, what once passed for character is now seen to be only a stereotyped set of masks.

You can thank the cinema and television for accelerating this process. The cinema degenerated because, like many a great empire, it stood still; it repeated its rituals identically again and again—but time passed and the meaning went out of them. Then television arrived at the very instant when the dramatic clichés of the cinema were being dished up for the nine millionth time. It began showing old movies—and rotten movie-like plays—and enabled audiences to judge them in a completely new way. In the cinema the darkness, the vast screen, the loud music, the soft carpets added unquestionably to the hypnosis. On television the clichés are naked: the viewer is independent, he is walking about his room, he hasn't paid (which makes it easier to switch off), he can voice his disapproval out loud without being sssshed. Furthermore, he is forced to judge, and to judge fast. He switches on the set and immediately judges from the face that he sees (a) whether it's an actor or someone "real"; (b) whether he's nice or not, good or bad, what his class or background, etc., are; (c) when it's a fictional scene, he draws on his experience of dramatic clichés to guess at the part of the story he has missed (because, of course, he can't sit round the program twice, as he used to do at the movies). The smallest gesture identifies the villain, the adulteress, and so on. The essential fact is that he has learned—from necessity—to observe, to judge for himself.

And this is where Brecht comes in. (There is so much of Brecht's work I admire, so much of his work with which I disagree totally.) I am convinced that almost all that Brecht was saying about the nature of illusion can be applied to the cinema—and only with many reservations to the theatre. Brecht claimed that audiences were in a state of trance, of sloppy, dreamlike surrender to illusion. I believe that this form of semi-drugged surrender did occur between audience and screen in the heyday of the movies. We all have had the experience of being moved by a film and afterwards feeling ashamed, tricked.

I believe that the new cinema unconsciously exploits the new independence of the viewer that television has brought about. It is catering to an audience capable of judging an image—I'd quote *Hiroshima Mon Amour* as the supreme example of this. The camera is no longer an eye; it does not track us into the geographical reality of Hiroshima as that famous tracking shot at the beginning of *La Bête Humaine* that sucked us out of our seats into some French railway station. The camera in *Hiroshima* presents us with a succession of documents which bring us face to face with the whole vast historical, human and emotional reality of Hiroshima in a form that is only moving to us through the use of our own objective judgment. We go into it as it were with our eyes open.

And this, surprisingly enough, gets me straight to *The Connection.* When you go to *The Connection* in New York you are aware, as you enter the building, of all the denial aspects of the evening. There is no proscenium—(illusion? Well, yes, insofar as the stage is arranged like a squalid room, but it is not like a set; it is more as though the theatre were an extension of this room)—there is no conventional playwriting, no exposition, no development, no story, no characterization, no construction and, above all, no tempo. This supreme artifice of the theatre —this one god, whom we all serve, whether in musicals or in melodramas or in the classics—that marvellous thing called pace—is there thrown right out of the window. So, with this collection of negative values, you seem to have an evening as boring as life must seem to a young and reluctant devotee sitting on the banks of the Ganges. And yet, if you persevere you are rewarded—from the zero you get to the infinite.

How does it work? Well, the mental process is roughly this. At first, you cannot believe that the reaction against all the "lies" of theatre can be total. After all, in Pinter, in Wesker, in Delaney, there are new artifices to replace the old, even if they seem for the moment to be closer to the "truth." In *Roots,* we know the washing up won't go on for ever, because we sense the presence of a dramatist with purpose. In *A Taste of Honey,* we know that a dialogue will cease at the moment when Shelagh Delaney's instinct tells her it is played out. But in *The Connection,* the tempo is the tempo of life itself. A man enters—for no reason—with a gramophone. (Oh yes, there is a reason. He wants to plug it into the light socket.) He wants (apparently—he doesn't say so) to play a record. And as it's an LP we have to wait for it to finish—a quarter of an hour or so later. At first, our attitude as audience is fouled by our expectations. We can't truly savor the moment (enjoy the record for what it is worth, as we would in a room) because years of theatre convention have conditioned us to a different tempo: man puts on record, story point made, now what? (Amazingly, we cannot enjoy a record we would enjoy at home, because we have paid for our seat.) We sit waiting for the next contrivance that will—with seeming natural-ness—interrupt the record and let us get on with . . . with what? That's the point.

For, in *The Connection* there's nothing to get on with. And as we sit there, baffled, irritated and bored, suddenly we put ourselves in question. Why are we baffled, why are we irritated, why are we bored? Because we are not being spoon-fed. Because we are not told what to look at, because we are not having our emotional attitudes and judg-ments prepared for us, because we are independent, adult, free. Then suddenly we realize what is actually in front of us. *The Connection*—as I should perhaps have said earlier—is a play about dope addicts. What we see is a roomful of junkies waiting for a fix. They are passing the time playing jazz, occasionally talking, mostly sitting. The actors who are portraying these characters have sunk themselves into a total, beyond Method, degree of saturated naturalism, so that they aren't acting, they are being. And then, one realizes that the two criteria—boredom or interest—are not in this case possible criticisms of the play, but criticisms of ourselves.

Are we capable of looking at people we don't know, with a way of life different from our own, with interest? The stage is paying us the supreme compliment of treating us all as artists, as independent crea-tive witnesses. And the evening is as interesting as we choose to make it. It is as though we were really taken into a room of far-gone drug addicts: we could be Rimbaud and spin our own fantasies from their attitudes; we could watch like a painter or a photographer the extraor-dinary beauty of their bodies slumped in their chairs; or we could relate their behavior to our own medical, psychological or political beliefs. But if we shrug our shoulders before this collection of warped, strange, miserable mankind, it's hard to feel that the lack is other than on our side. After all, *The Connection,* though "anti" in terms of stage convention, is supremely positive—it is assuming that man is passionately interested in man . . .

As I was saying earlier, we react against "lies" in the name of truth —but are in effect putting fresher conventions in the place of antiquated ones, and so long as they're fresh, they'll seem "truer." Now *The Connection* seems absolutely "real." Yet the fact that something does happen in *The Connection*—the man with the dope arrives and in the second act gives everyone a shot, and one character gets violent—is a form of plot. Equally, the choice of subject is in itself bizarre, theatrical, romantic. In twenty years, *The Connection* will seem plot-ridden and contrived. By then, we may be capable of watching a normal man in a normal state with equal interest. Maybe . . .

Note in passing that this is a Brechtian show in one particular sense—we look, we relate to our own prejudices, we judge. And note the interesting corollary: the stage picture is a sort of illusion—it is a room and the actors try to pass themselves off as real people; it is the ultimate development of the utterly naturalistic theatre and yet we are completely "distanced" all through the evening. In fact, were a few Brechtian slogans to be hung up to help us find our emotional attitude, then we might be caught up in illusion.

The Connection proves to me that the development of the tradition of naturalism will be toward an ever-greater focus on the person or the people, and an increasing ability to dispense with such props to our interest as story and dialogue. I think it shows that there is a supernaturalistic theatre ahead of us in which pure behavior can exist in its own right, like pure movement in ballet, pure language in declamation, etc.

The film I've just made, *Moderato Cantabile,* is an experiment in this. It is an attempt to tell a story with a minimum of fictional devices by using and relying on the actors' powers of characterization in the mediumistic sense of the word. In other words, the actors were not instructed in the aspects of character that were useful for the story, they saturated themselves in the characters by rehearsing scenes which do not exist in the film. The actors became other people in fictional relationship; however, from then on we observed—the camera recorded their behavior. The interest—if it's there—is in the eye of the beholder. The experiment is that the entire plot, exposition, narrative, exists in details of behavior which we have to find and evaluate for ourself—as we do in life.

You see the subject is vast—and I really would like to move on from *The Connection*. I believe that the future of the theatre must lie in its transcending the surface of reality, and I believe that *The Connection* shows how naturalism can become so deep that it can—through the intensity of the performer (I'm sure *The Connection* is nothing much on paper)—transcend appearances. Here it falls into place with the whole new school of French novel writing—Robbe-Grillet, Duras, Sarraute—which refutes analysis and puts concrete facts, i.e., objects or dialogues or relationships or behavior, before you, without comment or explanation.

But there are other ways of transcending appearances. I'm interested in why the theatre today in its search for popular forms ignores the fact that in painting the most popular form in the world today has become abstract. Why did a Picasso show fill the Tate Gallery with all manner of people who would not go to the Royal Academy? Why do his abstractions seem real, why do people sense that he is dealing with concrete, vital things? We know that the theatre lags behind the other arts because its continual need for immediate success chains it to the slowest members of its audience. But is there nothing in the revolution that took place in painting fifty years ago that applies to our own crisis today?

Do we know where we stand in relation to the real and the unreal, the face of life and its hidden streams, the abstract and the concrete, the story and the ritual? What are "facts" today? Are they concrete, like prices and hours of work—or abstract, like violence and loneliness? And are we sure that in relation to twentieth-century living, the great abstractions—speed, strain, space, frenzy, energy, brutality—aren't more concrete, more immediately likely to affect our lives than the so-called concrete issues? Mustn't we relate this to the actor and the ritual of acting in order to find the pattern of the theatre we need?

HAPPY SAM BECKETT
· · ·

I wanted to write about the new Beckett play *Happy Days* because I had just seen it, was full of excitement and enthusiasm and was shocked to find New York so indifferent. In the meantime I went to see Alain Resnais's film *L'Année dernière à Marienbad*. Then I read

Robbe-Grillet's statements in defense of his script and found that the more I thought about Beckett, the more I wanted to talk about *Marienbad*. The link between Beckett and *Marienbad* seems to me that both are attempting to express in concrete terms what would at first sight appear to be intellectual abstractions. My interest is in the possibility of arriving, in the theatre, at a ritual expression of the true driving forces of our time, none of which, I believe, is revealed in anecdote or characterization by the people and situations in so-called realistic plays.

The marvel of the Beckett play was its objectivity. Beckett at his finest seems to have the power of casting a stage picture, a stage relationship, a stage machine from his most intense experiences that in a flash, inspired, exists, stands there complete in itself, not telling, not dictating, symbolic without symbolism. For Beckett's symbols are powerful just because we cannot quite grasp them: they are not signposts, they are not textbooks nor blueprints—they are literally creations.

Years ago I directed a production of Sartre's *Huis Clos*. Today I cannot remember one word of the dialogue, not one detail of the philosophy. But the central picture of this play—the hell made up of three people locked in an eternal hotel room—is still with me. It was cast not from Sartre's intelligence, as his other plays have been, but from somewhere else—in a creative flash, the author found a stage situation which I think has actually entered into the terms of reference of our whole generation. I think that to anyone who saw the play, the word "hell" is more likely to evoke that closed room than fire and pitchforks.

Before Oedipus and Hamlet were born in their authors' minds, all the qualities these characters reflect must have been in existence as nebulous, formless currents of experience. Then came a powerful generative act—and characters appeared, giving shape and substance to these abstractions. Hamlet is there: we can refer to him. Suddenly the first "angry young man," Jimmy Porter, was there—we can't throw him off. At a given moment Van Gogh's Provence came into existence—inescapably—as did Dali's desert.

Can we define a work of art as something that brings a new "thing" into the world—something we may like or reject, but which annoyingly continues to be, and so for better or for worse becomes part of our field of reference? If so, this brings us back to Beckett. He did just this with those two tramps under a tree. The whole world found something vague made tangible in that absurd and awful picture. And those parents in the dustbin.

Now he's done it again. A woman is alone in the middle of the stage. She is up to her (ample) bosom in a mound of earth. Beside her is a large handbag, out of which she produces all the little things she might ever need, including a gun. The sun shines. She is, where—in a sort of no-man's-land? after the Bomb? We cannot tell. Somewhere at the back in a dubious anal region, her husband ekes out some sort of existence. Occasionally, on all fours—and once in top hat and tails—he emerges; for the most part he is a grunt, a mutter, or just a thin squeak. A bell chimes: it is morning. Bell chimes: it is night. The lady smiles. Time, she fancies, does not pass. Every day is a happy day.

By the last act the mound has risen to her neck, her arms are imprisoned but her head is free, and it remains as plump and cheery as before. Does she have intimations that all may not be for the best? Yes, fleetingly—in tiny seconds wonderfully caught. Her husband crawls out for the last time. He reaches up longingly—toward her face? Toward the gun a few inches away? We never know.

What does it all mean? If I attempt any sort of explanation, let me hasten to say that it will not be *the* explanation; my admiration for the play is that it is not a treatise—and so any explanation is a partial view of the whole. Certainly this is a play about man throwing his life away; it is a play about possibilities lost: comically, tragically, it shows us man atrophied, paralyzed, three-quarters useless, three-quarters dead —but grotesquely it shows he is only aware of how lucky he is to be alive. This is a picture of us ourselves endlessly grinning—not as Pagliacci once grinned, to conceal a broken heart, but grinning because no one has told us our heart stopped beating long ago.

This is a disturbing enough theme, real and vital to any audience today—more than anywhere in New York, which has rejected it. I do not see how this subject matter can be expressed by any more "realistic" means. It is a desperate cry, but at the same time it is implying something very positive, perhaps more positive than any other Beckett work. It is a paradise lost that is about man, only man, not about any other state, and in showing man bereft of most of his organs it is implying that the possibilities were there, are there still, buried, ignored. Unlike the other Beckett plays this is not only a vision of our fallen condition, it is an assault on our fatal blindness.

It contains its own answer to the obvious reproach that it is just another piece of pessimism and gloom. For the lady looking at us ensconced in her mound as comfortably as ourselves in our stalls is the very picture of facile optimism. Here is the audience (and the critics) at any play (or film) which after two hours finds the answers, which glibly asserts that life is good, that there is always hope and that all will be well. Here are most of our politicians grinning from ear to ear and buried up to their necks.

It is a long jump and a short step to *L'Année dernière à Marienbad*. For those who haven't seen it, this film is an attempt to split open the pure convention that time is consecutive. The authors of the film, speaking from a mid-twentieth-century sensibility and experience, refute the notion that the past is the past and that events in the present follow one another in chronological order. This is how time passes in films, they would claim, and this is a very arbitrary, shallow and unreal convention of film makers. Time for man can be an overlapping of fugitive experiences and in no way resembles the time of objects, for these remain untouched by the passage of events. Time in the cinema is the moment of watching a shot—and there can be no difference between a shot taking place in the past or the future. The act of watching a film is a chain of "nows." A film is a passionate assembly of "nows"—montage is not order, but relationships.

In Marienbad, in a wildly over-ornate Bavarian castle—ostensibly a hotel—a man and a woman exchange broken fragments of pure relationships; the sequence is not one of time or sense, but of the growth from attitude to attitude. The past and the present exist side by side, at once playing with one another, against one another, in endless repetitions and modulations.

The film is a time experiment—and attempts things I have been longing to see. I wish I could say I liked the result. But curiously, between a (in my view) totally right starting point and unquestionably superb execution (direction, photography and cutting are magnificent), it falls completely flat. I found it empty and pretentious, arty and imitative.

The trouble is that the authors were moved by the fascination of their experiment, nothing more. The set of images they present to us —and here I would compare them unfavorably to Beckett—is meaningless; this is the abstract/abstract as against the abstract/real. It may be said that my reaction is completely subjective, that what are meaningless pictures to me may be very disturbing to someone else. Maybe, but the point I am trying to establish is that there is a giant difference —which we are all very well equipped to judge—between the real and the meaningless, between the Picasso and the brush tied to the donkey's tail.

I feel that the world of *Marienbad*—in which the deadly monotony of riches is symbolized by zombie-faced figures in dinner jackets and Chanel dresses sitting in elegantly frozen groups or playing endless silent games—is an intellectual illustration using visual material that we've grown used to over the years in the ballet, in Cocteau's films, and so on. This is far from the haunting, worrying, challenging images struck by Beckett.

Yet the film is a radical experiment and its interest to me is its relation to the theatre.

It convinces me again that in the theatre, even more than in the cinema, we need no longer be bound at all by time, character or plot. We need not use any of these traditional crutches—and yet we can still be real, dramatic and meaningful.

The art of serial music is that of taking a series of notes—like a discipline—and then confronting this discipline with the sensibility and the wish of the composer. The burning shapelessness meets a rigid shape—and a new chain of order is forged. Take a stage, four characters: in this atom there is already an infinity of possibilities. (In one sense, this is *Beyond the Fringe,* and look what brilliant variations it spins.) Four characters—four actors, rather, for an actor can be old and young, consistent and inconsistent, one person or many—and here is already a set of relationships out of which like Chinese boxes, other relationships—tender, farcical and dramatic—can grow. Here the value of the work—as in abstract painting, as in serial music— would be directly a reflection of the nature of the dramatist himself: his nature in the deepest sense, his imagination, his experience and the endless interplay in him between society and his temperament.

BOUNCING

• • •

It's no use making plans. In the theatre we spend every free moment meeting, dining, drinking and phoning, by day and by night, dreaming up projects—and although we believe in them and announce them, they are never what we finally do. We are ping-pong balls bouncing off the net of events. I'm always finding myself in the most unexpected places, volleyed from one spot to another by obstacles that suddenly arise.

This year, 1958, I've spent in the air flying between London, Paris and New York, and it is all because of the French police, a shocked audience on Christmas Eve, the citizens of Dublin, and a heavy fog over the English Channel.

If my friend Simone Berriau, directress of the Théâtre Antoine in Paris, where I was going to stage a play called *The Balcony* in January, had not happened to call at the police station to discuss parking problems, I might well have landed in a French jail. For while she was with the police, a hand beckoned her into an inner room and she was told, off the record, that if she proceeded with this play, a riot would be organized (by the police, naturally!) and the theatre would be closed. This incidentally was a play that had run in London without scandal, but as it showed a priest and a general in a brothel it was more than the French could take.

So, faced with this threat, we were forced to postpone *The Balcony* by Jean Genet and put in its place Arthur Miller's *View from the Bridge*. This was a play I had produced in England a year before, when it had been banned by our authorities because two men kiss in it—a situation which the French took in their stride.

I never let anyone into my rehearsals. However, when we were doing the play in London, I discovered one night that Marilyn Monroe had smuggled herself into the dress circle. I went up, furious, to turn her out, but was disarmed by her wide-eyed look—"I've never seen a rehearsal before," she said. At once, she added her criticisms. "That girl," she pointed down at Mary Ure, "she's a marvellous actress. But in Arthur's play she's meant to be a girl of sixteen. No girl of sixteen wiggles." I thought Marilyn ought to know and toned Mary down accordingly.

Then I found myself sitting at rehearsal at the Théâtre Antoine with Marcel Aymé, the distinguished French writer, shocked at the excessive innocence of Evelyne Dandry playing the same part. "The girl must move as though she feels she is attractive," he cried, clutching my arm. "After all, at sixteen one knows about life." And of course he was right. These were not different aspects of the same truth. In France one can be more honest, more true to life than in England. Here we are all caught up in a conspiracy to hide the truth from ourselves in a cloud of hopefulness and charm.

That's why the English wouldn't take *The Visit*. While working in France I had found *The Visit,* a play by a Swiss author, Friedrich Dürrenmatt, which we opened, starring the Lunts, in Brighton on

Christmas Eve. An audience of uncles and aunts, already full of port, nuts and good cheer, virtually in paper hats, assembled to see the Lunts. They had made up their minds that this would inevitably be a sweet tale of candles and champagne, carrying a nostalgic reassurance that the aristocratic virtues of elegance and taste still rule the world. Instead, they got a bitter and important play about the evasions and dishonesty of provincial minds. When the curtain fell on Alfred Lunt's corpse being carried away under twinkling Christmas lights, it was a blow in the teeth for the audience, and they filed out of the theatre in angry silence.

Wherever we did this play there was an outcry, and in London theatre managers hurriedly discovered reasons for preventing our having a stage. The day came when we had to make a final decision as to what to do about getting a theatre for the Lunts and that day a thick fog descended on Paris, grounding all the planes. I took the Golden Arrow train ferry, furious at the loss of a full day in either town. The ship sailed across the Channel at a dead slow pace, the foghorn moaning, and I walked impatiently round the deck.

Suddenly I saw a figure, motionless, a vast jaw silhouetted against the white mist, a man I had not seen since I'd last been in New York, a real-estate tycoon, a man who pulls down and rebuilds entire cities. "I'm completing a new theatre on Broadway," he said. "It's costing us a million dollars. I wish I could find something really exciting for the opening." A few days later I was in Dublin, where the Lunts were now playing, with another tycoon, Roger Stevens—the man who had once bought the Empire State Building, and who adored theatre. The box office manager explained to us that business was bad because Catholic opinion was shocked. "It's the coffin," he said gloomily. Roger Stevens watched a dreary performance in an almost empty theatre. "This show'll be a sensation in New York," he said.

So all plans were turned upside down, London abandoned, *Irma la Douce* postponed, and to get to New York in time I had to catch a plane from Paris in the middle of the first night of *A View from the Bridge*. From Orly Airport I phoned the theatre and heard the applause that indicated all had gone well. A few weeks later that same heart-warming sound meant that New York had accepted this harsh, violent play in the new theatre to which the Lunts have now given their name.

The next day I was back in London at work on *Irma la Douce*. It is here that the wheel comes full circle. If I hadn't worked in London I would never have come upon *A View from the Bridge* to take to Paris;

if I hadn't worked in Paris I might never have found *Irma la Douce* to bring to London.

Again the discussions start. The Americans this time are shocked by it; many saw it in Paris and found that, though Broadway can take tough and violent plays, it would flinch at this innocent tale of a tart's adventures. We go to the Lord Chamberlain's office and he to everyone's surprise passes our script intact. He only cuts, without explanation, one word, "*Kiki*"—and I haven't the heart to tell him that this in Paris slang simply means the neck. We opened the play in Bournemouth. The journalists swarmed down—would Bournemouth be shocked, they wanted to know. But of course not, Bournemouth took it in its stride. Then it opened in London and there's uproar again. Uproar of those who are shocked and uproar of those who expect to be shocked and find out that there is nothing to be shocked by, at all.

But tomorrow I'll be in an airplane again, flying with no other plans than the firm resolve that for at least a year, whatever happens, I won't set foot in a theatre again. And like all plans this will most likely be changed at a moment's notice.

GROTOWSKI

• • •

Grotowski is unique. Why? Because no one else in the world, to my knowledge, no one since Stanislavsky, has investigated the nature of acting, its phenomenon, its meaning, the nature and science of its mental-physical-emotional processes as deeply and completely as Grotowski.

He calls his theatre a laboratory. It is. It is a centre of research. It is perhaps the only avant-garde theatre whose poverty is not a drawback, where shortage of money is not an excuse for inadequate means which automatically undermine the experiments. In Grotowski's theatre as in all true laboratories the experiments are scientifically valid because the essential conditions are observed. In his theatre, there is absolute concentration by a small group, and unlimited time. So if you are interested in his findings you must go to a small town in Poland.

Or else do what we did. Bring Grotowski to London.

He worked for two weeks with our group. I won't describe the work. Why not? First of all, such work is only free if it is in confidence, and confidence depends on its confidences not being disclosed. Secondly, the work is essentially non-verbal. To verbalize is to complicate and even to destroy exercises that are clear and simple when indicated by a gesture and when executed by the mind and body as one.

What did the work do?

It gave each actor a series of shocks.

The shock of confronting himself in the face of simple irrefutable challenges. The shock of catching sight of his own evasions, tricks and clichés. The shock of sensing something of his own vast and untapped resources. The shock of being forced to question why he is an actor at all. The shock of being forced to recognize that such questions do exist and that—despite a long English tradition of avoiding seriousness in theatrical art—the time comes when they must be faced. And of finding that he wants to face them. The shock of seeing that somewhere in the world acting is an art of absolute dedication, monastic and total. That Artaud's now-hackneyed phrase "cruel to myself" is genuinely a complete way of life—somewhere—for less than a dozen people.

With a proviso. This dedication to acting does not make acting an end in itself. On the contrary. For Jerzy Grotowski, acting is a vehicle. How can I put it? The theatre is not an escape, a refuge. A way of life is a way *to* life. Does that sound like a religious slogan? It should. And that's about all there was to it. No more, no less. Results? Unlikely. Are our actors better? Are they better men? Not in that way, as far as I can see, not as far as anyone has claimed. (And of course they were not all ecstatic about their experience. Some were bored.)

But as John Arden writes in *Sergeant Musgrave's Dance:*

> For the apple holds a seed will grow,
> In live and lengthy joy
> To raise a flourishing tree of fruit,
> For ever and a day.

Grotowski's work and ours have parallels and points of contact. Through these, through sympathy, through respect, we came together.

But the life of our theatre is in every way different from his. He runs a laboratory. He needs an audience occasionally, in small numbers. His tradition is Catholic—or anti-Catholic; in this case the two

Peter Brook *(left)* with Jerzy Grotowski

extremes meet. He is creating a form of service. We work in another country, another language, another tradition. Our aim is not a new Mass, but a new Elizabethan relationship—linking the private and the public, the intimate and the crowded. the secret and the open, the vulgar and the magical. For this we need both a crowd on stage and a crowd watching—and within that crowded stage individuals offering their most intimate truths to individuals within that crowded audience, sharing a collective experience with them.

We have come quite a way in developing an overall pattern—the idea of a group, of an ensemble. But our work is always too hurried, always too rough for the development of the collection of individuals out of whom it is composed.

We know in theory that every actor must put his art into question daily—like pianists, dancers, painters—and that if he doesn't he will almost certainly get stuck, develop clichés, and eventually decline. We recognize this and yet can do so little about it that we endlessly chase after new blood, after youthful vitality—except for certain of the most gifted exceptions, who of course get all the best chances, absorb most of the available time.

Grotowski's work was a reminder that what he achieves almost miraculously with a handful of actors is needed to the same extent by each individual in our two giant Royal Shakespeare companies in two theatres ninety miles apart.

The intensity, the honesty and the precision of his work can only leave one thing behind: a challenge. But not for a fortnight, not for once in a lifetime. Daily.

ARTAUD AND THE GREAT PUZZLE
• • •

All work is intended to raise questions. When we discover that some of the questions we raise are also being put by other people, our interest is immediately aroused. The fact that at the other end of the earth someone else is trying the same experiment makes us want to know the results. It is very simple.

When we founded our own theatrical research group, at LAMDA, in London in 1964, it was well before Grotowski's first visit and at that time group work was not yet fashionable. I well remember that at one point in our work, which was on sounds, voice, gestures and movements, a friend told me: "I was in Poland recently and I met someone there who is doing experimental work that you would find very interesting." Of course, I was interested: I had to know what Grotowski was doing.

Grotowski, in turn, told me that while he was working on subjects he found interesting, someone said to him, "Everything you do is based on Artaud!" At that time, Grotowski had no idea who Artaud was. Nor had I. In fact, it was while I was filming *Lord of the Flies* and had just finished directing a play in New York that a woman contacted me, to ask whether I would write her a short article on Artaud for a small avant-garde paper; she also invited me to give a lecture and answer questions about the influence Artaud had on me and our theatre.

As always, I was so far from any theoretical approach to theatre that I had not the remotest idea who Artaud might be. But the fact that this woman wrote, not only with passion, but with the firm conviction that I was bound to have heard of Artaud, made me think. One day I went into a bookshop, saw a book by Antonin Artaud and bought it: that is how I first became acquainted with Artaud. Without realizing it, for years the ground had been being prepared and so I was ready to be deeply impressed. At the same time, a voice warned me that even the most striking vision could only bring out one further aspect, one more fragment of the great puzzle.

With Grotowski, a deep friendship arose; we saw we shared the same aim. But our paths were different. Grotowski's work leads him deeper and deeper into the actor's inner world, to the point where the actor ceases to be actor and becomes essential man. For this, all the dynamic elements of drama are needed, so that every cell of the body can be pushed to reveal its secrets. At first, director and audience are necessary to intensify the process. However, as the action goes deeper, everything external must wither away until at the end there is no more theatre, no more actor, no more audience—only a solitary man playing out his ultimate drama alone. For me, the way of the theatre goes the opposite way, leading out of loneliness to a perception that is heightened because it is shared. A strong presence of actors and a strong presence of spectators can produce a circle of unique intensity in which barriers can be broken and the invisible become real. Then public truth and private truth become inseparable parts of the same essential experience.

HOW MANY TREES MAKE A FOREST?

. . .

Neither Brecht nor Artaud stands for ultimate truth. Each represents a certain aspect of it, a certain tendency, and at our time perhaps their respective viewpoints are the most diametrically opposed. To try to discover where, how, and at what level this opposition ceases to be real is something I have found very interesting, particularly during the period in 1964 between the season of the "Theatre of Cruelty" and the production of *Marat/Sade.*

During my first meeting with Brecht (in Berlin in 1950, while we were touring a production I had directed of *Measure for Measure* with what was then called the Shakespeare Memorial Theatre), we discussed the problems of theatre together, and I found I did not really agree with his view of the difference between illusion and non-illusion. In his production of *Mother Courage* by the Berliner Ensemble, I found that however much he tried to break any belief in the reality of what happened on the stage, the more he did, the more I entered whole-heartedly into the illusion!

I think that there is a surprising and very interesting connection between Craig and Brecht. Craig, by putting the question: "How much is it essential to put on the stage to convey a forest?" suddenly exploded the myth that it was necessary to show an entire forest, trees, leaves, branches and all the rest. And the moment the question was put, suddenly the doors opened to the bare stage and the single stick, suggesting whatever is needed.

Now it seems to me that one aspect of Brecht follows that same line of thinking, but relates it to acting. Actors landed with what's called a character role usually feel that to do their job honorably they've got to paint in a bit of every aspect of that character, in the round. The actor is there in rehearsal, wanting to do well, seeing descriptions in the text that relate to characterization, and he feels that he must do as much as possible. Well, when you're dealing with a naturalistic play, you can cheat yourself into thinking that you can do it all with makeup and hunched shoulders and false noses and the right voice imitated from life. When you have a richer text, like Shakespeare, the reality of the characters is denser. At one and the same time you see what the person looks like, you get the sound of his voice and you see how he thinks. You also know what sort of feelings are going through him. Here all is more complex—more real—there is more information. If you were a computer, you'd be getting more stuff in about the reality of that person, that situation.

To get that over in the same space of time—because a non-naturalistic play lasts the same length of time on the stage as a naturalistic play—you, the actor, have to do more in each moment. Consequently, simplification is your strongest tool. If you can then look at your characterization, which is what Brecht throws open—if, say, you're an old man, do you need to quaver your voice as well as shudder and jiggle? —if you can get that physical side down to a simple outline, not for any virtue in itself but because in doing so you can also put more emphasis on something else which is part of this reality, then you have more means at your disposal. I think it is in that area that the visual revolution of Craig relates to an acting revolution through Brecht.

I think there's a tremendous danger here. Stanislavsky has been misunderstood and Brecht has been misunderstood, and the danger in misunderstanding Brecht is to take a completely analytical, unspontaneous, anti-acting approach to the work in rehearsal, to think that you can sit down in cold blood and define intellectually the aims of a scene. The aim of a scene, the nature of a scene, have to be found by the rehearsal process. This is always a question of searching by a whole mixture of means; by discussion, by improvising, by feeling the elements and playing them out, and inevitably going through a stage where you have no simplicity, where you have an over-richness of material which eventually has to be simplified. And this is where Brecht's insistence on clear thought comes into play.

For Artaud, theatre is fire; for Brecht, theatre is clear vision; for Stanislavsky, theatre is humanity. Why must we choose among them?

IT HAPPENED IN POLAND

• • •

I first met Jan Kott in a nightclub in Warsaw. It was midnight. He was squashed between a wildly excited group of students: we became friends at once: a beautiful girl was arrested by mistake under our eyes.

Jan Kott leaped to her defense and an evening of high adventure followed which ended at about four o'clock in the morning with Kott and myself in the supreme headquarters of the Polish police trying to secure her release. It was only at this point when the tempo of events was slowing down that I suddenly noticed that the police were calling my new friend "Professor." I had guessed that this quick-witted and combative man was an intellectual, a writer, a journalist, perhaps a Party member. The title "Professor" sat ill on him. "Professor of what?" I asked as we walked home through the silent town. "Of drama," he replied.

I tell this story to point to a quality of the author of *Shakespeare Our Contemporary* which is to my mind unique. Here we have a man writing about Shakespeare's attitude to life from direct experience. Kott is undoubtedly the only writer on Elizabethan matters who assumes without question that every one of his readers will at some point or other have been woken by the police in the middle of the night. I am sure that in the many million words already written about Shakespeare—almost precluding anything new ever being said by anyone anymore—it is still unique for an author discussing the theory of political assassination to assume that a producer's explanation to his actors could begin: "A secret organization is preparing an action . . . You will go to Z and bring a case with grenades to house No. 12."

His writing is learned, it is informed, his study is serious and precise, it is scholarly without what we associate with scholarship. The existence of Kott makes one suddenly aware how rare it is for a pedant or a commentator to have any experience of what he is describing. It is a disquieting thought that the major part of the commentaries on Shakespeare's passions and his politics are hatched far from life by sheltered figures behind ivy-covered walls.

In contrast, Kott is an Elizabethan. Like Shakespeare, like Shakespeare's contemporaries, the world of the flesh and the world of the spirit are indivisible. They coexist painfully in the same frame: the poet has a foot in the mud, an eye on the stars and a dagger in his hand. The contradictions of any living process cannot be denied. There is an omnipresent paradox that cannot be argued, but must be lived: poetry is a rough magic that fuses opposites.

Shakespeare is a contemporary of Kott, Kott is a contemporary of Shakespeare—he talks about him simply, first-hand, and his book has the freshness of the writing by an eyewitness at the Globe or the immediacy of a page of criticism of a current film. To the world of scholarship this is a valuable contribution, to the world of the theatre an invaluable one. Our greatest problem in England where we have the best possibility in the world for presenting our greatest author is just this—the relating of these works to our lives. Our actors are skilled and sensitive, but they shy away from over-large questions. Those young actors who are aware of the deadly issues at this moment at stake in the world tend to shy away from Shakespeare. It is not an accident that at rehearsals our actors find plottings, fights and violent ends "easy"—they have clichés ready to deal with these situations which they do not question—but are deeply vexed by problems of speech and style which though essential can only take their true place if the impulse to use words and images relates to experience of life. England in becoming Victorian lost almost all its Elizabethan characteristics; today, it has become a strange mixture of Elizabethan and Victorian worlds. This gives us a new possibility of understanding Shakespeare side by side with an old tendency to blur and romanticize him.

It is Poland that in our time has come closest to the tumult, the danger, the intensity, the imaginativeness and the daily involvement with the social process that made life so horrible, subtle and ecstatic to an Elizabethan. So it is quite naturally up to a Pole to point us the way.

PETER WEISS'S KICK

• • •

For a play to seem like life, there must be a constant movement that goes back and forth between the social and the personal view; in other words, between the intimate and the general. For instance, Chekhov's plays contain this movement. He brings into focus the emotions of one character only to reveal a moment later a social aspect of the group. There is also another movement. It alternates between the superficial aspects of life and its most secret ones. If this is also present, then the play takes on an infinitely richer texture.

From the start, the cinema discovered the principle of changing perspectives, and audiences in every corner of the world accepted with-

Marat/Sade

out any difficulty the grammar of the long shot and the close-up. Shakespeare and the Elizabethans made a similar discovery. They used the interplay between everyday and heightened language, between poetry and prose, to change the psychological distance between the audience and the theme. The important thing is not the distance itself, but the constant in-and-out movement between various planes. This was the quality that most struck me when I first read Peter Weiss's *Marat/Sade* and found it a very good play.

What's the difference between a poor play and a good one? I think there's a very simple way of comparing them. A play in performance is a series of impressions; little dabs, one after another, fragments of information or feeling in a sequence which stirs the audience's perceptions. A good play sends many such messages, often several at a time, often crowding, jostling, overlapping one another. The intelligence, the feelings, the memory, the imagination are all stirred. In a poor play, the impressions are well spaced out, they lope along in single file, and in the gaps the heart can sleep while the mind wanders to the day's annoyances and thoughts of dinner.

The whole problem of the theatre today is just this: how can we make plays dense in experience? Great philosophical novels are often far longer than thrillers, more content occupies more pages, but great plays and poor plays fill up evenings of pretty comparable length. Shakespeare seems better in performance than anyone else because he gives us more, moment for moment, for our money. This is due to his genius, but also to his technique. The possibilities of free verse on an open stage enable him to cut the inessential detail and the irrelevant realistic action; in their place he could cram sounds and ideas, thoughts and images which make each instant into a stunning mobile.

Today we are searching for a twentieth-century technique that could give us the same freedom. For strange reasons, verse alone no longer does the trick. Yet there is a device. Brecht invented it, a new device of quite incredible power. This is what has been uncouthly labelled "alienation." Alienation is the art of placing an action at a distance so that it can be judged objectively and so that it can be seen in relation to the world—or rather, worlds—around it. Peter Weiss's play is a great tribute to alienation and breaks important new ground.

Brecht's use of "distance" has long been considered in opposition to Artaud's conception of theatre as immediate and violent subjective experience. I have never believed this to be true. I believe that theatre, like life, is made up of the unbroken conflict between impressions and judgments—illusion and disillusion cohabit painfully and are inseparable. This is just what Weiss achieves. Starting with its title *(The Persecution and Assassination of Jean-Paul Marat As Performed by the Inmates of the Asylum of Charenton Under the Direction of the Marquis de Sade),* everything about this play is designed to crack the spectator on the jaw, then douse him with ice-cold water, then force him to assess intelligently what has happened to him, then give him a kick in the balls, then bring him back to his senses again. It's not exactly Brecht and it's not Shakespeare either, but it's very Elizabethan and very much of our time.

Weiss not only uses total theatre, that time-honored notion of getting all the elements of the stage to serve the play. His force is not only in the quantity of instruments he uses; it is above all in the jangle produced by the clash of styles. Everything is put in its place by its neighbor—the serious by the comic, the noble by the popular, the literary by the crude, the intellectual by the physical; the abstraction is vivified by the stage image, the violence illuminated by the cool flow of thought. The strands of meaning of the play pass to and fro through its structure and the result is a very complex form. As in Genet, it is a hall of mirrors or a corridor of echoes—and one must keep looking front and back all the time to reach the author's sense.

One of the London critics attacked the play on the ground that it was a fashionable mixture of all the best theatrical ingredients around —Brechtian, didactic, absurdist, Theatre of Cruelty. He said this to disparage but I repeat it as praise. Weiss saw the use of every one of these idioms and he saw that he needed them all. His assimilation was complete. An undigested set of influences leads to a blur. Weiss's play is strong, its central conception startlingly original, its silhouette sharp and unmistakable. From our practical experience I can report that the force of the performance is directly related to the imaginative richness of the material. The imaginative richness is the consequence of the number of levels that are working simultaneously: and this simultaneity is the direct result of Weiss's daring combination of so many contradictory techniques.

Is the play political? Weiss says it is Marxist, and this has been much discussed. Certainly it is not polemical in the sense that it does not prove a case nor draw a moral. Certainly its prismatic structure is such that the last line is not the place to search for the summing-up idea. The idea of the play is the play itself, and this cannot be resolved in a simple slogan. It is firmly on the side of revolutionary change. But it is painfully aware of all the elements in a violent human situation and it presents these to the audience in the form of a disturbing question.

> "The important thing is to pull yourself up by your own hair. To turn yourself inside out and see the whole world with fresh eyes."
> —Marat

"How?" someone is bound to ask. Weiss wisely refuses to tell. He forces us to relate opposites and face contradictions. He leaves us raw. He searches for a meaning instead of defining one and puts the reponsibility of finding the answers back where it properly belongs. Off the dramatist and onto ourselves.

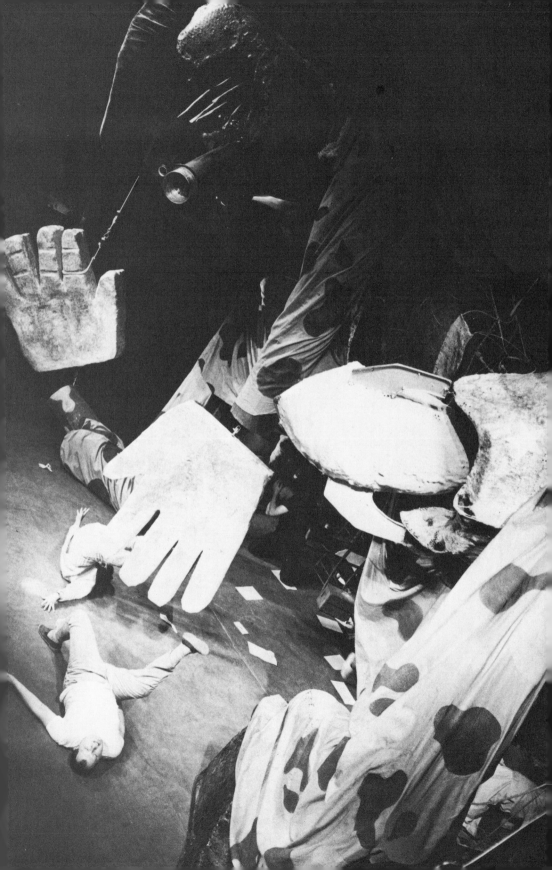

part III

PROVOCATIONS

Cruelty, Madness and War

. . .

MANIFESTO FOR THE SIXTIES

. . .

Culture has never done anyone any good whatsoever. No work of art has yet made a better man.

•～•

The more barbaric the people the more they appear to appreciate the arts.

•～•

Doing the repertoire of classical plays is in itself useless. There is no spiritual difference between a revival of Ibsen and a musical.

•～•

The trouble is not that we want entertainment, but that we don't. If audiences truly insisted on nothing but entertainment, the world's theatres would: (a) be completely emptied, once and for all; (b) start delivering much more serious work.

•～•

The curse of Stratford is that it is always full. People applaud the worst performances just as they applaud the best. Why don't they insist on entertainment? We'd be forced to give them better sense.

•～•

Nobility is nonsense. No one knows what Shakespeare's moral values were. We can only go by what we find in his texts today. In no folio is there a guarantee to move audiences to tears or to lead them to a finer life.

•～•

When someone says, "I was not moved," what gives him the illusion that his feelings are a reliable Geiger counter? There is always one critic who claims he wasn't moved. Perhaps it's true.

•～•

Intelligence is nonsense. We are producing a race of actors scared of extremes. Ham is hollow, naturalism is flat, so he walks intelligently in between. In acting the spark is in the middle but the poles are apart.

•∿•

An actor mustn't only present what he understands: he will pull the mystery of his part to his own level. He must let the part sound out in him all that he could never reach alone.

•∿•

The Berliner Ensemble is the best company in the world. They have exceedingly long rehearsals. In Moscow some plays rehearse for two years and are terrible. This is bad luck: it doesn't prove that long rehearsals are a bad thing.

•∿•

Some people spend money wisely, some waste it: this doesn't prove that a permanent company is better off if it is short of cash.

•∿•

When the Surrealists talked about the meeting of the umbrella and the sewing machine, they had something. A play is the meeting of opposites. This is theatrical harmony. Coziness is discord.

•∿•

If a play does not make us lose our balance, the evening is unbalanced.

•∿•

If a play confirms anything that we already believe, it is useless to us. Unless of course it confirms the real belief that theatre can help us to see better.

•∿•

Social theatre is dead and buried. Society needs changing—urgently—but at least let's use good tools. Television is a real implement: to use a play to fight a war is taking a taxi to the Marne.

•∿•

Social theatre can never get quickly enough to the point. The time it spends on illustration forces it to simplify the argument—which is its enemies' just complaint. The Berliner Ensemble has taken London by storm. What will we remember, skill or meaning?

•∿•

We need to look to Shakespeare. Everything remarkable in Brecht, Beckett, Artaud is in Shakespeare. For an idea to stick, it is not enough to state it: it must be burnt into our memories. *Hamlet* is such an idea.

•∿•

This is an acid test: ten years later, do we carry in us a trace from which we can reconstruct the play? This trace is an acid burn, it forms itself into a silhouette—not just a picture, an image with emotional and intellectual charge. From this hard kernel the meanings of the whole work can be found again. Examples: Mother Courage drawing her cart, two tramps under a tree, a sergeant dancing.

•~•

In Shakespeare there is epic theatre, social analysis, ritual cruelty, introspection. There is no synthesis, no complicity. They sit contradictorily, side by side, coexisting, unreconciled.

It is no use taking slices of Shakespearean values and dealing them to dramatists like cards. A dramatist who has Shakespeare's sense of history without his introspection is as dead a duck as the director who has the pageantry without the meaning.

Yet we are all sick to death of Shakespeare. We've now seen all the unknown plays. We cannot live on revivals of the masterpieces.

We cannot reconstruct a Shakespearean theatre by imitation. By the time we have decided on a Shakespearean technique, we are wrong. The dead man moves, we stay still. Modern staging is already as musty as the traverse curtain.

•~•

It is not the Shakespearean method that interests us. It is the Shakespearean ambition. The ambition to question people and society in action, in relation to human existence. Quintessence and dust.

•~•

I thought I knew by heart every single phrase of the Advice to the Players. The other day I heard the words, "Form and pressure...." What is our form and pressure?

Who cares?

Why?

•~•

We can talk about housing on TV. We can talk about heaven in the empty churches. In the theatre we can ask why it's worth living in the house and if we want to go to heaven. Where else can we do this? We can talk about shorter hours of work in the weeklies and about leisure. If we don't examine the living of our leisure in the theatre, where else will we do so? In the loony bin?

•~•

Are the dramatists scared? If they aren't, lucky men, let them tell us their secret. If they are, then let them dig into their terror. If they dare dig below the psychological they will find a volcano.

If they simply describe their volcano, they will be calling us back to the Dark Ages. If they bring the inner volcano up into the light of society, the explosion will be worth seeing.

•〜•

In Paris, a rehearsal is called a repetition. No accusation could be more deadly. In Paris there is a company called the Théâtre Vivant. There is no better name. "Vivant" is so vague a word, it means nothing; to make it precise, it must all the time be redefined.

•〜•

Thank God our art doesn't last. At least we're not adding more junk to the museums. Yesterday's performance is by now a failure. If we accept this, we can always start again from scratch.

THE THEATRE OF CRUELTY

• • •

We have spent most of 1965 working with a small group behind locked doors. Now, in presenting some of our experiments in public, we are calling these performances "Theatre of Cruelty" as a homage to Artaud. Artaud used the word "cruelty" not to invoke sadism, but to call us toward a theatre more rigorous, or even, if we could follow him that far, pitiless to us all.

This program is a collage, a kind of revue made up of shots in the dark, of shots at distant targets. It is not a series of texts; we have not tried to present new forms of theatrical writing. This is not a literary experiment. As we felt very strongly that certain essential resources of theatrical expression were being neglected, Charles Marowitz and I decided to gather together a group of actors and actresses to study these problems.

We believe that a healthy theatre should consist of three parts: the national theatre, kept alive by a constant renewal of old and modern classics; musical comedy, with its vivacity, its ability to project joy and amusement through music, with color and laughter pursued purely for what they are; and experimental theatre. Now, because of many actors moving over to the big commercial successes, we have lost our avant-garde theatre. The musical field has its composers of concrete music, of serial and electronic works, who are far ahead of their times, but who pave the way for all the young musicians who will follow them. Similarly, in painting, of the many experiments in form, space and abstraction, today's Pop art is only one of the most accessible. But where is the avant-garde of the theatre? Certainly, at their typewriters, playwrights can explore form and search for new ways of writing for the stage, perhaps even find a way for their pieces to be performed. But where are those—at times even disastrous—experiments from which actors and directors can learn how to move away from the static, rigid and often inadequate forms of today?

In order to face new audiences with new creative formulas, we must first be able to face empty seats.

And yet the touchstone of our theatre today is still the size of the audiences. Even the best of our impresarios, our actors, directors and writers truly believes that this is a good standard of judgment, and maintains in all honesty that a successful performance should at least pay its cost. This often happens, and if it does, it's a good thing. But in our system, every theatre is obliged at least to break even, because no one, however idealistic, can afford to stay in business and keep on losing money. Therefore, while the ones who want to make money say flatly: "We're only interested in the profits," the best anyone can possibly say is: "I want to cover expenses." And this is wrong. A theatre which always has to cover its expenses is a blunted theatre.

The Royal Shakespeare Company has sponsored our experiment completely. Since we have a small theatre, the sponsorship can be total; it would cover us if we never had even one seat filled at any performance. Under these conditions, failure would mean the inability to keep this kind of theatre alive, or to be limiting it, in too drastic a way, to only one line of experimentation.

Artaud found confirmation for his theories in Oriental theatre, in the life of Mexico, in the myths of Greek tragedies, and above all in the Elizabethan theatre.

Elizabethan theatre allows the dramatist space in which to move freely between the outer and the inner world. The strength and the miracle of Shakespearean texts lie in the fact that they present man simultaneously in all his aspects. We can in turn feel identified or take our distance, abandon ourselves to the illusion or refuse it; a primitive situation can disturb us in our subconscious, while our intelligence watches, comments, meditates. We identify emotionally, subjectively, and at the same time we evaluate politically, objectively, in relation to society. Because deep roots are sunk beyond the everyday, poetic language and a ritualistic use of rhythm show us those aspects of life which are not visible on the surface.

Nevertheless, with a break in rhythm, a sudden move toward

prose, by slipping into dialect or an aside directed at the audience, Shakespeare also manages to remind us where we are, and thus bring us back to the solid and familiar world where, when all is said and done, a spade is a spade. His characters have the complex consistency of one who is absorbed in his own fluid, interior life, yet at the same time presents a precise and recognizable outline.

Shakespeare's principal mode of expression was verse, a rich and agile instrument, formed and matured at an exceptionally favorable time when the English language was flexing its muscles and entering into its renaissance. Every subsequent attempt to equal Shakespeare's results by bringing back blank verse has failed.

From a certain point of view, the "cruelty" of Artaud could be considered an effort to recover, by other means, the variety of Shakespeare's expression, and our experiment, which uses the work of Artaud more as a springboard than as a model for literal reconstruction, may also be interpreted as the search for a theatrical language as flexible and penetrating as that of the Elizabethans.

Our search begins with a look at two milestones: Jarry and Artaud. Jarry, an elegant force of destruction, dragged French literature from fin-de-siècle symbolism into the Cubist age. Extracts from his chaotic and scatological masterpiece *Ubu Roi* are used as pretexts for improvisation, to show among other things that this experiment does not necessarily exclude humor. Artaud is represented by the first performance of the only part of his work which is written in dialogue form, *The Spurt of Blood.*

This current of cruelty is then investigated with the help of specially written texts, with the presentation of rehearsals and special exercises, or with efforts to reopen discussions on the relation between theatre and film, between theatre and sound. In all these cases, what we are looking for is the intensity, the immediacy and the density of expression.

In this spirit, we have approached the greatest experimental work of all: *Hamlet.* It seemed appropriate that a program launched in January 1964 should celebrate the fourth Shakespeare centenary by working on one of his plays in the most radical way possible.

Why do we present this experiment to the public? Because no theatrical experience is complete without people who observe, because we need their reactions, because we want to see at what point we meet.

Ubu Roi

We need to put their reactions to the test, just as much as our own actions.

This group is not a showcase for people looking for future stars, but one which hopes to be accepted per se. It isn't trying to make news; it hopes to provoke wide discussion.

We are presenting our program at a time in which all theatrical conventions are being challenged and rules no longer exist. Our group has in turn taken apart story, construction, characters, technique, rhythm, grand finale, great scene, dramatic high point, starting from the premise that the turmoil and complexity of our lives in 1965 must cause us to question all accepted forms.

Then what?

THE THEATRE CAN'T BE PURE

· · ·

When our theatre is serious, it is never very serious. What do we mean by words like "true," "real," "natural"? We use them as shields to prevent ourselves being hurt by a theatrical experience. Because a real experience would be so painful and so strange that it would seem "unreal," "untrue," "unnatural."

From time to time the theatre gets conscious of its tameness and words like "poetry" are bandied about. "Tragedy," "catharsis," "where are the poets?" are the cries. And yet what happens? There begins an exclusive, esoteric, solemn search for high or hidden values—a search thrilling and ennobling until anyone starts to laugh, after which all art founders in a cold shower of simple sense.

Our only hope is in extremes—in marrying opposites—so that the smashing of the conventions that cozy out the terrors and the pains be accompanied by laughter—so that explorations of time and consciousness, of rituals of love and death be accompanied by the coarse grain of life and living. The theatre is the stomach in which food metamorphoses into two equalities: excrement and dreams.

U.S. MEANS YOU, U.S. MEANS US

. . .

The Royal Shakespeare Theatre is using public money to do a play about Americans at war in Vietnam. This fact is so explosive, and has brought out so many contradictory reactions, that for once some explanation seems necessary.

There are times when I am nauseated by the theatre, when its artificiality appals me, although at the very same moment I recognize that its formality is its strength. The birth of *US* was allied to the reaction of a group of us who quite suddenly felt that Vietnam was more powerful, more acute, more insistent a situation than any drama that already existed between covers. All theatre as we know it fails to touch the issues that can most powerfully concern actors and audiences at the actual moment when they meet. For common sense is outraged by the supposition that old wars in old words are more living than new ones, that ancient atrocities make civilized after-dinner fare, whilst current atrocities are not worthy of attention.

We started *US* from what for us was a great need—to face up to the call, the challenge of this present Vietnamese situation. We recognized that no finished, formed work of art about Vietnam existed; we knew you can't go to an author, give him a sum of money and say, We order from you, as from a shop, the following masterpiece about Vietnam. So one either does nothing or one says, Let's begin!

Twenty-five actors in a close relationship with an authors' team set out to do an investigation of the Vietnamese situation, and this took a number of months. Over fifteen weeks' rehearsal the actor acquired a relationship with Vietnam which was perhaps more intense than you expect from a person without that time and opportunity. Now any performance (and this is true for all forms of theatre) gives you, the spectators, one possibility. The actor is paid by you as your servant, your protagonist, to go through something very exacting so that you can in a short space of time acquire in concentrated form what he has actually gathered over a long period of time. The actor becomes a filter, translating this bewildering chaos of material, coming back and back to Vietnam and relating it to what he can experience for real in himself. Eventually, for three hours, he relives this with you.

I have been asked if I find anything scaring in the sequence of work we have done, from *Lear* to *US*. One of the things we all find scaring in our work is the way things change from year to year when we do acting exercises, improvisations. Ten years ago, to get a group of English actors to improvise on any theme would have been extremely difficult; the most prominent thing you'd come up against would be the English actor's unwillingness to throw himself into something uncharted. Today we find that to ask a group of actors who have worked together to do scenes of torture, brutality, violence and madness is frighteningly easy and frighteningly pleasurable for all of us. The thing takes off and moves and develops with quite alarming ease.

When the actors sit in silence at the end of *US*, they are reopening the question, each night, for all of us, of where we stand at this moment here and now in relation to what is going on in ourselves and the world around us. The very end of *US* is certainly not, as some have taken it to be, an accusation or reproach to the audience from the actors. The actors are truly concerned with themselves; they are using and confronting what is most scary in themselves.

US made no claims. It arose from experimental laboratory work, which is another way of saying that it was turned up by a series of attempts to probe a certain problem.

The problem was, How can current events enter the theatre? Behind this lies the question, Why should they enter the theatre? We had rejected certain answers. We did not accept the idea of the theatre as television documentary, nor the theatre as lecture hall, nor the theatre as vehicle for propaganda. We rejected these because we felt that from TV set to classroom, via newspaper, poster and paperback, the job was being done already through media perfectly adapted to the task. We were not interested in Theatre of Fact.

We were interested in a theatre of confrontation. In current events, what confronts what, who confronts whom? In the case of Vietnam, it is reasonable to say that everyone is concerned, yet no one is concerned: if everyone could hold in his mind through one single day both the horror of Vietnam and the normal life he is leading, the tension between the two would be intolerable. Is it possible then, we ask ourselves, to present for a moment to the spectator this contradiction, his own and his society's contradiction? Is there any dramatic confrontation more complete than this? Is there any tragedy more inevitable and more terrifying? We wanted actors to explore every aspect of this contradiction, so that instead of accusing or condoling an audience, they could be what an actor is always supposed to be, the audience's representative, who is trained and prepared to go farther than the spectator, down a path the spectator knows to be his own.

US used a multitude of contradictory techniques to change direction and to change levels. It aimed to put the incompatible side by side. But this wasn't drama. This was in a way seduction—it used a contemporary, highly perishable fun-language to woo and annoy the spectator into joining in the turning over of basically repellent themes. All this was preparation, like all the many phases of a bullfight that precede the kill. We aimed not at a kill, but at what bullfighters call "the moment of truth." The moment of truth was also our one moment of drama, the one moment perhaps of tragedy, the one and only confrontation. This was when at the very end all pretenses of play-acting ceased and actor and audience together paused, at a moment when they and Vietnam were looking one another in the face.

I am writing this just after doing a production of *Oedipus.* It seems the opposite pole from *US* and yet to me the two pieces of theatre are strangely related. There is nothing in common in their idiom, but the subject matter is almost identical: the struggle to avoid facing the truth. Whatever the cost, a man marshals everything at his disposal to skid away from the simple recognition of how things are. What is this extraordinary phenomenon at the very root of our way of existing? Is any other subject so urgent, so vital for us to understand now, today? Is Oedipus' dilemma something to do with the past?

Out of the two experiences, I am left with one vast unresolved query of my own. If the theatre touches a current issue so burning and so uncomfortable as Vietnam, it cannot fail to touch off powerful and immediate reactions. This seems a good thing, because we want our theatre to be powerful and immediate. However, when the trigger is so light, when the ejaculation comes so soon, when the first reaction is so strong, it is not possible to go very deep. The shutters fall fast.

With *Oedipus,* a Roman play at a national theatre, all the references are reassuring and so the audience's barriers are down. Hundreds of years of safe and insulated culture make any *Oedipus* a harmless exercise. So there is no opposition from the audience and it is possible for actors armed with a probing text to go very deeply into the nether lands of human evasion. The audience follows down these dark alleys, calm and confident. Culture is a talisman protecting them from anything that could nastily swing back into their own lives.

The contemporary event touches raw nerves but creates an immediate refusal to listen. The myth and the formally shaped work has power, yet is insulated in exact proportion. So which in fact is more likely to be useful to the spectator? I want to find the answer.

A LOST ART

· · ·

Seneca's play, Oedipus, has no external action whatsoever. It may never have been acted during the author's lifetime, but possibly it was read aloud in the bath house to friends. Anyway, it takes place nowhere, the people are not people, and the vivid action, as it moves through the verbal images, leaps forward and back with the technique of the cinema and with a freedom beyond film.

So this is theatre liberated from scenery, liberated from costume, liberated from stage moves, gestures and business. We may not wish to observe this, but at least we know where to begin. All the play demands is the ear of an exceptional musician with theatre in his veins—in this case my inseparable collaborator, Richard Peaslee, and a group of actors, standing stock-still. However, these motionless actors must speak. They must set their voices in motion. To do so, many other motions must invisibly be activated: the still exterior must cover an extraordinary inner dynamism. Today, a body-conscious theatre has liberated a generation of actors who can express a powerful emotional charge through intense physical activity. This text demands not less than that, but more: it asks physically developed actors not to go backward but to push forward in the most difficult direction to the discovery of how leaps, rolls and somersaults can turn into acrobatics of larynx and lung, while standing still. Above all, this text demands a lost art—the art of impersonal acting.

How can acting be impersonal? I can see at once what would happen if a trusting actor hearing this word and trying to be faithful to its suggestion tried to depersonalize himself: his face a set of taut muscles, his voice a foghorn, he could produce unnatural rhythms. Perhaps he might believe that he was taking his place in ritual theatre—but while seeming hieratic to himself he would just seem phoney to us. And yet if he simply allows free rein to his personality, if he sees acting as a form of personal expression, another phoneyness can easily appear, which swamps the text in a morass of groans and cries, all stemming from a ready exposure of his own phobias and fears. The worst features of the experimental theatre come from a sincerity that is essentially insincere. Such a state is at once revealed when words appear, for a false emotion clogs clarity.

Of course, all acting is made by people and so is personal. Yet it is very important to try to distinguish between the form of personal expression that is useless and self-indulgent and the sort of expression in which being impersonal and being truly individual are one and the same thing. This confusion is a central problem of contemporary acting, and the attempt to stage this text of *Oedipus* brings it into focus.

How can the actor approach this text? One common method would be to identify himself with the character of the play. The actor looks for psychological similarities between Oedipus and himself. If I were Oedipus, he would say, I would do X, Y or Z because I remember that when my father . . . He tries to analyze Oedipus and Jocasta as "real people" and is bound to discover the total failure of this approach. Jocasta and Oedipus may be concentrations of human meaning—but they are not personalities.

There is another approach to acting which throws psychology aside, and seeks only to release the irrational in the actor's nature. He tries to cultivate a form of trance to awaken his subconscious and it is easy for him to think that he is getting closer to the level of universal myth. He can easily imagine that out of these he can draw valid dramatic material. But he must beware of being taken for a ride by a dream—the trip into the subconscious can be an illusion that feeds an illusion, and his acting remains where it was.

It is not enough for the actor to find his truth—it is not enough for him to be open blindly to impulses from sources inside himself that he cannot understand. He needs an understanding that must in turn ally itself to a wider mystery. He can only find this link through a tremendous awe and respect for what we call form. This form is the movement of the text, this form is his own individual way of capturing that movement.

It is not for nothing that the greatest of poets always have needed to work on existing material. *Oedipus* was never "invented": before the Greek dramatists there were the legends—the Roman writer reworked the same material—Shakespeare often reworked Seneca—and now Ted Hughes reworks Seneca and through him reaches the myth. And an interesting question arises: Why in great drama is there a wish amongst creative and inventive men not to invent? Why do they put so little store on personal invention? Is there a secret here? In serving a pre-existing pattern, it is not himself and his own meaning that the dramatist is trying to impose—it is something he is seeking to transmit. Yet to transmit properly he realizes that all of him—from his skills, his associations, to the deepest secrets of his subconscious—has to be potentially ready to leap into play, into rhythmic order, to act as carrier. The poet is a carrier, the words are carriers. So a meaning is caught in a net. Words drawn on paper are the mesh of the net. It is not for nothing that Ted Hughes, most individual of poets, is also the most concentrated. It is by his rigorous eliminating of all unnecessary decoration, all useless expressions of personality, that he gets to a form that is his own and not his own.

So we return to the actor. Can he be a carrier too—in the same way? It involves his understanding of two very difficult concepts: distance and presence. Distance as Brecht has described it means keeping his personality at arm's length. It means the individual voluntarily subduing many subjective impulses, because he wishes something to appear that for him is more objective. What can help to do this? Not a moral nor an artistic decision. Willful dehumanizing is mechanical, and many Brecht productions have shown how easy it is to fall into this trap—using the willpower of the intellect as a sort of Pentagon holding rebel elements at bay.

The only help is understanding; the more the actor understands his exact function on all levels, the more he finds the right performance pitch. To take a very simple example, a radio newsreader is intuitively impersonal and distant because he understands his function—he is a voice put at the disposal of making a news sheet clear—he needs clarity and tempo—his intonations must be neither too warm nor too dry—and yet for him to bring his personal emotions to bear on the information, coloring it according to whether the news makes him bright or sad, would be silly.

The actor's task is infinitely more complex than that of the newsreader. The way opens when he sees that presence is not opposed to distance. Distance is a commitment to total meaning: presence is a total commitment to the living moment; the two go together. For this reason, the most eclectic use of rehearsal exercises—to develop rhythm, listening, tempo, pitch, ensemble thinking or critical awareness—is most valuable provided none of them is considered a method. What they can do is to increase the actor's concern—in body and in spirit—for what the play is asking. If the actor truly feels this question to be his own he is unavoidably caught in a need to share it: in a need for the audience. Out of this need for a link with an audience comes an equally strong need for absolute clarity.

This is the need that eventually brings forth the means. It forges the living link with the poet's matrix, which in turn is the link with the original theme.

part IV

WHAT IS
A SHAKESPEARE?

. . .

SHAKESPEARE ISN'T A BORE
. . .

If my production of Romeo and Juliet has done nothing else, it has at least aroused controversy, which in itself is a good thing; the theatre has had too little of it lately. I have been criticized on many counts—some of them quite contradictory—but the significant thing is that in 1946 we are attempting a clean break with the accepted style of Shakespearean production, and the storm of controversy is some measure of our success.

The worldwide appeal of Shakespeare lay originally in the tremendously exciting, fast-moving, dramatic quality of the plays. But—let us confess it—however faithful to the text may have been the productions of the last century, Shakespeare has become, for the ordinary playgoer, a bit of a bore.

Each moment in Shakespeare should be as important as every other: each speaker should be the "lead" as he speaks—but what has happened? In the course of time, as the theatre developed, and with the advent of the picture-frame stage, the "star" and the actor-manager, supporting scenes have been trimmed, and single moments exploited. Thus, *Romeo and Juliet,* originally intended, mark you, to be played by two young boys as part of a team, has become the vehicle for the exercise of the talents of a pair of "great" artists.

It has been said that Shakespeare's poetry suffers from too "harsh" treatment at our hands: we have tried to convey the true feeling of poetry as understood by Raleigh, Sydney, Marlowe and Essex—not Tennyson and Coventry Patmore. To the Elizabethans, violence, passion and poetry were quite inseparable.

What I have attempted is to break away from the popular conception of *Romeo and Juliet* as a pretty-pretty, sentimental love story, and to get back to the violence, the passion, and the excitement of the stinking crowds, the feuds, the intrigues. To recapture the poetry and the beauty that arise from the Veronese sewer, and to which the story of the two lovers is merely incidental.

We knew before we started that to attempt anything so radical as a complete break with tradition in a play so well loved and popular was bound to arouse fierce antagonism. We were right—it has. And we welcome the criticism—it is healthy and it is helpful—but it is only by the judgment of people coming to Stratford-on-Avon purely to enjoy the performance, and with no preconceptions about Shakespearean production, that we shall be able to tell to what extent our attempt to find a new path for the 1940s is justified and is the right one.

AN OPEN LETTER TO WILLIAM SHAKESPEARE, OR, AS I DON'T LIKE IT . . .

· · ·

Dear William Shakespeare,

What has happened to you? We used to feel we could depend on you. We were prepared for our own efforts on stage sometimes to be approved of, sometimes not, in the normal run of things. Now it's you who are always getting such a terrible press. When the notices of *Titus Andronicus* came out, giving us all full marks for saving your dreadful play, I could not help feeling a twinge of guilt. For to tell the truth it had not occurred to any of us in rehearsal that the play was so bad.

Of course, we soon learned how wrong we were, and I for one would have accepted the view that this was your worst effort had I not been disturbed by certain other memories. When I staged *Love's Labor's Lost,* for instance, didn't a critic write that this was you at your "feeblest and silliest"? And *The Winter's Tale*—I can remember a review that said, "This is Shakespeare's worst play—preposterous longwinded rubbish." At the time I had labored under the delusion that *The Winter's Tale* was beautiful and wondrous, deeply moving in its unreality, a fable whose happy end, the statue coming to life, was a true miracle brought about by Leontes's new-found wisdom and for-

Titus Andronicus

giveness. I am afraid I had lost sight of the fact that no miracle counts, if it is too unlikely.

I suppose that bit by bit I should have been preparing myself to realize that *The Tempest* was your gravest mistake. I of course had wrongly held that it was your finest play; I had imagined it to be a *Faust* in reverse, the last in your final cycle of plays about mercy and forgiveness, a play that is throughout its length a storm, reaching calm waters only in its final pages. I had felt that you were in your right mind when you made it hard, craggy and dramatic. I felt that it was no accident that in the three plots you contrast a lonely, truth-seeking Prospero with lords crude and murderous, with greedy and darkly wicked clowns. And I felt that you had not suddenly forgotten about the rules of playwriting, such as the one of "making every character like someone-or-other in the audience," but you had deliberately put your greatest masterpiece a little farther away from us onto a higher level.

Now, after reading all the notices, I find that *The Tempest* is your worst play—the very worst, this time—and I must apologize to you for failing to disguise its weakness more thoroughly. Fortunately, I became aware of my mistake while still at Stratford and as I had a few days to spare before leaving, I thought I would go and see one of your accepted masterpieces. I looked up the program. *King John,* it said, and I was just about to book my ticket when I remembered reading that this play was a "shapeless mess"; so I decided not to waste time on it.

There was *Julius Caesar* the following night, but they had said this was "one of the dreary ones," so I skipped on to *Cymbeline* (I confess I've always had a sneaking love for the glowing fantasy of this tale). However, in the nick of time I took a glance at the theatre's press-cuttings book and found it universally agreed that although saved by the production, this was "as downright silly a piece of nonsense as *Titus Andronicus,*" and though normally I'd love to see fine production and acting, you'll understand that this time I just wanted to see a good play.

Then my eye was caught by the words *As You Like It.* There it was in bold letters: Matinee half-past two, *As You Like It,* the only play of yours against which I have never heard a word, the play above suspicion. So I paid my money and went in. Now I must confess it. I don't like your *As You Like It.* I'm sorry, but I find it far too hearty, a sort of advertisement for beer, unpoetic and, frankly, not very funny. When you have one villain repenting because he's nearly been eaten by a lion and another villain at the head of his army "converted from the world" because he happens to meet an "old religious man" and has "some question" with him, I really lose all patience.

So now, dear author, I don't know what to say. I find most of your plays miraculous—except *As You Like It.* The critics find most of your plays a bore—except *As You Like It.* The public loves them all—including *As You Like It.* Why this odd division? What links these strangely contradictory attitudes? Could the fact that I did *As You Like It* for School Certificate have anything to do with it? Would going as a professional duty to every new Shakespeare production, willy-nilly year in and year out, make them all merge into a nightmare School Certificate blur? I wonder.

WHAT IS A SHAKESPEARE?
• • •

I think that one of the things that is very little understood about Shakespeare is that he is not only of a different quality, he is also different in kind.

So long as one thinks that Shakespeare is just Ionesco but better, Beckett but richer, Brecht but more human, Chekhov with crowds, and so on, one is not touching what it's all about. If you can talk about cats and a bull, one sees that these are different species. In modern scientific analysis you would beware of the dangers of mixing categories, and talking about a person in category A as though he really belonged to category B. I think that this is what happens with Shakespeare in relation to other playwrights, and so I'd like to dwell for a moment on what this particular phenomenon is.

To me, this phenomenon is very simple. It is that authorship as we understand it in almost all other fields—in the way that one talks about the authorship of a book or poem, and today the authorship of a film when directors are called authors of their films, and so on—almost invariably means "personal expression." And therefore the finished work bears the marks of the author's own way of seeing life. It's a cliché of criticism that one comes across very often, "his world," "the world of this author." Now it's not for nothing that scholars who have tried so hard to find autobiographical traces in Shakespeare have had so little success. It doesn't matter in fact who wrote the plays and what biographical traces there are. The fact is that there is singularly little of the author's point of view—and his personality seems to be very hard to seize—throughout thirty-seven or thirty-eight plays.

If one takes those thirty-seven plays with all the radar lines of the different viewpoints of the different characters, one comes out with a field of incredible density and complexity; and eventually one goes a step further, and one finds that what happened, what passed through this man called Shakespeare and came into existence on sheets of paper, is something quite different from any other author's work. It's not Shakespeare's view of the world, it's something which actually resembles reality. A sign of this is that any single word, line, character or event has not only a large number of interpretations, but an unlimited number. Which is the characteristic of reality. I could say that is the characteristic of any action in the real world—say, the action you're doing now, at this moment, as we are talking together, of putting your hand against your head. An artist may try to capture and reflect your action, but actually he interprets it—so that a naturalistic painting, a Picasso painting, a photograph, are all interpretations. But in itself, the action of one man touching his head is open to unlimited understanding and interpretation. In reality, that is. What Shakespeare wrote carries that characteristic. What he wrote is not interpretation: it is the thing itself.

And if we're very bold, and think not in very constricting verbal terms, "He's an author, he wrote plays, the plays have scenes," and so on, but think much more broadly and say, "This creator created an enormous skein of interrelated words," and if we think of a chain of several hundred thousand words unfolding in a certain order, the whole making an extraordinary fabric, I think that then one begins to see the essential point. It is that his fabric reaches us today, not as a series of messages, which is what authorship almost always produces, but as a series of impulses that can produce many understandings. This is something quite different. It is like tea leaves in a cup. Think of the chance arrangement of tea leaves in a cup—the act of interpretation is a reflection of what is brought to the cup by the person looking at it. The whole act of interpreting tea leaves—or the fall of a sparrow, for that matter—is the unique meeting, at one point in time, between an event and the perceiver of the event.

I think two things come out of this. On the one hand, it is obvious that every interpretation of this material is a subjective act—what else could it be?—and that each person, whether it's a scholar writing, an actor acting, a director directing or a designer designing, brings to it— and always has and always will—his subjectivity. Which means that even if he tries to bridge the ages and say, "I leave myself and my century behind, and I'm looking at it with the eyes of its own period," this is impossible. A costume designer tries to interpret one period and at the same time he reflects his own epoch—so he produces a double image. We look at photographs of, say, Granville-Barker's productions —or we look at any production anywhere—and the double image is always there.

This is an unavoidable human fact. Each person brings what he is; there's no one walking around this world who has somehow dropped his personality. How you use your personality is the question. You can willfully and blindly give your ego free rein, or you can put your ego into play in a way that can help a truth to appear. For instance, the history of leading acting. The actor who's crude, bombastic, self-inflated, seizes on Shakespeare's plays because he sees, in their million facets, the facets which are food for his "me." He certainly gets a powerful energy out of what he finds, and the demonstration may be dazzling. But the play has gone, and the finer content, and many other levels of meaning are steam-rollered out of existence.

Of course, the theatre artist's relations with his material are basically affective, they come out of a love for and affinity with what he's doing. Doing a play as a solemn duty, with the highest level of respect, won't work. The mysterious and essential creative channel will not be opened by respect alone. So obviously for a director as for an actor the decision to do a certain play is purely instinctive and affective.

On the other hand, the danger that also has to be watched is when any of the artists or scholars dealing with a play by Shakespeare allow their love and excitement and enthusiasm to blind them to the fact that their interpretation can never be complete. There's an enormous danger that takes very precise form and leads to a form of acting that one's seen over many years, a form of directing, a form of designing, which proudly presents very subjective versions of the play without a glimmer of awareness that they might be diminishing the play—on the contrary, a vain belief that this is the play and more . . . not only Shakespeare's play, but Shakespeare's play as made into sense by such-and-such an individual. And that's where the virtue of having a feeling of love and enthusiasm has to be tempered by a cool sense that anybody's personal view of the play is bound to be less than the play itself.

I saw the other day an interview on French television with Orson Welles, on Shakespeare, where he started by saying something like "We all betray Shakespeare." The history of the plays shows them constantly being reinterpreted and reinterpreted, and yet remaining untouched and intact. Therefore they are always more than the last interpretation trying to say the last word on something on which the last word can't be said.

One of the first productions of Shakespeare that I did was *Love's Labor's Lost,* and at that point I felt and believed the work of a director was to have a vision of a play and to "express" it. I thought that's what a director was for. I was nineteen or twenty. I had always wanted to direct films, and in fact I started in films before going into the theatre. A film director shows his pictures to the world, and I thought a stage director did the same in another way. Even before I did *Love's Labor's Lost,* when I was up at Oxford I terribly wanted to do *Coriolanus,* and I remember very strongly that my way of wanting to do *Coriolanus* was sitting at a table and drawing pictures. I drew images of *Coriolanus,* which is the film director's way of wanting to bring into life a personal picture one has, a picture of Coriolanus walking away in brilliant sunlight—things like that.

When I did *Love's Labor's Lost,* I had a set of images in mind which I wanted to bring to life, just like making a film. So *Love's Labor's Lost* was a very visual, very romantic set of stage pictures. And I remember that from then all the way through to *Measure for Measure* my conviction was that the director's job, having found an affinity between himself and the play, was to find the images that he believed in and through them make the play live for a contemporary audience. In an image-conscious time, I believed designing and directing to be inseparable. A good industrial designer has to sense just what the shapes are for a particular moment, and therefore he produces the right car body, and so on. In exactly the same way I understood that a director studies deeply, is as in tune with the play as he can be, but that his real work is the making of a new set of images for it.

Since then, my view has changed, evolved, through a growing awareness that the overall unifying image was much less than the play itself. And eventually, as I worked more and more outside proscenium theatres and in forms of theatre where the overall image proved to be less and less necessary and important, it became clear that a play of Shakespeare, and therefore a production of Shakespeare, could go far beyond the unity that one man's imagination could give, beyond that of the director and designer. And it was only through discovering that there was far more to it than that that my interest moved from just liking the play, and therefore showing my own image of the play, to another process, which starts always with the instinctive feeling that the play needs to be done, now.

This is a big change of attitude: without thinking consciously or analytically, there is this sense that this play is meaningful in many ways at this moment which opens a new awareness. It's not only that it's meaningful for me autobiographically at this moment. At certain points in one's life one can identify with and wish to do a youthful play, a bitter play, a tragic play. This is fine, but one can then go beyond to see how a whole area of living experience that seems close to one's own concerns is also close to the concerns of the people in the world around one. When these elements come together, then is the time to do that play, and not another.

Fortunately, I've never been in the position of having to do lots of plays systematically. I think it's always destructive to have to do plays in this way. For years I wanted to do *Lear,* I wanted to do *Antony and Cleopatra,* and I did them. I never wanted to do a *Twelfth Night.* These are purely personal things. I think that every director has them that way, plays he's more drawn to, and every actor too. But I would now say that that's our loss: choosing plays is a Rorschach test by which you can tell the openness and blinkeredness of each individual. Because if I could sympathize and empathize with every one of Shakespeare's plays, and every one of his characters, I would be that much the richer, and I think that goes for any actor. And if a theatre were to take on the task of doing the entire work of Shakespeare, out of an absolute conviction that this is the greatest school of life that they know, that group would be an astonishing group in human terms.

A fuller attitude begins to shape itself when we have not only a response to what we like and dislike, but when we respond to what we can discover through working on the play. This is a very big step, because as long as one's in the first instinct, "I like this, I want to do it," one is most likely within the closed circle of wishing to illustrate what one likes. "I like it, and I'll show you why I like it." The next step is, "I like it, because it parallels all that I need to know about the world." If I spend three months on a play, at the end of that time my wish to understand will have taken me further into its complexity, and it will do the same for an audience. So personal expression ceases to be an aim and we go toward shared discovery.

THE TWO AGES OF GIELGUD

• • •

We had assembled for the first reading of *Measure for Measure* at Stratford. It must have been about 1951. I had never worked with John Gielgud before, nor had most of the actors. The occasion was nerve-wracking, and not only because this time the reading was going to take place in the presence of a legend. Gielgud's reputation at the time inspired both love and awe, and as a result each actor was thrilled to be there and dreading the moment when he would have to be seen and heard.

To break the ice I made a short speech, then asked the actor playing the Duke to begin. He opened his text, waited for a moment, then boldly declaimed the first line. "Escalus!"

Gielgud listened attentively.

"My lord?" came the answer, and in those two words, hardly audible, one could hear the panic of a young actor, wishing for the ground to open and playing safe with a token murmur.

"Peter!" From John came an impulsive, agonized cry of alarm. "He's not really going to say it like that, is he?"

The words had flown out of John's mouth before he could stop them. But just as swiftly he sensed the dismay of his poor fellow actor and immediately was contrite and confused. "Oh, I'm so sorry, dear boy, do forgive me. I know, it'll be splendid. Sorry everyone, let's go on."

In John, tongue and mind work so closely together that it is sufficient for him to think of something for it to be said. Everything in him is moving all the time, at lightning speed—a stream of consciousness flows from him without pause. His flickering, darting tongue reflects everything around and inside him: his wit, his joy, his anxiety, his sadness, his appreciation of the tiniest detail of life and work. In fact, every observation once made is spoken; his tongue is the sensitive instrument that captures the most delicate shades of feeling in his acting and just as readily produces gaffes, indiscretions and outrageous puns which are as much part of the very special complex called John.

John is a mass of contradictions which happily have never been resolved and which are the motors of his art. There is in him an actor-reactor, quick on the draw, answering before the question is put, highly strung, confusing and ever so impatient. Yet tempering his

John-in-perpetual-motion is the John-of-intuitions, who winces at every excess, his own or others.

It is always thrilling to work with the impatient John. Directing him is a dialogue, a collaboration—it has to be, it could not be anything else. You begin to suggest something, "John, perhaps you could enter from the right and . . ." Before you can finish your sentence, he has applauded the idea, agreed, is ready to try it, but before he has taken two steps he has seen five objections, ten new possibilities and is proposing, "But, what if I come from the left . . ." and if that in turn

Irene Worth and John Gielgud

suggests something new to you, he will already have discarded his thoughts to explore your own.

He loves "changing the moves" in rehearsals and of course he is right. "Moves" in the theatre are just the outer expression of ideas and, hopefully, ideas change and develop all the time. But many actors have difficulty keeping up with his tempo, become resentful, long to be told once and for all what they have to do and then be left alone. For such actors, John sometimes seems maddening, impossible. It is said that as he leaves the stage after a last performance he is still changing the moves.

He seems to have no method, which is in itself a method that has always worked wonders. His inconsistency is the truest of consistencies. He is like an aircraft circling before it can land. He has a standard, intuitively perceived, whose betrayal causes him deep pain. He will change and change indefinitely, in search of rightness—and nothing is ever right. For this reason, it has always been absolutely necessary for him to work with the best actors and his generosity toward them in performance comes from his need for quality, which has always been infinitely more important to him than his own personal success. When he directs, often he neglects his own performance and one has grown accustomed to seeing him in a leading role standing to the side, back turned to the audience, an observer, deeply involved in the work of others.

Despite his great gifts as a director, as an actor he needs to be directed. When he develops a part, he has too many ideas: they pile in so fast, hour after hour, day after day, that in the end the variation on top of variation, the detail added to details all overload and clog his original impulses. When we worked together, I found that the most important time was just before the first performance, when I had to help him ruthlessly to scrap ninety percent of his over-rich material and remind him of what he had himself discovered at the start. Deeply self-critical, he would always cut and discard without regret. When we did *Measure for Measure,* he was inspired by the name of Angelo and spent long, secret hours with the wigmaker, preparing an angelic wig of shoulder-length blond locks. At the dress rehearsal no one was allowed to see him, until he came onto the stage, delighted at his new disguise. To his surprise, we all howled our disapproval. "Ah!" he sighed. "Goodbye, my youth!" There were no regrets and the next day he made a triumph, appearing for the first time with a bald head.

The last time we worked together was Seneca's *Oedipus* at the Old

Vic. I accepted to do the play uniquely for the pleasure of working with John again after many years, although in the meantime my own way of approaching theatre had greatly changed. Instead of starting with the first reading, I now spent a long period doing exercises, largely involving bodily movement. In the company, there were a number of young actors very eager to work in this way and there were also several older actors for whom all these methods seemed dangerous new fads. The young actors angrily despised the older actors in return and to my horror, they regarded John as a symbol of a theatre they had rejected.

On the first day, I suggested some exercises that demanded considerable physical involvement. We sat in a circle and the actors tried the first exercise one by one. When John's turn came, there was a moment of tension. What would he do? The older actors hoped he would refuse.

John knew that after the confident young actors he could only appear ridiculous. But as always, his reaction was immediate. He plunged in. He tried, he tried humbly, clumsily, with all he could bring. He was no longer the star, a superior being. He was quite simply there, struggling with his body, as the others would be later with their words, with an intensity and a sincerity that were his own. In a matter of seconds, his relation with the group was transformed. It was no longer the name or the reputation of Gielgud that mattered. Everyone present had glimpsed the real John, he had bridged the generation gap and from that moment he was held in true admiration and respect.

John is always in the present; he is modern in his restless quest for truth and new meaning. He is also traditional, for his passionate sense of quality comes from his understanding of the past. He links two ages. He is unique.

SHAKESPEAREAN REALISM

• • •

Everyone has a sort of shrewd suspicion that all great art is "real," but nobody agrees on what the word means. As a result, the very precise work involved in staging a play can easily get muddled by a large band of people valiantly seeking completely different things.

Any child today knows that at any given moment through his living room disembodied images are invisibly floating toward the television set; he knows that the substance he breathes called air (which he cannot see but believes exists) is throbbing with equally concealed vibrations of musicians, comedians and BBC announcers. As he grows older, he learns about the subconscious. Long before he is out of school, he is aware that his father's stolid silences may be concealing a volcanic flow of pent-up hates, that his sister's blithe chatter may be a counterpoint to an inner rumble of obsessive guilt.

By the time he is old enough to be a theatregoer he will have already learned from films if not from life that space and time are loose and meaningless terms: that with a cut the mind can flick from yesterday to Australia.

So he will realize that the distinction between the realistic play and the poetic one, between the naturalistic and the stylized is artificial and very old-fashioned. He will see that the problem of the play that takes place in a living room or in a kitchen is no longer that it is *too* realistic but that it is not realistic at all. He will realize that although the chairs and tables are undoubtedly genuine, everything else smells false. He will sense that the so-called real dialogue and the so-called real acting do not actually capture that totality of information, visible and invisible, that corresponds to what he instinctively knows as reality.

So we come to Shakespeare. For centuries our practical understanding of Shakespeare has been blocked by the false notion that Shakespeare was a writer of far-fetched plots which he decorated with genius. Too long we have considered Shakespeare in separate compartments, dividing the story from the characters, the verse from the philosophy. Today we are beginning to see that Shakespeare forged a style in advance of any style anywhere, before or *since,* that enabled him, in a very compact space of time, by a superb and conscious use of varied means, to create a realistic image of life.

Let me take a far-fetched parallel. Picasso began to paint portraits with several eyes and noses the day he felt that to paint a profile—or to paint full face—was a form of lie. He set out to find a technique with which to capture a larger slice of the truth. Shakespeare, knowing that man is living his everyday life and at the same time is living intensely in the invisible world of his thoughts and feelings, developed a method through which we can see at one and the same time the look on the man's face and the vibrations of his brain. We can hear the particular rhythm of speech and choice of slang by which we would know him at once as a character in real life, with a name, as though we met him on the street. But in the street his face might be blank and his tongue silent—Shakespeare's verse gives density to the portrait. This is the purpose of the striking metaphor, the purple passage, the ringing phrase. It can no longer be held for one second that such plays are "stylized," "formalized" or "romantic" as opposed to "realistic."

Our problem is to bring the actor, slowly, step by step, toward an understanding of this remarkable invention, this curious structure of free verse and prose which a few hundred years ago was already the Cubism of the theatre. We must wean the actor away from a false belief: that there is a heightened playing for the classics, a more real playing for the works of today. We must get him to see that the challenge of the verse play is that he must bring to it an even deeper search for truth, for truth of emotion, truth of ideas, and truth of character—all quite separate and yet all interwoven—and then as an artist find, with objectivity, the form that gives these meanings life.

The problem for the actor is to find a way of dealing with verse. If he approaches it too emotionally, he can end up in empty bombast; if he approaches it too intellectually, he can lose the ever-present humanity; if he is too literal, he gains the commonplace and loses the true meaning. Here are great problems, related to technique, imagination, and living experience that have to be solved in creating an ensemble. Eventually, we want to have actors who know with such certainty that there is no contradiction between the heightened and the real that they can slide effortlessly between the gears of verse and prose, following the modulations of the text.

We must move the productions and the settings away from all that played so vital a part in the postwar Stratford renaissance—away from romance, away from fantasy, away from decoration. Then they were necessary for shaking the ugliness and the boredom off these well-worn texts. Now we must look beyond an outer liveliness to an inner one. Outer splendor can be exciting but has little relation with modern life: on the inside lie themes and issues, rituals and conflicts which are as valid as ever. Any time the Shakespearean meaning is caught, it is "real" and so contemporary.

In the same way, in a country that has become very theatre-conscious, and which happens also to possess such a fantastic heritage, one question must be why no present-day English dramatist approaches the beginnings of Shakespearean power and freedom. Why, we must ask in the mid-twentieth century, are we more timid and more constipated in the ambition and scope of our thinking than the Elizabethans?

When we perform the classics, we know that their deepest reality will never speak for itself. Our efforts and our technique are to make them speak clearly through us. I think our responsibility toward the modern drama is to see that the reality of everyday life will not speak for itself either. We can record it, film it, jot it down, but we will be far from catching its nature. We see that Shakespeare in his day found the answer in his verse and prose structure related to the peculiar freedom of the Elizabethan stage. This can teach us something, and it is no coincidence that the modern theatre is moving toward open stages and is using surrealism of behavior in the place of verse as a technique for cracking open surface appearances. Our great opportunity and our challenge in Stratford and London is to endeavor to relate our work on Shakespeare and our work on modern plays to the search for a new style—dreadful word, I would prefer to say anti-style—which would enable dramatists to synthesize the self-contained achievements of the Theatre of the Absurd, the epic theatre and the naturalistic theatre. This is where our thinking must go and where our experiments must thrust.

LEAR—CAN IT BE STAGED?

• • •

Peter Brook talks to Peter Roberts during rehearsals of King Lear *at Stratford-on-Avon in 1962.*

ROBERTS: The Lear of Shakespeare cannot be acted, said Charles Lamb. "To see Lear acted is to see an old man tottering about the stage with a walking-stick, turned out of doors by his daughters in a rainy night!" Obviously you wouldn't agree with this, otherwise you would not be staging it. But do you think there is at least some truth in what Lamb said?

BROOK: No, none at all. Lamb was talking about the stage of his day and the way plays were staged in his time. Who said that Shakespeare laid down that you have to see a poor old man tottering with a stick into the storm? I think that's absolute nonsense.

I would say that *King Lear* is probably Shakespeare's greatest play and for this reason it's the most difficult. The terrible thing one finds all the time is that it's harder to do masterpieces than anything else. We were complaining of this the other evening at rehearsal and there was James Booth with a skipping rope saying, "Would it be amusing if we did the whole scene skipping?" and I replied, "The tragedy of having to do a play that is so marvellous is that you can't do that kind of thing. Only where you really feel confident that bits are badly written or boring does one have the freedom to invent skipping ropes and so forth." You know I once did a production of *King John* years ago where we had a medieval newsreel and a man who was the equivalent of the King's newsreelman following the King everywhere. Alas, you can't do this with a masterpiece. It has to be done only one way: the right way. And because of that it's very difficult to find.

We're now coming back more and more to appreciating that not only do the later plays of Shakespeare have marvellous things to be found in them but that so also do the lesser roles. *Lear,* for example, has been very much mishandled and mistreated because people haven't recognized the fact that *King Lear* is not a play about King Lear and the others in the way that, from a certain point of view, *Hamlet* is about Hamlet. All the other characters are essential and are marvellous playing parts but they all relate to Hamlet. Hamlet is the pivot of all activity in the play while, in *Lear,* the total structure of the play is the composite meaning of eight or ten independent and eventually equally important strands of narrative. The strands that start in the whole subplot about Gloucester eventually become, when they intertwine, the complete play. The result is that one comes up against the fact that the play as written by Shakespeare to be truly revealed on the stage needs not only a capital performance in the part of Lear but equally illuminating acting all the way through. And I think that it is here— rather than in the problem of staging the storm—that the real challenge and the real difficulty of *Lear* lie.

I've examined the traditional cuts (you know, around the theatre here there are books with all the cuts that have been made over the years) and have been interested to find that while lots of them make sense, they all lose something. Cutting prevents the actors of smaller parts having the material to build three-dimensional figures and so the net result is the destruction of the real texture of the play.

I've found that there are lots of places where, through filling in the traditional cuts, one suddenly sees—oh, the whole fascination of the play. For instance, one finds that most times one sees the play done in the cut version, one lumps together Goneril and Regan as two identical women and their husbands, Cornwall and Albany, as just two chaps. Yet the difference between them is quite amazing. For example, the Goneril-Regan relationship is a completely Jean Genet one, where Goneril is consistently dominant and where Regan is soft and weak. Goneril wears the boots and Regan wears the skirt. Goneril's masculinity continually fires Regan, whose squelchy softness of core is very opposed to the steely hardness of her sister. This relationship develops very interestingly through the second part of the play (I'm dividing it into two parts) because one sees that disaster and troubles make Goneril more and more dominant and harder. Regan, on the other hand, completely goes under and in the end creeps ignominiously off the stage poisoned in the stomach like a squashed spider, whereas Goneril takes her leave defiantly.

There is, too, a tremendous difference between Albany in all his weakness, tolerance and confusion, and Cornwall—impetuous, fiery and sadistic. All this interesting character material comes to light when you don't cut.

The key problem, one that I have been pondering upon for the year I've been preparing this production, is whether to fix the production specifically in a certain place at a certain time. You can't say that *Lear* is timeless, which is what the interesting but unfortunate Noguchi experiment at the Palace in 1955 proved. In his program note to that production, George Devine wrote, "We're trying to show with timeless costumes and timeless sets the timelessness of the play"—an apology which didn't actually touch the core of the problem. Although in a sense it is timeless (that's a sort of critic's comment), in actual fact it is taking place in big, violent and therefore very realistic circumstances, with flesh and blood actors in very harsh, cruel and realistic situations.

The key problem is—how are they dressed, what do they wear? Looking at the evidence of the play, one has got two contradictory necessities: the play has to take place, unless you put it into science fiction, in the past; yet it cannot take place in any period after William the Conqueror. Even though I've long since forgotten the kings and queens of England, I roughly remember the order, and I know that ninety percent of our audiences know that sandwiched between Henry VI and someone else there didn't happen to be a King Lear.

So there is something that is shocked in one's belief if one acts *Lear* Elizabethan or Renaissance, particularly as there is another element that is strong in the play—its pre-Christian nature. The ferocity and horror of the play is destroyed if you try to tip it into Christianity. The imagery of the play and the gods who are continually invoked are pagan ones.

Lear's society is primitive. On the other hand, it is clearly not primitive Stonehenge because if you go back to that you find another falsity, which is that *Lear* is, at the same time, a very sophisticated society. For it is not a society of people that live in the open air surrounded by ceremonial stones. To put the play back to that period is to lose the essential cruelty, which is the cruelty of turning a man outdoors. The people who are indoors feel the difference between the elements and the man-made solid world from which Lear is expelled. If the King is used to sleeping out of doors, the play is shattered. Furthermore the language of the play is not the language of that book of William Golding's where the inhabitants just say "Og" and "Gug." It is true language of high Renaissance. So it seems to me that the problem one has to face is that one has to create a pre-Christian society which for present-day audiences has the smell of belonging to an early part of history. At the same time, that early part of history has to be a moment of history where, for these people, they were in as high a state of development as was the Mexican society before Cortés or ancient Egypt at its peak.

So *Lear* is barbaric and Renaissance; it's those two contradictory periods.

Then we come back to the modern, the timeless school. It is not that the issue of the play is about a king and a fool and cruel daughters. In a way it is so much loftier than any historical setting that the only thing one can equate it to is a modern play such as Beckett might write. Who knows what is the period of *Waiting for Godot?* It is happening today and yet it has its own period in reality. That is also essential to *Lear* because *Lear* for me is the prime example of the Theatre of the Absurd, from which everything in good modern drama has been drawn.

The aim again of the setting is to produce a degree of simplification which enables the things that matter to be more apparent, because the play is hard enough without the added problem that any form of romantic decoration adds. Why does one decorate a bad play? For that purpose—to decorate it. With *Lear,* on the contrary, one has to withdraw everything possible.

With Keegan Smith, who runs the wardrobe at Stratford, we've evolved costumes which carry the minimum necessary real statement that each character needs. For instance, King Lear himself has to wear a robe because I think that you can't go round this point. There are certain necessities for an actor as Lear. Even if you take everything else away from him, he has to enter with something that covers his legs for a certain regality of the character to appear. He has a robe, therefore, which no one else has. There's no one else in the play who needs one. At the very beginning of the play, then, he has a robe which is very rich, and after that he goes into a very simple costume made of leather. All the other costumes we have simplified so that only the essential remains. When in a Shakespeare production you have thirty or forty equally elaborate costumes, the eye is blurred and the plot becomes hard to follow. Here, we only gave important costumes to eight or nine central characters—the number one can normally focus on in a modern play. It is interesting to hear people saying, "How clear the play seems!" without realizing that the secret was related to the clothes.

And the setting has also been immensely simplified. My real aim is to try to give ourselves conditions in which we can in the modern theatre follow what Shakespeare does on the page, which is to put completely different styles and conventions side by side without any feeling of uncomfortable anachronism. One needs to accept the very anachronisms as a strength of this form of theatre and as a pointer to the methods we have to find to stage it.

ROBERTS: How have you approached music and sound effects in this production?

BROOK: I don't think there is any place for music in *Lear* at all. As regards sound effects, the storm is the key problem. If you try to stage it realistically, you have to go the full Reinhardt way. Yet if you go to the other extreme, which is to have the storm taking place in the audience's imagination, it cannot work because the essence of drama is conflict and the drama of the storm is Lear's conflict with it. Lear needs the wall of the storm to fight against and this cannot be done if the storm is indicated intellectually—i.e., by flying in placards saying "This is the storm." That would be giving the conflict of the storm to the minds of the audience, whereas it must also be an emotionally charged thing.

After months of working on this problem it suddenly struck us how effective would be a thunder sheet on view on the stage. The vibrations of a large sheet of rusty metal have, as anybody knows who has watched a stage manager shaking a thunder sheet, a curiously disturbing quality. The noise is, of course, disturbing but so also is the fact that you see it vibrating. The thunder sheets on view in this production of *Lear,* then, give the King a firm source of conflict without at the same time attempting to stage the storm realistically, which never really works.

ROBERTS: Over the years you have come more and more to design your own productions as you are doing with this *King Lear.* Why?

BROOK: Although I have loved working with designers, I find that it is terribly important in Shakespeare in particular that I design myself. You never know whether your ideas and the designer's are evolving at the same rate. You come to a portion of the play that you cannot find your way through. At that point the designer finds a solution which seems to fit and which you are bound to accept, with the result that your own thinking on that scene becomes frozen. If you are doing it yourself, it means that over a long period of time your imagery and your staging evolve together.

Anyway, I doubt whether there is any designer living who would have the patience to work with me. After working for a year on this *King Lear* I scrapped the whole of my original set when the production was postponed. As it happened the new set cost about £5,000 less, so nobody minded.

EXPLODING STARS

• • •

Just as in astronomy a certain planet swings closer to the earth in its orbit, and all the astronomers get out their telescopes because this is the moment to study it to advantage, in the same way for the first time in four centuries the Elizabethan era with all its values has swung closer to us than it has ever been.

Similarly within the galaxy of plays, there are plays that move closer to us at certain moments of history, and some that move away. As I write, the bitterness and cynicism of *Timon of Athens* is bringing it nearer, out of oblivion, whilst Othello's jealousy seems to be drifting away.

So we have every reason today to wish to throw off all influences that still reach us from the nineteenth century, for that happens to be the time when the Elizabethan age was at its farthest point from us— virtually in total eclipse.

As I write this, we are on tour with *King Lear* in European countries where the nineteenth-century tradition is even more firmly embedded than in England. This is for two reasons. One is that all these countries know Shakespeare through translations, and the golden age of Shakespearean translating has been within the last hundred years. In Germany, for instance, a child's first encounter with Shakespeare is in the Schlegel-Tieck version, which is early nineteenth-century and very romantic. It's as though *Hamlet* were only known as translated by Byron, *Lear* by Shelley or *Romeo and Juliet* by Keats. So that the tendency which is already there of regarding Shakespeare as a great Victorian poet is enhanced: that it's all about castles and cliffs and brooding storms.

Also, before the war it was universally accepted that everyone in the world knew how to produce and act Shakespeare except the English, who, apart from a few lonely exceptions, had nothing to compare with the grand old-fashioned European productions.

I think we made a dent in a number of traditions. Our audiences were often surprised, but, happily, they came away convinced. They were surprised by the fact that Lear is not a feeble, but a strong old man; that he isn't pathetic, sentimental, but hard and obstinate, powerful and often wrong. They discovered that Regan and Goneril aren't villainesses, but women shown in depth who, although their deepest motives have no justification, always manage to find some apparent, and even sincere, reason for the small incidents that build up to the final cruelties. They are surprised by the different strands running through the production, because the tradition has always been that it's the story of Lear alone. Here they see the story of Edmund, Edgar, Gloucester, and so on. Cordelia has the same strength and weight as her sisters, just as the genetic resemblance between the three is clear. They are all Lear's daughters; Cordelia's goodness is uncompromising and tough in an inherited, Lear-like way.

The cruelty caused controversy. There were those who said it wasn't in the play, and others who were forced to admit that it came from nowhere else.

One of the things that makes Elizabethan plays so relevant today is that the deeper you go into Europe, the more related they are to contemporary history. In the countries which have known constant revolutions and coups d'état, the violence of *King Lear* has a more immediate meaning. In Budapest, when Lear comes on in the last scene—the cruelest scene, because the hanging of Cordelia is gratuitous and not in any way the result of classic tragic causes—he carries Cordelia dead in his arms, and there are no words, only that great howl. At that moment I felt the audience was moved by something much more considerable than the sentimental image of a poor old father howling. Lear was suddenly the figure of old Europe, tired, and feeling, as almost every country in Europe does, that after the events of the last fifty years people have borne enough, that some kind of respite might be due.

The last line of the play is unique in Shakespeare. All his other plays suggest an optimistic future; no matter how terrible the events that have passed, there is hope that they will not happen again. In *Lear,* the last line poses a question. Edgar says: "We that are young shall never see so much, nor live so long," and no one can give a simple explanation of this. It is loaded with inexplicable hints of tremendous meanings. It forces you to look at a young man, his eye naturally on the future, who has lived through most horrifying times.

POINTS OF RADIANCE
• • •

The unique nature of the Shakespearean material is that it's endlessly moving, endlessly changing. The plays in themselves seem to be static objects because you see them on a shelf. One says, "If that book's on a shelf, and I go out of the room, when I come back it will still be there," and it's still there—therefore one believes it's static. It isn't. I've just been reading *Tarzan* to my little son, and when Tarzan first discovered a book he saw little squiggles on a page, and he felt they were little bugs. He looked at them: "What are these little bugs?" and he came back and there were more little bugs. It's marvellously right, because I think that Shakespeare's plays, deceptively in hard covers, are big bugs within which there are smaller and smaller bugs. And when the grown-ups go to bed, they move.

I'll give you an example. I've been working in France on a translation of *Timon of Athens,* for the French. Most French audiences have only seen four or five plays of Shakespeare. They have seen *Coriolanus* and therefore conclude that Shakespeare is a Fascist. He's a great writer, they say, but he's a Fascist. I know that when they go to see *Timon,* it's going to be very disturbing for them because suddenly this same author, who's proved to them that he only likes generals, who despises the crowd, has now written a play in which you see that the only honest people are the servants. So the Fascist is a democrat after all. And if you put one play next to another, or one character beside another, or one thought against another, it's like a fortune teller dealing out again and again the same pack of cards. As they fall on the table, always in a fresh order, patterns shift, new images arise, meaning, content and implication are always on the move.

This comes out even further working on a translation. I'm working with a very imaginative and intelligent French writer, Jean-Claude Carrière, and he asks constantly, "What does this mean? What exactly does this word mean?" He knows English very well, he brings out a dictionary: Does it mean this, or this? And I say: Both. And so the word begins to take on more and more dimensions, until he says, "Ah, now I understand. These are 'des mots rayonnants.' "

I thought this was very interesting, because that was how he understood the different sort of syntax he was trying to translate, finding what words in a language where the mot juste has only one sense could match the many-levelled ambiguities of the original. When you have a word that has these resonances, you can see how from it you can draw a line to a level of meaning in the third word, or you can draw a line to the fifth word, or another line to the fifteenth word, and once again you get into infinite combinations.

When I started work on Shakespeare, I did believe to a limited extent in the possibility of a classical word music, that each verse had a sound that was correct, with only moderate variations; then through direct experience I found that this was absolutely and totally untrue. The more musical the approach you bring to Shakespeare, which means the more sensitive you are to music, the more you find that there is no way, except by sheer pedantry, that can fix a line's music. It just can't exist. In exactly the same way, an actor who tries to set his performance is doing something anti-life. While he has to keep certain consistencies in what he's doing or it's just a chaotic performance, as he speaks it, each single line can reopen itself to a new music, made round these radiating points.

DIALECTICS OF RESPECT

• • •

Should we respect the text? I think there is a healthy double attitude, with respect on the one hand and disrespect on the other. And the dialectic between the two is what it's all about. If you go solely one or the other way, you lose the possibility of capturing the truth. I think that Shakespeare's plays are not all written with the same degree of finish. Some plays are looser and some plays are tighter. In *A Midsummer Night's Dream* I didn't have the least wish to cut a word, to cut or transpose anything, for the simple and very personal reason that it seemed to me an absolutely perfect play. In treating it as something you don't pull around, you have a much greater chance of getting into its depths. It helps to have the absolute conviction that each word is there because it has to be; by total belief in a text you find its rightness.

Alan Howard played over two or three years with an ever-greater sense of secret meanings, on many levels endlessly discovered and rediscovered, of vibrations passing through Theseus into Oberon and back again across the whole play. And the play was at its best when the whole cast was at its most sensitive, so that it became like those sculptures made out of tight wires in a complex pattern; when the wires aren't tight, you don't get the pattern. So, with the *Dream,* although I can well imagine being very entertained by somebody taking a totally iconoclastic view of the plot and turning it upside down, I'm certain I would find it a diminishing of the play itself because I don't think you can change a word without losing something.

However, in other plays you can move words and scenes, but you have to do it in full recognition of how dangerous it is. And I think that this is really something for which there are no rules. What in one line doesn't really matter, in another line matters like hell. One must trust one's judgment and take the consequences.

SHAKESPEARE IS A PIECE OF COAL

• • •

History is a way of looking at things, but not one that interests me very much. I'm interested in the present. Shakespeare doesn't belong to the past. If his material is valid, it is valid now.

It's like coal. One knows the whole process of the primeval forest and how it goes down into the ground and one can trace the history of coal; but the meaningfulness of a piece of coal to us starts and finishes with it in combustion, giving out the light and heat that we want. And that to me is Shakespeare. Shakespeare is a piece of coal that is inert. I could write books and give public lectures about where coal comes from—but I'm really interested in coal on a cold evening, when I need to be warm and I put it on the fire and it becomes itself. Then it relives its virtue.

Now take this one step further. I think that today our understanding of perception is changing greatly, and we are beginning to recognize that the human faculty of perception is not static, but is a second-by-second redefining of what it sees. Look at those visual conundrums where you don't know if something is upside down—you know, black and white squares that seem to be jumping inside out. You can actually see how the mind copes with something which it is trying to re-understand, as it tries to verify whether the cube is upside down or not. The mind is constantly trying to remake a coherent world out of such impressions.

To me, the total works of Shakespeare are like a very complete set of codes, and these codes, cipher for cipher, stir in us vibrations and impulses which we immediately try to make coherent. If we accept this way of looking at Shakespeare's writing, we see that our present-day consciousness is our own aid. And this consciousness into which we plunge has of course its own dark forests, its own underground, its own stratosphere. The strange corners of Shakespeare's work that at first sight seem archaic or remote can, if we let them, awake secret zones in ourselves. This is the approach that can help one to discover a sense behind the apparently senseless brutalities in *Titus Andronicus.* In *The Tempest* or *A Midsummer Night's Dream,* the unavoidable question, "How do we stage fairies and spirits?" cannot be solved by aesthetic devices, because on an immediate level "fairy" suggests nothing to the modern mind, so there would be nothing to dress up. However, by dwelling on the image "fairy," it gradually becomes clear that the fairy world is a manner of speaking in symbolic language of all that is lighter and swifter than the human mind. "Swift as meditation," says Hamlet. A fairy is the capacity to transcend natural laws and enter into the dance of particles of energy moving with incredible speed. What theatre imagery could enable human bodies to suggest bodilessness? Certainly not gossamer schoolgirls.

Sitting with Sally Jacobs the designer, seeing Chinese acrobats, we found the key: a human being who, by pure skill, demonstrates joyfully that he can transcend his natural constraints, become a reflection of pure energy. This said "fairy" to us. A new imagery could begin to flow from Sally's rich creativity.

This is just one example. The word "fairy," passed through the analytical, culture- and history-conscious lobes of our brain, can only throw up dead associations. But if we listen differently, far behind we can perceive living values! If we can touch them, the coal begins to burn.

THE PLAY IS THE MESSAGE

• • •

People have often asked me: "What is the theme of *A Midsummer Night's Dream?*" There is only one answer to that question, the same as one would give regarding a cup. The quality of a cup is its cupness. I say this by way of introduction, to show that if I lay so much stress on the dangers involved in trying to define the themes of the *Dream* it is because too many productions, too many attempts at visual interpretation are based on preconceived ideas, as if these had to be illustrated in some way. In my opinion we should first of all try to rediscover the play as a living thing; then we shall be able to analyze our discoveries. Once I have finished working on the play, I can begin to produce my theories. It was fortunate that I did not attempt to do so earlier because the play would not have yielded up its secrets.

At the center of the *Dream,* constantly repeated, we find the word "love." Everything comes back to this, even the structure of the play, even its music. The quality the play demands from its performers is to build up an atmosphere of love during the performance itself, so that this abstract idea—for the word "love" is in itself a complete abstraction—may become palpable. The play presents us with forms of love which become less and less blurred as it goes on. "Love" soon begins to resound like a musical scale and little by little we are introduced to its various modes and tones.

Love is, of course, a theme which touches all men. No one, not even the most hardened, the coldest or the most despairing, is insen-

A Midsummer Night's Dream

sitive to it, even if he does not know what love is. Either his practical experience confirms its existence or he suffers from its absence, which is another way of recognizing that it exists. At every moment the play touches something which concerns everyone.

As this is theatre, there must be conflicts, so this play about love is also a play about the opposite of love, love and its opposite force. We are brought to realize that love, liberty and imagination are closely connected. Right at the beginning of the play, for example, the father in a long speech tries to obstruct his daughter's love and we are surprised that such a character, apparently a secondary role, should have so long a speech—until we discover the real importance of his words.

What he says not only reflects a generation gap (a father opposing his daughter's love because he had intended her for someone else), it also explains the reasons for his feeling of suspicion toward the young man whom his daughter loves. He describes him as an individual prone to fantasy, led by his imagination—an unpardonable weakness in the father's eyes.

From this starting point we see, as in any of Shakespeare's plays, a confrontation. Here it is between love and its opposing qualities, between fantasy and solid common sense—caught in an endless series of mirrors. As usual, Shakespeare confuses the issue. If we asked someone's opinion on the father's point of view, he might say, for example, that "The father is in the wrong because he is against freedom of the imagination," a very widespread attitude today.

In this way, for most present-day audiences, the girl's father comes over as the classical father figure who misunderstands young people and their flights of fancy. But later on, we discover surprisingly that he is right, because the imaginative world in which this lover lives causes him to behave in a quite disgusting way toward the very same daughter: as soon as a drop of liquid falls into his eyes, acting as a drug which liberates natural tendencies, he not only jilts her but his love is transformed into violent hate. He uses words which might well be borrowed from *Measure for Measure,* denouncing the girl with the kind of vehemence that, in the Middle Ages, led people to burn one another at the stake. Yet at the end of the play we are once more in agreement with the Duke, who rejects the father in the name of love. The young man has now been transformed.

So we observe this game of love in a psychological and metaphysical context; we hear Titania's assertion that the opposition between herself and Oberon is fundamental, primordial. But Oberon's acts deny this, for he perceives that within their opposition a reconciliation is possible.

The play covers an extraordinarily broad range of universal forces and feelings in a mythical world, which suddenly changes, in the last part, into high society. We find ourselves back in the very real palace: and the same Shakespeare who, a few pages earlier, offered us a scene of pure fantasy between Titania and Oberon, where it would be absurd to ask prosaic questions like "Where does Oberon live?" or, "When describing a queen like Titania did Shakespeare wish to express political ideas?" now takes us into a precise social environment. We are present at the meeting point of two worlds, that of the workmen and the court, the world of wealth and elegance, and alleged sensitivity, the world of people who have had the leisure to cultivate fine sentiments and are now shown as insensitive and even disgusting in their superior attitude toward the poor.

At the beginning of the court scene we see our former heroes, who have spent the entire play involved in the theme of love, and would no doubt be quite capable of giving academic lectures on the subject, suddenly finding themselves plunged into a context which has apparently nothing to do with love (with their own love, since all their problems have been solved). Now they are in the context of a relationship with each other and with another social class, and they are at a loss. They do not realize that here too scorn eliminates love.

We see how well Shakespeare has situated everything. Athens in the *Dream* resembles our Athens in the sixties: the workmen, as they state in the first scene, are very much afraid of the authorities; if they commit the slightest error they will be hanged, and there is nothing comical about that. Indeed, they risk hanging as soon as they shed their anonymity. At the same time they are irresistibly attracted by the carrot of "sixpence a day" which will enable them to escape poverty. Yet their real motive is neither glory nor adventure nor money (that is made very clear and should guide the actors who perform this scene). Those simple men who have only ever worked with their hands apply to the use of the imagination exactly the same quality of love which traditionally underlies the relationship between a craftsman and his tools. That is what gives these scenes both their strength and their comic quality. These craftsmen make efforts which are grotesque in one sense because they push awkwardness to its limit, but at another level they set themselves to their task with such love that the meaning of their clumsy efforts changes before our eyes.

The spectators can easily decide to adopt the same attitude as the courtiers: to find all this quite simply ridiculous; to laugh with the complacency of people who quite confidently mock the efforts of others. Yet the audience is invited to take a step back: to feel it cannot quite identify with the court, with people who are too grand and too unkind. Little by little, we come to see that the craftsmen, who behave with little understanding but who approach their new job with love, are discovering theatre—an imaginary world for them, toward which they instinctively feel great respect. In fact, the "mechanicals" scene is often misinterpreted because the actors forget to look at theatre through innocent eyes, they take a professional actor's views of good or bad acting, and in so doing they diminish the mystery and the sense of magic felt by these amateurs, who are touching an extraordinary world with the tips of their fingers, a world which transcends their daily experience and which fills them with wonder.

We see this quite clearly in the part of the boy who plays the girl, Thisbe. At first sight this tough lad is irresistibly absurd, but by degrees, through his love for what he is doing, we discover what more is involved. In our production, the actor playing the part is a professional plumber, who only took to acting a short while ago. He well understands what is involved, what it means to feel this nameless and shapeless kind of love. This boy, himself new to theatre, acts the part of someone who is new to theatre. Through his conviction and his identification we discover that these awkward craftsmen, without knowing it, are teaching us a lesson—or it might be preferable to say that a lesson is being taught us through them. These craftsmen are able to make the connection between love for their trade and for a completely different task, whereas the courtiers are not capable of linking the love about which they talk so well with their simple role as spectators.

Nonetheless, little by little the courtiers become involved, even touched by the play within the play, and if one follows very closely what is there in the text we see that for a moment the situation is completely transformed. One of the central images of the play is a wall, which, at a given moment, vanishes. Its disappearance, to which Bottom draws our attention, is caused by an act of love. Shakespeare is showing us how love can pervade a situation and act as a transforming force.

The *Dream* touches lightly on the fundamental question of the transformations which may occur if certain things are better understood. It requires us to reflect on the nature of love. All the landscapes of love are thrown into relief, and we are given a particular social context through which the other situations can be measured. Through the subtlety of its language the play removes all kinds of barriers. It is therefore not a play which provokes resistance, or creates disturbance in the usual sense. Rival politicians could sit side by side at a performance of *A Midsummer Night's Dream* and each leave with the impression that the play fits his point of view perfectly. But if they give it a fine, sensitive attention they cannot fail to perceive a world just like their own, more and more riddled with contradictions and, like their own, waiting for that mysterious force, love, without which harmony will never return.

part V

THE WORLD AS
A CAN OPENER

. . .

THE INTERNATIONAL CENTRE

• • •

In 1970, I moved to Paris. It wasn't a sudden decision. A workshop done in 1968, when Jean-Louis Barrault had invited me to be part of the Théâtre des Nations, had given me the first taste of working with actors from many different cultures. But at least twenty years before, I had come to know a remarkable person, Micheline Rozan. She had worked in every branch of theatre, had produced her own shows, and we found we understood one another, usually without need of words.

Together, we confronted the difficulties of theatre in its present form and felt the need to re-explore it through a new structure. We wanted to get away from the idea of a company and yet we did not want to shut ourselves away from the world, in a laboratory.

From the start, the word "centre" seemed to correspond with what we needed. At first, we set up a Centre of Research, then later we added a Centre of Creation, which were two names for an overlapping series of activities. We felt that research in the theatre needs constantly to be put to the test in performance and performing, and needs all the time to be refreshed by research with the time and conditions it demands —and which a professional company can seldom afford.

To begin with, what we needed was money, a space and people. The money came generously from international foundations; our earliest sponsors were the Ford and the Anderson foundations from the United States, the Gulbenkian Foundation from Europe, and the Shiraz Festival from Iran. The space was a tapestry gallery lent to us by the French government, the people were actors from all over the world. The Centre was a point where different cultures could converge; the Centre was also a nomad, taking its mixed group on long journeys to interact with peoples never touched by a normal theatrical tour. Our first principle, we decided, was to make culture, in the sense of culture that turns milk into yoghurt—we aimed to create a nucleus of actors who could later bring ferment to any wider group with whom they worked. In this way, we hoped that the special privileged conditions we were making for a small number of people could eventually enter into the theatre's mainstream.

When we began working with our international group, everyone outside who was interested in our work thought it was an attempt at synthesis, that each member was going to display his tricks and that we would operate an exchange of techniques. This was not the case at all. No synthesis based on technical exchange was either desirable or possible. Perhaps making actors more skillful might be the aim of a school for virtuosi, but it cannot be that of a center for research.

We are seeking for what gives a form of culture its life—not studying the culture itself but what is behind it. For this, the actor must try to step back from his own culture and, above all, from its stereotypes. Life constantly tends to label even the most intelligent and flexible African as an African, and every Japanese just as a Japanese; this phenomenon occurs also inside a group, where the honest admiration of his friends may thrust one of its members into a constant repetition of his superficial tricks.

Our first task was to try to put an end to the stereotypes, but certainly not to reduce everyone to a neutral anonymity. Stripped of his ethnic mannerisms a Japanese becomes more Japanese, an African more African, and a point is reached where forms of behavior and expression are no longer predictable. A new situation emerges which enables people of all origins to create together, and what they create takes on a color of its own. This is not unlike what happens in a piece of orchestral music, where each sound keeps its identity while merging into a new event.

If we occasionally achieve this, it is because in the microcosm of our little group a possibility of contact exists at a very deep level. It becomes possible for people who have no common language or references, no shared jokes or grumbles, to establish real contact by what could be decribed as telepathic intuition. But all our work shows us that this can be achieved only if certain conditions are fulfilled: if there is sufficient concentration, sincerity, creativity. If this microcosm of people is capable of collective creativity, then the object it produces can be received in a similar way by other people. Our aim is to seek something in the theatre which touches people as music does.

In order to establish a relationship with its audience, an international group must be a small world, not consisting of people who understand each other easily, but dependent on diversity and contrast—

a diversity which mirrors the audience. When I began to build up an international group, I tried to revert to a basic principle which has always accompanied the establishment of a company of actors: if it is to be a mirror of the world, it must be composed of highly varied elements. Look at Roman comedy, at the companies that played Plautus, and other companies over hundreds of years; there was always an old man, a very beautiful girl, a very ugly woman, an agile boy, a coarse character (a sort of Falstaff), a miser, an irrepressible joker, etc. And this keyboard, this range of colors was the reflection of a certain society. Within our society today the difference between types is not so marked—you have only to compare faces in the subway or in a pub with those in the engravings of Hogarth or Goya to realize this. Today the conditions of urban life have buried bold expressions of "type" beneath a bland exterior, so that conflicts, differences and struggles are more and more concealed. This softening of our outside world is very bad for theatre. Often theatre groups are formed which seek mutual agreement as their basis instead of looking for conflicts. It seemed to me that, on the contrary, founding an international group gave us the chance to discover in a new way the strong and healthy differences between people.

So, of course, everyone asks, "What exactly do you do?" We call what we are doing "research." We are trying to discover something, to discover it through what we can make, for other people to take part in. It demands a long, long preparation of the instrument that we are. The question always is: Are we good instruments? For that we have to know: What is the instrument for?

The purpose is to be instruments that transmit truths which otherwise would remain out of sight. These truths can appear from sources deep inside ourselves or far outside ourselves. Any preparation we do is only part of the complete preparation. The body must be ready and sensitive, but that isn't all. The voice has to be open and free. The emotions have to be open and free. The intelligence has to be quick. All these have to be prepared. There are crude vibrations that can come through very easily and fine ones that come through only with difficulty. In each case the life we are looking for means breaking open a series of habits. A habit of speaking; maybe a habit made by an entire language. A mixture of people with lots of habits and without even a common language have come together to work.

This is where we begin . . .

STRUCTURES OF SOUND

• • •

The theme of the first year's work of the International Centre of Theatre Research was to be a study of structures of sounds. Our aim was to discover more fully what constitutes living expression. To do this, we needed to work outside the basic system of communication of theatres, we had to lay aside the principles of communication through shared words, shared signs, shared references, shared languages, shared slang, shared cultural or subcultural imagery. We accepted the validity of these very workable language systems and yet we deliberately cut ourselves off from them in the way that in some fields filters are used to eliminate certain rays so that others can be seen more clearly. In our case, a form of cerebral understanding for both the actor and the audience was discarded so that another understanding might take its place.

For instance, the actors were given a passage in ancient Greek. It was not divided into verses, nor even into separate words; it was just a long series of letters, as in the earliest manuscripts. The actor was confronted with a fragment: ELELEUELELEUUPOMAUSFAKELOS-KAIFREENOPLEGEIS . . .

He was asked to approach this like an archeologist, stumbling over an unknown object in the sand. The archeologist would use one science, the actor another; but each would use his knowledge as a detecting and deciphering instrument. The actor's truly scientific tool is an inordinately developed emotional faculty with which he learns to apprehend certain truths, to discriminate between real and false. It was this capacity that the actor brought into play, tasting the Greek letters on the tongue, scanning them with his sensibility. Gradually, the rhythms hidden in the flow of letters began to reveal themselves, gradually the latent tides of emotion swelled up and shaped the phrases until the actor found himself speaking them with increasing force and conviction. Eventually, every actor found it possible to play the words with a deeper and richer sense of meaning than if he had known what they were meant to say. A deeper sense for him and for any listener. But whose meaning was it? The actor's? Not exactly—plain improvisation could never reach this point. The author's? Not exactly—for the meaning was different every time it was spoken. And yet it was the quality of the text that charged the actors. A theatrical truth is a joint truth made up of all the elements that are present at a given moment if a certain combustion takes place.

When Ted Hughes first came to Paris to a session of our work, we improvised for him on random syllables, then on a piece by Aeschylus. He at once began his own experiments, searching to create first of all roots of language and then what he described as "great blocks of sound."

From here to Orghast was of course a long and intricate journey. But in taking on the incredible task of inventing a phonetic language, in an odd way Ted Hughes was doing what poets do all the time. Every poet works through several semi-conscious levels—let's call them A to Z. At level Z energies are boiling inside him, but they are completely out of the range of his perceptions. At level A they have been captured and shaped into a series of words on paper. In between, at levels from B to Y, the poet is half-hearing, half-making syllables that drop in and out of swirls of inner movement. Sometimes, he perceives these pre-words and preconcepts as moving forms, sometimes as murmurs, as patterns of sound that are on the brink of words, sometimes as musical values that are becoming recognizable and precise. But in fact, they are not strangers to him—he lives with them all the time. The great originality and daring of Ted Hughes lay in working openly in an area that gained a control and freedom that makes the subsequent Orghast impossible to separate into sense and sound.

The situation is not unlike that of the abstract painter. At first, abstract painting unleashed on the world angry protesters convinced that their little boy or their ass's tail could do better. Now the expensive difference between, say, de Stael and an ass's tail is unmistakable. Our work also has shown us the difference between random letters, Ted Hughes's letters and Aeschylus' letters. The principles of authorship and of creative writing are unchanged: only the level of expression and the degree of concentration differ. A poem written in familiar words at level A may compress years of experience into ten lines. Writing between levels B and Y is more condensed; the principle of compression is taken to its limit. Ted Hughes crystallizes his deepest experiences in the decision that leads to the root syllable being GRA and not MNO. But of course, for a writer to plunge into the depths of personal experience is not necessarily a virtue. After all, every man's experience is always woefully incomplete.

A private world can reveal itself in fine poetry, but drama needs something quite different. The theatre tries to reflect the real world, and theatre of any consequence must reflect more than one man's world, however fascinating his obsessions may be. An author has to be true to himself and yet he knows he must create material that reflects more than himself. Before this Zenlike contradiction it is hardly surprising that the man who got through remains unique—no one has yet succeeded in nailing Shakespeare down to his own viewpoint; it is the open-ended nature of his writing that is the measure of his genius.

Deeply conscious of this dilemma, Ted Hughes introduced into *Orghast* the play sections of ancient Greek and Avesta with corresponding conflicting thematic material to extend the range of Orghast the language beyond private and personal limits.

When we first encountered Avesta through a remarkable Persian scholar, Mahin Tojaddod, who has done considerable research into the nature of its sound, we realized that we had come close to the source of our study. Avesta came into being some two thousand years ago uniquely as a ceremonial language. It was a language to be declaimed in a certain manner in rituals whose sense was sacred. The letters of Avesta carry within them concealed indications of how the particular sounds are to be produced. When these indications are followed, the deep sense begins to appear. In Avesta, there is never any distance at all between sound and content. In listening to Avesta, it never happens that one wants to know "what it means." In fact, translations at once lead one into the colorless and flavorless world of religious clichés. But as spoken, Avesta is meaningful directly in relation to the quality made by the act of speaking.

Avesta proved that what we were looking for could be found, but it has to be approached with great care. It cannot be copied, it cannot be reinvented. It can only be explored—and the exploration threw light on the questions with which we had lived all year. We printed them in the program of *Orghast,* and I cannot do better than to reproduce them here:

What is the relation between verbal and non-verbal theatre? What happens when gesture and sound turn into word? What is the exact place of the word in theatrical expression? As vibration? Concept? Music? Is any evidence buried in the sound structure of certain ancient languages? . . .

LIFE IN A MORE
CONCENTRATED FORM
● ● ●

For many hundreds of years, the motivating force as much in classical
as in commercial theatre was making an effect on an audience. The
reaction of the experimental theatre today has been to go to the opposite extreme. For the theatrical machine to work properly, its relationship with the audience forms the belt that holds the machine together.
And it is not just a question of getting laughs or applause. Too easily,
actors and directors can fall into thinking of the audience as an enemy,
as a dangerous, fickle animal, and even serious artists approach an
audience on one of two bases: to "win," "seduce," "dominate," "lick,"
"silence," "get" them—or else to ignore them: "Let's work for ourselves,
as though they're not there."

The way to learn a different relationship is to make a very long
series of improvisations far away from audiences accustomed to theatre, in the thick of life, with nothing prepared at all, like a real dialogue, which can start anywhere and can go off in any direction.

In this sense, improvisation means that the actors come before an
audience prepared to produce a dialogue, not to give a demonstration.
Technically, to produce a theatrical dialogue means to invent subjects
and situations for that particular audience, in a way that allows it to
influence the development of the story during performance.

An actor starts by feeling out the audience in the simplest possible
way. He may play with an object, he may speak; he may show fragments
of human relationships—through music, singing and dancing. In
doing so he is probing the audience's reaction—just as in conversation
we soon feel what concerns and interests the other person. As the actor
finds common ground and he develops it, he takes into account all the
little signs which indicate the audience's response. The audience feels
this at once, understands that it is a partner in unfolding the action,
and feels surprised and happy to discover that it is taking part in the
event.

We have discovered through our experience in Africa, in America
and France—playing in isolated villages and tough urban areas, for
racial minorities, old people, children, delinquents, the mentally
handicapped, the deaf, the blind—that no two performances can ever
be identical.

We have learned that improvisation is an exceptionally difficult and precise technique and very different from the generalized idea of a spontaneous "happening." Improvisation requires great skill on the part of the actors in all aspects of theatre. It requires specific training and also great generosity and a capacity for humor. Genuine improvisation, leading up to a real encounter with the audience, only occurs when the spectators feel that they are loved and respected by the actors. We have learned that for this reason improvised theatre must go to where people live. We have also learned that groups of people living in a form of isolation, like immigrants in France, are astonished and touched when actors come to them quite simply and play in their familiar places. The greatest tact and sensitivity are needed to avoid giving the impression that their intimacy is invaded. If there is no sense of an act of charity, only the feeling that one group of human

Exercises at the Bouffes du Nord

beings wants to make contact with the other, then theatre becomes life in a more concentrated form. Without theatre, a lot of strangers meeting one another would not get very far in a short time. But the additional energies released by singing, dancing and playing out conflicts, and by excitement and laughter, are so great that in a single hour amazing things can happen.

This effect is particularly intense if the group of actors includes people with different backgrounds. With an international company, a deep understanding can be touched between people who seem to have nothing in common.

At this time, when every aspect of culture is being challenged, such events, even on a small scale, bring back the feeling that theatre can be useful. Even necessary.

BROOK'S AFRICA
An Interview by Michael Gibson
· · ·

On December 1, 1972, a group of thirty people—actors, technicians and auxiliaries—left France for Africa with director Peter Brook. It was the start of a three-month journey of experimental work and research sponsored by the International Centre of Theatre Research in Paris. With the group went a movie crew; a photographer, Mary Ellen Mark; and John Heilpern, an English writer and journalist.

GIBSON: Tell me about the geographical situation of the journey. Then, let's discuss the contact between you and the people you encountered.

BROOK: We set out from Algiers, went straight through the Sahara into northern Niger, to Agades, where we stayed a week. From there we went down to the south of Niger, which is Zinder, across the frontier into Nigeria, to Kano. Then down to the middle of Nigeria to Jos, which is on the Benin Plateau, the center of Nigeria. From there we branched across Nigeria to Ife, where the university is, not far from Lagos, and to Cotonou in Dahomey, which is where we hit the sea, and where the whole group sprang out of the Land Rovers and rushed headlong straight into the sea, fully dressed, out of sheer hysteria at the sight of the water after all this time!

From Cotonou we went up through Dahomey into Niger again, to the capital, which is Niamey, then north, cutting across a bit of Mali and Gao and then across the Sahara, a different way, back to Algiers.

We played in Algeria, both coming and going. Our first performance was in Algeria and was the most moving moment of the whole journey. We had just crossed the first part of the Sahara when we came into this little town called In-Salah. Nobody was prepared for us, but we came. It was morning; there was a tiny market, and I suddenly said: "Let's play for the first time, here!" And everyone responded because we liked the place.

We got out, unrolled our carpet, sat down, and an audience assembled in no time. And there was something incredibly moving—because it was the total unknown, we didn't know what could be communicated, what couldn't. All we discovered after was that nothing resembling this had ever happened before in the market. Never had there been a strolling player or some little improvisation. There was no precedent for it. There was a feeling of simple and total attentiveness, total response and lightning appreciation. Something that, perhaps in a second, changed every actor's sense of what a relation with an audience could be.

We did little, fragmentary improvisations. The first was done with a pair of shoes. Somebody took off a big, heavy, dusty pair of boots that he'd worn through the desert, and put them in the middle of the carpet. This was already a very intense moment, everybody staring at these two objects which were loaded with many sorts of meanings. And then one person after another came in and did various improvisations with them, on a really shared premise: that first of all there was the empty carpet—there was nothing—then a concrete object. And its appearance wasn't based on anything being thought or prepared beforehand, but actually at that moment, everybody, the actors and the audience, saw these boots as though for the first time. Through the boots a relationship was established with the audience, so that what developed was shared in a common language. We were playing with something that was real to everybody, and therefore the things that came out of it, the use that was made of them, was an understandable language.

GIBSON: Are the improvisations describable?

BROOK: You can never capture that sort of thing in a description. They played with the transformations that the boots made on different people wearing them in different ways—something that everyone could immediately feel and recognize.

GIBSON: Did you have contact with the people afterwards?

BROOK: Yes. We talked. In fact, there was a schoolteacher who took us back to his little house to sit on the floor and have mint tea. Everywhere we had the same sort of experience, which is that people were interested and pleased. This in itself (I mean, it's very pleasant, very warming) doesn't mean a great deal, because in a sense they couldn't be otherwise. It's too strange an event. One can't be taken in by that, because something would have to be radically wrong if people weren't interested by something that they'd never seen before.

But it teaches the actors a great deal. An actor can see how there is a permanent agitation in him, partly through the conditioning of Western society, and partly through the expectations of Western audiences. Something has to happen; a result has to be shown. This always produces things that aren't properly prepared.

But when you have an audience that is very much with you and *there*, but for whom the sense of hurry is absent ("If you don't get on with something, I'm going away. You'd better get a good result and get it fast because I expect that of you!"), whether it comes from oneself or the other, then you reach a completely different level of relaxation, out of which things can arise in a quite different and often more organic way.

GIBSON: Tell me something about the main stages of the journey.

BROOK: The first period for us, as we started playing, was like learning a new instrument. We knew of absolutely no experience to go by. In the first period you really have to discover what the actual conditions are by which you get an audience. What is the best way of gathering an audience? What is the best time of day? What happens if you have too few people? What happens if you have too many, and how long can you go on like this? Do you have to keep going? Can you stop? Can you wait?

It was the discovery of how free you can be. The actual learning of what it is (and even technically learning) to keep a relation with an audience in the hot sun in the marketplace. And the difference between that and playing at night (we had lamps and a little generator). And to discover the difference between theory and fact about what it means to bring electricity to a village that's never seen an electric light. And does that alienate one from the population? Because there, suddenly, one is no longer people like them, players strolling in and doing something, but, suddenly, the whole of the Western technocratic world. I mean, is this true or not?

In fact, we found it wasn't as true as we thought. We were very wary at first about using these lights. We thought that something precious would be spoiled, and found that this was sentimental and not true. One village we went into, we put up lights and started playing in daylight. And at a certain point we went through a twilight and, just as it got too dark to see, the lights came up. It was an extraordinary moment, after which all attention went back to what was going on, with a greater concentration because of the pooling effect of the light. I couldn't distinguish any difference, later, between the times we played by day, or at night with a couple of lamps. I couldn't find anything that was changed in the villagers' relations to us; except to the good, because at night the performances usually gained from the added concentration you get by having something lit in the surrounding darkness.

Nothing had a better effect on the actors than the stillness of the African audiences. It is very natural to most Africans not to manifest. The African isn't Mediterranean in his behavior. He is, of course, capable of enormous energy, but also of enormous stillness, and this still, concentrated attention was the most precious thing to play to.

We found there were laws of numbers: that when there were too many people, the audience itself was continually agitated. People were pushing from the back of the crowd because they were trying to see. This was a thing we never really dominated. We never found the technique to hold a big seething audience. That's particularly difficult when you're working without words.

Then we found that we'd prepared all sorts of bits and pieces of material, not necessarily to use, but so as not to come completely unprepared. And we found immediately that the more we took the total risk, and went into villages prepared for everything but having no idea at all of what we were going to do, the freer, in fact, we got from any sort of structure or idea, the better the result always was. The conditions were so unexpected.

Somebody would start, and everything developed from the fact that one person got up and walked. Or somebody started singing. It's very frightening, really, to take that risk. But the more that risk was taken, the better the results. Something always created itself, that really was influenced, second by second, by the presence of the people, the place, the time of day, the light—all of those reflected themselves in the best performances. And themes that we'd worked on in the past then would reoccur in a different place, a different order and a different manner. These were the best performances. And when, because something had worked, we tried to repeat it (often just through laziness, tiredness, or through not thinking), the result was less good. Very easily one came to a point where a barrier between oneself and the audience could be felt because one was within a form. You were in a form that made sense to you. I don't think it was a surprise to anyone, but it's quite different to have a first-hand experience of it, actually to experience how easily in theatre you can be on a different wavelength from the audience without anybody noticing it, because you haven't really created a full relationship, starting from zero.

And we found that in the best of cases each performance had to start from this zero point in which an audience makes a circle; and if you start with anything that has an assumption built into it, you're already out of touch.

You have to create this first assumption. An example was the thing with shoes. After we'd done it once, we developed it into a "shoe show." We rapidly found that we were skipping the first stage, and realized that in the first show what was good was that there had been just some people sitting on the ground playing music and singing a bit. The first dramatic step was a pair of shoes. You didn't have to have a conception of theatre. There was nothing to prepare. You didn't have to know what acting was, or that there was a form called theatre, because here was the first step: a pair of shoes. Everyone looked at them because there was already an interrogation mark over them. Something needed to happen. Everybody was looking at a spot where, someone having performed one action, a further action was expected.

And we found then how many things one takes for granted. In one or two places, we came to a point that was very interesting, which was to see that even make-believe, in the sense of a story, can't be taken for granted. By that I mean that an actor takes for granted that if he steps into the circle and somebody trips him, and he falls, this will be received without question as the first step in the story. Or a young actor steps forward, and bends himself to walk like an old person. This is clearly the first step in a make-believe theme about an old man. Now since we were sometimes in places where there had never been any theatre at all meant that even that couldn't be taken for granted, be-

In Africa

cause if somebody who's walking straight suddenly doubles up, he
might genuinely at that moment have been taken ill, or he might be
doing a strange movement for its own sake.

A very interesting thing is to strike a point where the mental
habits have not been formed that accept the linear development of a
story, so that, in fact, events are received as a set of disconnected
impressions. Therefore, they are suddenly taken really for what they
are. At that moment the values change, because at that moment one
can see that maybe their only living value resides in what the sequence
is building up to, while second for second they're not all that interesting. At that moment the actor senses that the story is nothing to lean
on, because if, as the old man walking on, he does not produce something complete in its own right, the attentiveness of the people surrounding it will be in no way heightened. And if he hasn't created,

then and there, the actual difference between something *for real* and something *for make-believe,* the language of what's going on will never be fully entered into.

It was very interesting, really starting from zero, to discover where an action becomes a story, and in what way a story. Or when thematic action is or is not a development. There are a million things one can take for granted without being aware of it, and these are all questions that were represented in a living way by the experience we had.

That's why one of my strongest impressions was that this sort of experience is perhaps the most necessary one in training for the theatre. If anybody on the verge of going to a drama school to learn about the theatre—actor, director, designer, writer—were first sent to play continually in these conditions, they would find that every question about their future work is raised for them directly. No process that can be done in rooms with theory or practice can bring the root questions into the open the way that going into these conditions does, and recognizing, second for second, that something is or isn't being made.

GIBSON: How did the fact that you were a very varied group from various countries in the world. with equipment and vehicles, how did this affect the way you were received?

BROOK: Things are a lot simpler in Africa than they seem to be at a distance. Most of the things that people would discuss and worry about before we went, completely dissipated in the reality of the extraordinary human quality that the Africans have. For example, many times before going I had to explain, struggling through a whole screen of questions, why a group should want to go and do this. Then we would come into a village where such a thing had never happened, and we'd see the chief of the village and, through some interpreter, perhaps just a child from the village, I would explain in very few words that a group of people, from different parts of the world, had set out to discover if a human contact could be made through a particular form called theatre, without a shared language. Everywhere this was understood without further explanation. It seemed unprecedented yet quite natural. Therefore our coming was not a complicated event.

It was an event that was always welcomed, and always taken directly on its own terms for what it was. I think the group brought the right sort of simplicity in its own approach in human terms.

You can't go anywhere pretending to be other than what you are, and this group set out with all the advantages for an expedition of this sort, and couldn't pass itself off as a group coming on foot and living in exactly the same human conditions as the people it was playing to. It was quite clear that this wasn't the case.

At the same time, this didn't represent a barrier; it didn't condition the attitude that was taken between the people who came and the people who were there. It fell into the expected. To see a group of Westerners, non-Africans rather, arriving in an African village having crossed the Sahara on foot would be really freakish. But for outsiders to come in, with what is accepted as being part of their natural way of life, cars and electrical equipment and such, this was as expected.

The thing that we were most wary about was cameras. (I long ago gave up carrying a camera because I dislike that sense of coming into a strange place and trying to snatch something away from the people with this ever-violating instrument.) I took the greatest care not to let still cameras, movie cameras and tape recorders appear in the insensitive, automatized way that is usual with Western tourists.

But gradually one found that the camera is a less aggressive instrument than one might feel if one is aware of it in this way. In fact, later, when we did start filming the things that we were doing, we found that the camera has become a normally accepted part of Western clothing, like shorts, pocket handkerchieves and ball-point pens. The thing that makes it aggressive is the way it is actually used.

Then, too, we came with our own food: first, because there was no accurate information on what foods were available, and because we wanted to be free to go anywhere we chose. At this time there was a terrible drought and food problems in lots of the places we visited. So we took a great deal of tinned and dried food with us. There were thirty of us, which is much too big a group to come into a village and hope to be given food, even in exchange for money.

But, in fact, we found more and more that one could live very simply there. On another trip we might try to really live off the land. When we sat in our camp eating stew that had come out of a tin and processed cheese out of a packet, it was self-evident that we conformed to our way of living the way they do to theirs. And when people from the village would come into our camp we could give them something of what we had to eat.

The externals did nothing. The relationship had to be made—or not made—in human terms. And when the performance worked well, what happened was something that could only happen through such a form. In other words, if thirty foreigners came into a village just like that and mooned around and stared at the inhabitants, either an artificial situation would be created, or the situation would in no way evolve. But through a performance it was possible within an hour for the relationship to be enormously warmed and enhanced and evolved because something had happened.

We were paid for it. One time in Nigeria they came with a little bag with shillings that they'd collected; another time they came with chicken; another time with a goat. Because we did something that was an offering created a bond at once.

What did it do? Certainly you can't go into a village, play for an hour, and go away having changed people's lives. But it is quite clear that the way is open to hundreds of companies. Hundreds of groups could, if they wished—very inexpensively, too—go up and down the continent, playing this way and meeting nothing but appreciation.

Then something very active could happen, quite different from what happens on the level of official culture. Because official culture is mostly ridiculous. All sorts of countries have sent ballet companies, opera companies—England has sent Shakespeare companies—but where to? To the big cities. So the performances unfold to an audience made up largely of government officials and the European diplomatic corps. And why they go there is highly suspect. In any event, no relation is made. And for an act of relation to be made that is different from the relation between outsiders and Africans over all the centuries *could* have meaning. If it were done on a quite different scale. If, in a year, a great number of groups from different countries were doing this, it could have a quite different meaning.

We explored, we opened up a trail, and found that it was a valid one. Of course there are economic problems, but they're not absolute, because people get to every part of the globe one way or another if they want to. All you need is a group of actors with nothing at all (we carried a carpet to play on, but you don't even need that). You've only to go there and start. The moment you accept that, it opens up a possibility.

It is something with enormous richness in all directions. You have to give and take. You're not showing and you're not teaching and you're not imitating.

For instance, the African can use his body marvellously—his capacity of movement and of rhythm is world famous. But within each culture this vast capacity is put to a very restricted use, because each culture works, in its dances and its music, in a very narrow set of rhythms. And so, although nobody in our group could move like an African—it was an object of envy and amazement and admiration to see an African in movement—the Africans, with great generosity, looked the other way round at this, and they would say how interesting it was for them to see movements that they just had never realized were within the natural scope of their bodies. One of the interests for them was to see unfamiliar movements, or to hear unfamiliar rhythms. Sometimes unfamiliar rhythms can be a barrier if you haven't gone through the process of building up to them. But if you have led up to them, they can be of enormous interest, because your range, both in terms of feeling and awareness of means of expression, is obviously widened. You see things that haven't occurred to you. You don't imitate them directly, but they show you something's possible that you hadn't actually realized before.

That is what we were continually doing in our contact with their ceremonies, dance, singing and rituals. And sometimes the opposite happened in a very interesting way. We would, for instance, produce certain sounds that we'd made in exercise, not because they're in our tradition, but because in searching to discover how the human voice can vibrate in a manner that matches a certain emotional experience, one finds certain sounds. Now we found that those sounds made by our group and the sounds made by Africans in some of their singing were the same.

Once we sat all afternoon in Agades in a small hut, singing. We and the African group sang, and suddenly we found that we were hitting exactly the same language of sound. We understood theirs and they understood ours. Something quite electrifying happened because, out of all sorts of different songs, one suddenly came upon this common area.

Another experience of that same sort occurred one night when we were camping in a forest. We thought there was no one around for miles, but as always, suddenly children appeared from nowhere and beckoned. We were just sitting and doing some improvised song, and the children asked us to come down to their little village, only a couple of miles away, because there was going to be some singing and dancing later in the night and everyone would be very pleased if we could come.

So we walked down through the forest, found this village, and found that, indeed, there was a ceremony going on. Somebody had just died and it was a funeral ceremony. We were made very welcome and we sat there, in total darkness under the trees, just seeing these moving shadows dancing and singing. And after a couple of hours they suddenly said to us: "the boys say that this is what you do, too. Now you must sing for us."

So we improvised a song for them. And this was perhaps one of the best works of the whole journey. Because the song that was produced for the occasion was extraordinarily moving, right and satisfying, and made a real coming together of the villagers and ourselves. It is impossible to say what produced it, because it was produced as much by the group that was working together in a certain way, as by all the conditions of the moment that bore their influence: the place, the night, the feeling for the other people, the feeling for death, so that we were actually making something for them in exchange for what they had offered us.

It was a remarkable song and, like all theatre things, something that once made is gone. One doesn't, in the theatre, create things for a museum or a shop, but for the moment. And there, an instance of that sort of theatre, actually happened. You ask: What did we leave? I think the truer question is: What did we share?

GIBSON: What then were your motives for undertaking this journey to Africa?

BROOK: To know those motives we'd have to discover the motives behind the International Centre of Theatre Research in Paris, and that goes back into the motives for making theatre in the first place.

The reason we started the Centre was to start working outside contexts. My own work, and the work I've been in contact with, has always been work within a context. The context is either geographical, cultural or linguistic, so that we work within a system. The theatre that works within a system communicates within a system of reference. The broadest of these is language in the general sense of the word. Spoken conversation in English is incomprehensible to someone whose ear is only tuned to spoken conversation in Finnish, say. This is the broadest barrier. And within English itself there are forms of "in" language, of argot, and there are local references that almost completely enclose the group of people who can share a common experience with the actors. The common experience, to a greater or lesser extent, relies on something that is not universal.

And this is not only language. It is every sort of manifestation that has a relative meaning created by modes of communication. Yet at the same time, for instance, through working in Shakespeare, one also has seen the opposite experience, which is that some of the most powerful performances of the works I have been connected with have taken place, paradoxically, where people have understood the language least. Which raises a strange question. This obviously doesn't deny the whole tremendous power and richness of language, but it suggests how many other signals are coming simultaneously; and in certain circumstances the performance is felt more powerfully if only a portion of the signals come through.

I wrote in *The Empty Space* about the experience of playing *King Lear* in Eastern Europe and in America, and how, in Eastern Europe, the people who didn't understand the language received more than the people of Philadelphia who theoretically understood the language but were not tuned toward the play. Now, out of those sorts of observations and paradoxical experiences and out of the central observation that nowhere in the world is there a complete theatre but only fragments of a theatre, we set out to explore what the conditions were through which the threatre could speak directly. In what conditions is it possible for what happens in a theatre experience to originate from a group of actors and be received and shared by spectators without the help and hindrance of the shared cultural signs and tokens?

All our work has been turning around this problem in different ways. In going to Africa, we didn't go in the hopes of finding something that we could learn, take away, or copy. We went to Africa because in the theatre the audience is as powerful a creative element in the primal event as the actor. Whether the audience participates in a way that has become fashionable, by showing it is participating because it is moving around, whether it participates by standing motionless, or whether it participates in a sitting position is only of secondary importance. What is of great importance is that the theatre phenomenon only exists when the chemical meeting of what has been prepared by a group of people, and is incomplete, comes into relationship with another group, a wider circle which is the people who are there as spectators. When that fusion takes place, then there is a theatre event. When the fusion doesn't take place, there is no event.

And this combustion, this chemical process depends very, very largely on certain elements that the audience brings.

So let's just talk for a moment about what the audience is in the Western theatre.

The basic attitude of theatre people, whoever they are, toward an audience is a shifty one. It's very hard for there to be a basis of trust—

and certainly not of love—toward an audience. The theatre would lose
its whole sense if an audience were selected, were handpicked—if you
had to show a moral passport at the gate before getting into the theatre.
I don't think one could imagine anything worse. Part of the splendor
of theatre, at least of the possible theatre, is that anyone can come. It
is always an unknown mixture of people coming together round a core.
You don't know who's going to be there, and at the moment of the
event all are welcome. So actually, at the moment of performance, the
actor is in an ambiguous relationship to the audience. He needs the
audience, he wishes the audience to be there, yet he doesn't trust it
and he feels it is basically hostile. The audience brings elements of
judgment that make the actor's work partly a fight for domination over
the audience. The clearest illustration of this is in the French theatre,
where one finds the expression *se défendre*. The actor's relationship
with the audience is seen as that of defending himself against that

An African audience

assumed hostility—assumed to be one that will annihilate him unless he, with his acting, his skills and his part, is in a position to defend himself gloriously.

Part of the work in our theatre has to be, rightly, the softening up, the actual working on the audience to get it to a state of readiness. And perhaps part of the work of production—production work in all its forms from the crudest onwards—is the actual preparation of an audience starting from zero, or even starting from subzero, starting maybe from a hostility, from an active coldness (which is what you have on a first night), something actively against the event coming from many sections. The overcoming of that and preparing the audience, and step by step bringing it to the point where an event can take place, is part of production techniques.

But what we are looking for is something infinitely more fragile. The reason one works a lot behind closed doors, the reason you restrict yourself to a small number of people, or perhaps sometimes to a tiny audience, is that you're attempting something that, because you are going a little further for the first time, is more fragile.

And here every experimental group has discovered something that is, I think, a dangerous and essentially unpleasant discovery—that there are things you can do among a group of actors behind locked doors that are better when you are alone and compromised when an audience is there.

This is a highly destructive and unhealthy discovery for any group of actors to make because out of it can come one of the worst phenomena of the last decade: that is, you have groups logically concluding that the whole idea of theatre being for anybody else is an insincere notion. Sincerity is to make a closed world where you use theatre forms, improvisations, etc., for exercises, for yourself. If audiences are let in, they are let in fairly contemptuously and offhandedly, as people who are privileged to come and watch other people who are making no effort to incorporate them, but just making the minimum effort of letting them in at the door to pick up the crumbs. Now this, I think, is a terrifying situation.

The discovery that the most imaginative and unexpected things happen when there's no one to witness them, and when a witness is there they don't happen, is a tragic discovery. It really denies the whole existence of theatre.

So what we wanted to do in Africa was to go to what could be considered an optimum audience—an audience vivid in its responses and having a total openness to forms, because it has not in any way been conditioned by Western forms.

Once you get outside a tiny set of people in the African cities, you have a whole continent that is competely free of theatre associations in our sense of the word. Yet it is an audience that, with this openness, is in no way naive—it is not a primitive audience. Primitivism is a completely false notion to apply to Africa, where the traditional civilizations are not only extremely rich and extremely complete, but in relation to the theatre they prepare the audience in a unique way.

The African who has been brought up in the traditions of the African way of life has a very highly developed understanding of the double nature of reality. The visible and the invisible, and the free passage between the two, are for him, in a very concrete way, two modes of the same thing. Something which is the basis of the theatre experience—what we call make-believe—is simply a passing from the visible to the invisible and back again. In Africa, this is understood not as fantasy but as two aspects of the same reality.

For that reason, we went to Africa to have the possibility of experimenting with our own work in relation to what one could consider an ideal audience.

GIBSON: Do you think there's any way of saying now whether what you gained in this experience is applicable in theatre in a Western context?

BROOK: What we're looking for is very simple, and very hard for us to come by. That is, how, in the theatre, to make simple forms. Simple forms which, in their simplicity, are both understandable and yet packed with meaning. I think we all know how to split that into two unattractive alternatives: "simple," meaning childish and simplistic, and "complex," meaning "only available to people of a particular intellectual formation," which makes the eternal distinction again between the elite and the popular.

Real simple is simple in the sense that a circle is simple, and yet it's the most charged symbol—a cat, a child and a sage can all play with a circle in their own manner. In the same way, the innocence one wants to find in theatre is one in which the forms can be simple— something that's very hard to come by in the theatre as we know it— simple and thus very accessible, and yet containing the full charge that a true simplicity should carry.

In that direction the African experience has, I think, increased everybody's level of preparation. It is something that we cannot share with other people on a theoretical level. If one says: "This is very unfair, that a small group of people should have an experience like this, that remains exclusive to them"—well, this is true. But in a way it is like any experience in life. You can't share it except through a form once removed.

We have made a film of it, which will capture something. But the actual experience itself can only be made accessible through the work we can do. Our form comes out of this journey and this experiment.

THE WORLD AS A CAN OPENER

. . .

In the middle of Africa, I scandalized an anthropologist by suggesting that we all have an Africa inside us. I explained that this was based on my conviction that we are each only parts of a complete man: that the fully developed human being would contain what today is labelled African, Persian or English.

Everyone can respond to the music and dances of many races other than his own. Equally one can discover in oneself the impulses behind these unfamiliar movements and sounds and so make them one's own. Man is more than what his culture defines; cultural habits go far deeper than the clothes he wears, but they are still only garments to which an unknown life gives body. Each culture expresses a different portion of the inner atlas: the complete human truth is global, and the theatre is the place in which the jigsaw can be pieced together.

In the last few years, I have tried to use the world as a can opener. I have tried to let the sounds, shapes and attitudes of different parts of the world play on the actor's organism, in the way that a great role enables him to go beyond his apparent possibilities.

In the fragmented theatre that we know, theatre companies tend to be composed of people who share the same class, the same views, the same aspirations. The International Centre of Theatre Research was formed on the opposite principle: we brought together actors with nothing in common—no shared language, no shared signs, no common jokes.

We worked from a series of stimuli, all coming from without, which provided challenges. The first challenge came from the very nature of language. We found that the sound fabric of a language is a code, an emotional code that bears witness to the passions that forged it. For instance, it is because the ancient Greeks had the capacity to experience certain emotions intensely that their language grew into the vehicle it was. If they had had other feelings, they would have evolved other syllables. The arrangement of vowels in Greek produced sounds that vibrate more intensely than in modern English—and it is sufficient for an actor to speak these syllables to be lifted out of the emotional constriction of the twentieth-century city life into a fullness of passion which he never knew he possessed.

With Avesta, the two-thousand-year-old language of Zoroaster, we encountered sound patterns that are hieroglyphs of spiritual experience. Zoroaster's poems, which on the printed page in English seem vague and pious platitudes, turn into tremendous statements when certain movements of larynx and breath become an inseparable part of their sense. Ted Hughes's study of this led to *Orghast*—a text which we played in collaboration with a Persian group. Though the actors had no common language they found the possibility of a common expression.

The second challenge, which also came to the actors from the outside, was the power of myths. In playing out existing myths, from myths of fire to myths of birds, the group was stretched beyond its everyday perceptions and enabled to discover the reality behind the fairytale trappings of mythology. Then it could approach the simplest everyday action, the gesture, the relation with familiar objects in the knowledge that if a myth is true it cannot belong to the past. If we know where to look we can find it at once, in a stick, a cardboard box, in a broom or a pack of cards.

The third challenge came from allowing the outside world—people, places, seasons, times of day or night—to act directly on the performers. From the start, we studied what an audience means, and deliberately opened ourselves to receive its influence. Reversing the principle on which theatre tours are based, where finished work remains constant although circumstances change, we tried, in our travels, to make our work fit the moment of playing. Sometimes this came from pure improvisation, such as arriving in an African village with no fixed plans at all and letting circumstances create a chain reaction out of which a theme would arise as naturally as in a conversation. Sometimes we let the audience dominate the actors completely—as in La-

In Africa

mont, California, where, one Sunday morning under a tree, a crowd of strikers who had been listening to César Chávez stimulated our actors into creating the images and characters that they needed passionately to cheer or hiss, so that the performance became a direct projection of what the audience had uppermost on its mind.

In Persia, we took *Orghast* away from its serious-minded audience and its setting of royal tombs and did a performance in a village, to see whether we could bring it down to earth. But the task was too difficult —we had not acquired the necessary experience. Two years later, in California, however, together with the Teatro Campesino, we played *The Conference of the Birds* to an audience of farmworkers in a park and it all fell into place: a Sufi poem translated from Persian to French, from French to English, from English to Spanish, played by actors of seven nationalities, had made its way across the centuries and across the world. Here it was no alien classic; it found a new and urgent meaning in the context of the Chicano struggle.

This was possible because we had learned many lessons on the way. From a shanty town near Paris to the villages of Africa, in front of deaf children, asylum inmates, psychiatrists, business trainees, young delinquents; on cliffs, in pits, in camel markets, at street corners, in community centres, museums, even a zoo—and also in carefully prepared and organized spaces—the question: What is theatre? had become for us a proposition that had to be faced and answered immediately. The constant lesson taught and retaught was respecting audiences and learning from them. Whether throbbing with excitement (I think of three hundred black teenagers in Brooklyn); or menacing, stoned on glue in the Bronx; or grave, immobile and attentive (in a Saharan oasis), the audience is always "the other person": as vital as the other person in speech or love.

And it is clear that just pleasing the other is not enough. The relationship implies an extraordinary responsibility: something has to take place. What? Here we touched the basic questions: What do we need from the event? What do we bring to the event? What in the theatre process needs to be prepared, what needs to be left free? What is narrative, what is character? Does the theatre event tell something, or does it work through a sort of intoxication? What belongs to physical energy, what belongs to emotion, what belongs to thought? What can be taken from an audience, what must be given? What responsibilities must we take for what we leave behind? What change can a performance bring about? What can be transformed?

The answers are difficult and ever-changing, but the conclusion is simple. To learn about theatre one needs more than schools or rehearsal rooms: it is in attempting to live up to the expectations of other human beings that everything can be found. Provided, of course, one trusts these expectations. This is why the search for audiences was so vital.

Another aspect of the process we were following was that of interchange between working groups. Groups of many nationalities had passed through our Centre in Paris, and this prepared the way for the eight-week experience of living together with the Teatro Campesino in San Juan Bautista. In theory, no two groups could be more different, and although we continually sought out opposites, obviously not every combination can work. Here we started with the advantage that between the director of the Teatro, Luis Valdez, and myself, there existed a miraculously close understanding. "In different ways," Luis said on the first day, "we are all trying to become more universal. But universal does not mean broad and generalized. Universal means, quite simply, related to the universe." It was on this point that the work of our two groups began—trying to relate the smallest specific detail to the widest framework. For instance, to the Teatro, as to Chávez, the word "union" not only means organized labor but also unity, with all its overtones.

The work with the Campesino was a major experiment, and it established that it is possible for different groups to help each other to search for the same goal. Once again it was the differences between the groups that made the strongest experiences occur.

In Paris, in 1972, we worked with deaf children, touched by the vividness, eloquence and speed of their body languages. The American National Theatre of the Deaf spent a very rich period with us, experimenting both in movement and in sound, and extending the possibilities of both companies.

Then there was the summer we worked intensively on a reservation in Minnesota with the American Indian group from La Mama. The remarkable sensitivity of these actors toward sign language convinced us that something important would take place if we could bring the Indian and the deaf groups together. So one day, in the quiet of our space in the Brooklyn Academy of Music, we all met. And as theatre is a far more powerful means of communication than any social form, we did theatrical work together. We began with direct communication through signs, which spread rapidly from conversational signs to poetic ones, and soon penetrated into the strange area where what to a hearing person is a vibrating sound, to a deaf person is a vibrating movement. These became one and the same channel of expression.

That same night we decided to perform together, and we rapidly prepared a special version of *The Conference of the Birds* in which all three groups took part. Performing in front of an audience produces the heat which makes every experience touch its peak; this performance technically was very rough, but slickness and professionalism were of little consequence. There was a direct power produced by the combustion of the three different elements. The audience that evening had no knowledge of what gave the performance its particular electricity but both the audience and the groups took away a very precious human experience. For over twelve hours the theatre had been a meeting place, and the evening had become an expression of the essence of that meeting.

We were five weeks in Brooklyn and we aimed at making a coherent whole of this time, bringing together all the different elements of our work into one process. We tried to make a cross-fertilization from the rough work in the streets, the concentrated and silent exercises, the performances, discussions and demonstrations that we held at the Brooklyn Academy of Music. We crammed into each day as much as it could hold and demanded of ourselves every reserve of energy. This led to incredible risks, and the workload was so heavy, the strain so great, the time so short, the changes so bewildering that the group was often punch-drunk, and the quality of the experiences varied like the weather.

What nearly led us all to the cracking point was that we were snatching every possible moment for our own rehearsals, as at the same time we were sustaining an experiment with *The Conference of the Birds.* This piece was in constant evolution—we had played several versions in Africa, others in Paris, and many across America before coming to Brooklyn. At the end we rotated the casts nightly so that each member of the group could bring a new understanding to each role and so add to the overall development of the piece. During the last week seven couples were responsible for seven different versions. The last night there were three performances: at 8:00 p.m., at midnight and at dawn. The first of these was improvised; the second grave and textual; the third ceremonial. Between them, they reflected the experiences of three years. They showed us that what we had been looking for is possible to reach.

I am constantly asked if I will "go back" to the legitimate theatre. But research is not a pot that one opens and then puts back in a cupboard, and all theatre has the possibility of being legitimate. For years, all the large-scale productions I have been involved with have been the result of extended periods of closed research. The two aspects of the process have to stay together like the swing of a pendulum. So there can be no renouncing of the principle of playing for large audiences. In the theatre, the small experiment and the big show both can have quality and meaning. All that matters is that they should aim at capturing truth and life. Captivity kills fast. For this reason, there are no conclusions. The methods must always change.

THE IK

• • •

The Ik is a story which shows a broken world. The wreckage is so clear, its silhouette so sharp, that it seems to draw out for us very vividly how life once was, in the good times. We see the misery and we feel how it could have been: this is the tragedy. And the actors cannot play this diminished, morally destroyed people with cold-blooded judgment. On the contrary, they have to enter as truly as possible into the Ik's emaciated, starving bodies.

We worked on this piece for a year and a half. We spent much of the time improvising scenes from Colin Turnbull's detailed anthropological studies in *The Mountain People,* but this time necessity forced us to evolve a completely new technique. We worked from photographs and made hundreds of lightning improvisations—never longer than thirty or forty seconds. The actors studied the photographs and tried to reproduce with ever-greater precision the details of each attitude, down to the last crook of the finger. When the actor was satisfied that he could capture the exact pose of the Ik in the photograph, then his task was to bring the image to life by improvising every movement just a few seconds before the shutter clicked and continuing for a few seconds after.

This was a far cry from what is usually understood by "free improvisation." We found it enabled European, American, Japanese, African actors to understand quite directly something about playing starving people, a physical condition none of us has ever experienced and therefore cannot reach by imagination or memory. When the actors began to find themselves close to the bones of the real-life characters, it was then possible to do realistic improvisations from Turnbull's material. But these improvisations were not in any way theatrical, they were fragments of Ik life, like shots from a documentary film. We ended with many hours of almost pure observed behavior, and it was with these elements that our three very professional authors, Colin Higgins, Denis Cannan and Jean-Claude Carrière, began to work almost like editors in a cutting room surrounded by thousands of feet of location shooting. Rigorously, they carved the essential out of this mass, and its eventual theatricality was the result of extreme compression.

According to Colin Turnbull, before the calamity that deprived them of all sources of food, the Ik were a normal, well-adjusted tribe, held together by the same bonds that structure every traditional African society. However, the effect of hunger was to erode all forms of community life, including ritual. At the end, the last surviving priest, Lolim, is turned out by his son and left to die alone, without ceremony, on the mountainside. Yet even then one last vestige of faith remained: the Ik would still contemplate the sacred mountain, Morongule.

In the same way, in our world, people who have long given up going to churches are still comforted by their secret prayers and private faith. We try to believe that family bonds are natural and close our eyes to the fact that they have to be nourished and sustained by spiritual energies. With the disappearance of living ceremony, with rituals empty or dead, no current flows from individual to individual and the sick social body cannot be healed. In this way, the story of a tiny, remote, unknown African tribe in what seems to be very special circumstances is actually about the cities of the West in decline.

The Ik

Turnbull lived for a long while amongst the Ik, passing from compassion to anger and disgust. Every conditioned fiber in him judged
and condemned what for a Westerner was the Iks' inhumanity. However, when some years later he saw the play for the first time, he was
overwhelmed, not only because he was taken back to his experience
with the Ik, but because he found he understood them differently. He
no longer judged: compassion returned. Why? I think this touches on
the core of what acting is about. No actor can look at the character he's
playing as a cool observer, he has to feel him from the inside, like a
hand in a glove, and if he once lets judgment in, he loses his way. In
the theatre, an actor defends his character and the audience goes along
with him. Our actors had come to be the Ik and thus to love the Ik;
and Colin Turnbull, as he watched, found himself transported out of
his trained professional stance of observer into something anthropo-
logically suspect, but so normal in the theatre—understanding
through identification.

AN ABORIGINE, I PRESUME

• • •

A *tiny airstrip* in the heart of Australia. The Aborigine who has been
waiting patiently all day for his plane looks up at the drawing, then
passes through the door to relieve himself, having correctly interpreted
the men's room symbol—a top hat, a cane, a pair of gloves.

A film unit that is recording our journey has brought a large party
of Aborigines from the interior to see us play *The Ik* because it is about
a people brought to the verge of extinction. My first impression is of
lumbering men, eyes puffed and half-closed, large stomachs bulging
over trousers, women equally overweight. They seem interested by the
performance and afterwards they dance for us. Their dances, for which
they prepare themselves slowly and carefully, only last a few moments;
some listless movements and that is all. "Give them a hand!" shouts
one of them, a crazy one who speaks some English. "Did you like it?"
asks another.

With the help of interpreters and much gesticulating, I tell them
the story of the Ik and realize that in telling them about an African

tribe brutally deprived of its land I am telling them their own story as well.

The Aborigines are fat for the same reasons the Ik are thin. A whole way of life has been shattered; for the starving Ik this means filling their stomachs with pebbles, for the Aborigines it means unemployment relief, white bread and over-sweetened tea. For the Ik, no hope, no future. Our Aborigines have been photographed in a supermarket, going up and down their first moving staircase, laughing and terrified. They were filmed as they filmed themselves on their first video machine. The Aborigines left us having traded their air tickets to buy a Toyota truck. Was their way of life ruined? What can they preserve? I wanted to know more. The Aborigines' lawyer, Phillip Toyne, was flying from station to station to discuss the Land Rights negotiations. He offered to take me with him.

Alice Springs, in the centre of the continent, is low, square and wooden. It is also white and reactionary. An English journalist, to the disgrace of British journalism and to the delight of the locals, recently described the Aborigines in Alice Springs as indistinguishable from plastic garbage bags on the sidewalks. When the blacks come into town from the reservations, they often end up in the jail, as they are as susceptible to drink as American Indians. When we arrived, an Aborigine community leader had just committed suicide. As a boy, he had been taken away from his tribe by force and put in a mission school, where he was taught English hymns and English history. He grew up full of hatred of all things white and one night he blew out his brains. We go to his funeral at a shining new Catholic church. A black congregation listens to a series of fulsome tributes. A little white lady in a nurse's cowl sings into a microphone in a proud, thin soprano. A violent halfcaste lay preacher assaults the congregation, Billy Graham style—then the priest glosses gently over the realities of the situation.

Outside the church, I learn of another black, wrenched away from his home in a similar manner, but who had returned to his people at the age of twenty and had done the arduous initiation of a boy of fourteen. He is now an elder and much respected, with a unique knowledge of white ways.

Alice Springs to Ernabella by one-engined Graumann with my lawyer friend Phillip at the controls. The landscape is a disc of scrubland, dented by waterless rivers, patched with sheets of salt, broken by great isolated rocks and ridges, intercut by long orange ribbons of track. The earth is powdered with gray and greenish dust, just like the tobacco the Aborigines mix with ash and keep in pellets behind their ears.

Ernabella has been a mission since 1928, when it was started as a buffer for Aborigines between their lands and the towns. Most missions insist: If you want our God, drop yours, but this one accepts people going to church and still maintaining their own ceremonies. In the centre of Ernabella, a pylon with a clock that does not work, a large church, a hall and a store, both decrepit, and a few low buildings separated by an ochre-red road. A voice is continually emerging from a radio, spreading information from village to village, and soon it is joined by a second loudspeaker calling everyone together.

Under a tree in a garden the old men with fine beards, flat noses and protruding bellies sit cross-legged. They wear red headbands and have a front tooth missing, as marks of initiation. The women join them. Dogs wander in and are driven off with stones and punches. Phillip talks, sometimes in English, sometimes in Pitjinjajare. The people listen, impassive. A strong woman, one arm in a plaster cast, bangs the ground from time to time with a long stick. An old man waves the children away, except one, no doubt his own, who packs the reddish dust into a doll's tea cup and pees on it to make a paste. A young man reads a comic called *For Lovers;* an old man, in a stained sweatshirt saying "Melbourne Medical School," wears a leprechaun-green cotton hat over a face so dark and a beard so streaked with dust that he is like a negative, like the Turin Shroud. Another old man, bare to the waist with impressive paunch, listens from a distance, for there are many complex interfamily taboos that could prevent his sitting with the others.

Phillip explains the latest developments in the struggle of the Aborigines to regain possession of the land that had been theirs for forty thousand years. This land had been stolen—or at best bought for a few trinkets—by the first settlers, and today the story of brutality, rape and murder sits uneasily on the liberal conscience of Australia. When the labor administration was in power, it had virtually agreed to return the tribal lands to the Pitjinjajara, and now that the conservatives are back there seems surprisingly an even greater hope of agreement. Phillip explores this warily, but for the Aborigine the issue is simple. The land is his.

At the end of the meeting the women are sent away, so that the men can speak to us alone. They say they wish to show us a sacred site. This is an unusual privilege, but also a practical gesture, as it is vital for some white people to see what the Land Rights dispute is really about.

We set off in a brand-new red truck. In a long prairie we get down and wait, while three men go ahead, as the order of approach to a sacred spot is of great importance. After an interval, we follow, winding round the ridges. There is a small hole in the rocks. The ritual objects have been brought out and laid on the ground for our inspection. There are a couple of iron bars, a mass of feathers, some wooden slats and a stone. They are all part of a story—the story that belongs to this portion of the landscape. The story here is a movement across the continent; you don't read stories, you walk them. A short story is a few miles long, but an epic can cover a great distance. If you ask, "How long is your story?" the answer could well be, "Fifty miles."

Aborigine stories come from an indefinite prehistory, when legendary figures moved through unformed space. Each of their adventures became fossilized into boulders, rocks and valleys, so that the landscape was created like a series of words in Braille. At first, a child learns just his and his family's tales, then through initiation he learns other fragments, until one day he is ready to take part in a ceremony with other tribes which fills in the gaps. By the time he is old, the many scattered pages bind together in a complete and coherent book and he becomes the possessor of the totality of tribal understanding.

Thus, for a people who are always on the move, life is a walk toward wisdom. The first anthropologists translated the Aborigine name for the pre-world of myth as "Dream-time," and the word has stuck. I feel it must be a poor translation—even a dangerous one—because it gives to white people a condescending image. At tourist spots, sacred places are even signposted as "Sites of Aborigine Fairy Tales." When Phillip speaks, he always uses another word for tradition, and I'm never sure whether he's saying "law" or "lore." In fact, he means both. To understand the Aborigines' passion for their soil, we must realize that it is their Book. The tribal lands are rich in minerals, even uranium. For white Australia, they mean wealth and employment. The Aborigine does not refuse to discuss mining, but he wants it to be on his own terms, as only he can determine what can be dug without blasting holes in his Gospel.

We fly on to Amata. Clear light, from a low sun. Hills like squat toads or early pyramids. We lose radio contact with Alice Springs and land on a strip of bulldozed grit. One recognizes images from Australian paintings: Surrealist stumps in desperately lonely deserts. We pass cemeteries of cars, more wrecks than inhabitants. The town, an unattractive set of square buildings and tin huts. A red-faced Englishman from Colchester greets us. In the dust, naked children fight and roll. One has a sheriff's hat and a pistol. "This didn't happen a year ago," the Englishman says. "It's the movies." There are Westerns three times a week, even horror pictures, and the effect is so strong that in Ernabella the people have decided to stop film shows altogether. A tin hut has a wire cage attached to one wall. It's the prison, and two bright-eyed grinning teenagers talk to passers-by as though they were in the stocks. They steal petrol to sniff and they owe $100 in fines. In some white settlements, the courts turn a blind eye on Aborigine delinquents, and black-bashing is becoming a white sport.

Morning in Amata. Various styles of house, tried and abandoned. For forty thousand years, the Aborigines had always been on the move. Like the Ik, they had only one tool, a sharp stick, for digging, cutting, hunting—no clothes, big fires for warmth, and as protection against the rain, "humpies," the roughest of huts made of branches. When the need for food made them move on, they discarded the humpies. The superfluous was always discarded. Today, the habit remains. Anything that's not needed is thrown on the ground, so every station looks like a garbage heap, although the instinct is not for squalor but for freedom. To the despair of white do-gooders, from missionaries to liberal government agencies, what is given with charity usually ends up on the ground. Everything has been done that in white eyes can "improve" the Aborigines. They have been given houses, but not only do they resent the separation from the others—and the early morning chatter which is the only way in which news is carried across each camp—but also tradition demands that after a death they move on.

We fly across more desert. From time to time, three or four lean-to corrugated iron shelters and a shining steel windmill, pumping out water. These are the homeland settlements, arising from the new back-to-the-land movement, stemming from a refusal to accept the erosion of tribal ways, yet based on twentieth-century ways, on trucks and rifles. Men still hunt and women forage, but they no longer stalk nor teach their children to stalk in the way they did when their only weapon was a sharp stick. They say that even the kangaroos have learned about rifles and now sense danger from much farther off.

We decide to sleep out in the dried-up riverbed. A fire is quickly made from dead branches: we cook bacon and potatoes and canned mushrooms. Two very young schoolteachers from the nearest settlement have joined us—they have come straight from Teachers' Training College to this lonely job, full of apprehension and a sense of inadequacy. The Aborigines do not welcome them, they prefer married teachers, for they dread the womanless white man. "It's either the misfits who find their way here," says Phillip, "or operators wanting to rip off the tribes."

In fact, the misfits are a very special breed. All through this trip, I've been meeting them, young, bright, at odds with the cities, dropping out into the bush with beards, books of philosophy and politics, cassettes of classical music. Still another sort of Australian, hiding his idealism under a lot of banter, but dedicated to making a bridge to the Aborigines.

Our last trip is by truck. Through sunset into darkness, through the bush on deep red earth roads, always straight to the horizon, to Utopia. Utopia, a white man's name for rich farmland, cows crossing the track, cows bellowing from thirst, and amongst the trees a brick-and-wood open cabin, bright oil lamps. Tolly, a young Australian with parents from the Ukraine, greets me in Russian and at once begins discussing the Ik. We sit round the fire and talk. Will the Aborigines also be destroyed? Or will they win their legal battles? Will they be preserved and assimilated? Will they survive in isolation as anthropological curiosities? Will they find a way of integrating their traditions into a new way of life?

In the plane to Melbourne, a young Australian who has lived with the tribes in the North tells of the beauty and complexity of their customs, of the force of their spirituality. "The Aborigines never meet white people of inner quality," he says. "They want to know if such people exist."

Back to the other Australia, the Australia of beautiful cities, of generous, friendly people, very appreciative of our performances. One of them says: "You're lucky! I've lived here all my life and I've never seen an Aborigine."

For him, it is easier to be deeply moved by the Ik, starving in the no-man's-land of a theatre performance, than by the plight of the over-fed Aborigine just out of sight.

part VI

FILLING THE
EMPTY SPACE

. . .

SPACE AS A TOOL

• • •

I don't like this space. This time yesterday we were at Caracas University, performing under a tree; at night, we are playing *Ubu* in a dilapidated, abandoned moviehouse, and the space feels fine. Today, you've invited me to join a conference on theatre spaces in your glamorous, ultra-modern hall and I'm ill at ease. I'm asking myself: Why?

I think we can all see right away that it is a difficult space. This is because what matters is for us to have a living contact with one another. If this contact isn't there, then everything we can possibly say about the theatre in theory just falls to pieces.

To my mind, the theatre is based on a particular human characteristic, which is the need at times to be in a new and intimate relationship with one's fellow men. However, at this moment, looking around me in this room, I get the impression that everyone is keeping his distance . . . If I had to act a part here, the first thing I'd have to do would be to break this distance. This reminds me of one of the first principles we discovered, when working in all sorts of conditions. Nothing is so unimportant as comfort; comfort in fact often devitalizes the experience. For example, you are all comfortably seated; if at this moment I want to say something in the hope of getting an immediate reaction out of you, I'll have to speak very loudly and try to send a charge of energy through the person nearest to me, and so on, all the way to the back of the room. Even if I were to succeed, your reaction would be very slow, retarded by the gaps between people imposed by the architects, no doubt to conform with regulations. As this is a new building, there have to be just so many seats, arranged in a certain way. Besides, new buildings are under new fire regulations, which each day get more and more strict. So the inhospitable nature of this room leads me to a very simple reference to measure the difference between a living and a dead space: the manner in which the human beings who are in it are placed, one in relation to the other.

Throughout all our experiments we were able to establish that the audience never suffers from lack of comfort if at the same time the acting becomes more dynamic. Take our present situation here: you are all seated in comfortable chairs—and you are in danger of falling asleep!

One of the difficulties caused by a space like this one is the distance—in all its meanings—which is involved. That is why the arrangement of your seats, which is the usual one, of course, the most logical way of accommodating a maximum number of people, results in each of us staring at the back of the neck of the person just in front. And I think you will agree that the back of the neck is the least interesting part of our neighbor's anatomy.

Here is another relevant phenomenon. My voice carries slowly round this hall, not only because of your system of simultaneous translation, but also because of the space it has to cross. If I were an actor this would force me to speak more slowly, more emphatically, less spontaneously. Now, if we were closer, if we were quite close together, our exchange would be all the more dynamic.

It is undeniable that spaces impose certain conditions, and it is easy to see the price we pay for each of the factors which determines our choice of space.

Suppose we had to perform a play in this hall. We should have two alternatives to choose from: one would be to place all the actors at a certain height above the audience, which would immediately create a new relationship between us; if I climb on to this table, watch!, you are now all forced to look up at me. I become a superman, a mystery, looking down at my audience like a politician delivering a speech. This is the arbitrary, artificial relationship which has been characteristic of the theatre for hundreds of years.

The other alternative would be to place the actor at the same level as his audience. Let me do so now—you see?—no, you can't, for most of you will not see me at all! My only possible contacts are reduced to a small number of people—that man in glasses, for example, sitting very close, or that one over there standing by those mirrors, or this lady sitting on the floor to my left. You others have the expressionless faces of people who are "out of it." It is not your fault, it's just that the way you are seated offers little chance of real contact between us.

One way of solving the problem in this particular space might be to push the audience higher. But a glance is enough to show us that it would be useless here, for though the hall has depth it has not enough height—in other words, the number of people who could be placed above the level of the actors would be extremely small.

Nevertheless, if we do place the audience higher than the actors, we shall see that the situation we have created is not without consequence. If you look down on the action, then a new dramatic relationship will be established and the very meaning of the theatrical event will be modified again. This kind of change must be studied with precision and not regarded as accidental.

In England, a country which had never had a national theatre, it was finally decided for strange reasons of national pride that one should be built. So I found myself a member of a committee that was responsible for guiding the architect's plans. At our first few meetings, questions like these were put to us: "What is the ideal angle for the stalls?" My reply was: "Don't exhaust yourselves making a plan of the theatre; forget mathematics and drawing boards for a while. Instead, devote three or six months to making contact with people who have different occupations—watch them in the street, in restaurants, during a quarrel. Be pragmatic, sit on the floor and look upwards, get as high as you can and look down, get at the back, in the middle, in front of people. Then deduce your scientific and geometrical conclusions from the experience you will have acquired."

We could try the same kind of thing in this room. For example, if I leave the microphone and try to project my voice it will give you no pleasure and no warmth, for this environment, the character of the ceiling and the walls, deprives words and sounds of their life. We are in a modern, hygienic building which sterilizes sound. The moviehouse in Caracas where we are performing is better in this respect, because its concrete walls allow more vibration. And the place where we played last week in France was better still, for we performed in the open air on a space with a stone floor and this produced an extraordinary resonance.

The important thing is not space in theory but space as a tool.

If our only aim at the moment were to communicate a precise text, in which each word had its sense, we would add a few partitions here and there and everyone would be gathered together into a small space so that the actors could speak fast and look in all directions. As a result this hall could be transformed into a suitable and satisfactory space. Although its acoustics are not the best nor the most romantic, it could be used just the same. And we would describe it as "functional."

Then we would have to examine different functions. If we wanted to play *Oedipus* and the audience had to be emotionally affected by the deep tones of the actor's voice, in this room it would be impossible. If the purpose of the play were precisely to evoke a cold, white world like the one here, we would be in the ideal premises. But if the purpose were to release the imagination and introduce the audience to a world of fantasy—well, as you can see, it would be uphill work.

The problem of space is relative. We could always rearrange this hall and we could employ a designer to hide and transform it all. If we did that, it would land us face to face with another question: in that case, why not play in a theatre? The relationship between the theatrical event and a place which has its own character disappears as soon as we begin to reconstruct the space.

In theatre there are things which help and things which obstruct. Outside the theatre, the same elements exist.

When we leave conventional spaces and move into the street, the countryside, the desert, a garage, a stable, or any place so long as we are in the open air, it can be both an advantage and a drawback.

The advantage is that a relationship can at once be established between the actors and the world, which could not come about in any other circumstances. This gives theatre a new breath of life. To invite the audience to break with its conditioned habits—which include going into a special room—is a great dramatic advantage.

The most important element to take into account, the one which really distinguishes one space from another, is the problem of concentration. For if there is a difference between theatre and real life, which may be hard to define, it is always a difference in concentration. An event in theatre may be similar or identical to an event in our lives, but thanks to certain conditions and techniques our concentration is greater. So space and concentration are two inseparable elements.

If the purpose of a performance were to create an image of confusion, then a street corner might be perfect. But if the object were to centre the interest on a single point, and there are extraneous noises, or if visibility is bad, or if events occur simultaneously above, below, behind and very near the spectator, he will obviously find concentration impossible.

We have sometimes carried out experiments in which the actor leaves the stage and moves among the spectators, taking great care to maintain the actor-audience relationship. This relationship will depend on the dimensions of the space, the speed of the movements, the way in which the actor speaks and the length of the experiment—for a moment will come when the contact is lost, all communication destroyed and the experiment reduced to nothing. That indicates the extent to which distance, duration and sound in a particular space totally condition the event.

There are no strict rules to tell us whether a space is good or bad. In fact, all this relates to a kind of rigorous and precise science which we can only develop by continuous experiment and empiricism based on fact.

That's it! Theorizing's over!

LES BOUFFES DU NORD

• • •

Three years of travel and experiment had taught us—the hard way— what was a good and what was a bad space. One day, Micheline Rozan said to me, "There is a theatre behind the Gare du Nord that everyone's forgotten about. I've heard that it's still there. Let's go and look!" So we jumped into a car, but when we reached the place where the theatre should have been, there was nothing, just a café, a shop and the many-windowed facade of a typical nineteenth-century Paris apartment block. However, we noticed some loose boarding covering a hole in the wall. We pushed it aside, crawled through a dusty tunnel and suddenly straightened to discover—wrecked, charred, streaked by rain, pock-marked, yet noble, human, glowing-red and breathtaking—Les Bouffes du Nord.

We made two decisions: one was to keep the theatre exactly as it was, not to erase a single trace of the hundred years of life that had passed through it; and the other was to bring new life back into it as quickly as possible. We were advised that it would be impossible. A Ministry official told us it would take two years to get money and permits. Micheline refused their logic, accepted the challenge. Six months later, we opened with *Timon of Athens*.

We kept the old wooden seats in the balcony, but we put fresh varnish on them. At the first performances, some people were literally glued to their seats and we actually had to pay compensation to some irate ladies who had been compelled to leave part of their skirts behind.

Fortunately there was a lot of applause, but it literally brought the house down, as large lumps of plaster decoration were dislodged by the vibration and fell, just missing the heads of the audience. Since then, the ceiling has been scraped, but an extraordinary acoustical quality remains.

Micheline and I formulated a policy: the theatre was to be simple, open, welcoming. There were to be no numbered seats, one price everywhere, and that price to be as low as possible, half or a quarter of boulevard prices. We aimed at making the theatre accessible to people from the outer suburbs, to families, not barred by cost from coming in fours and fives, and we made a Saturday matinee—always one of the best and warmest audiences—at even lower prices. This way elderly people could come, who were afraid to go out at night. Also, we resolved to give ourselves the freedom to close the theatre when we chose, or give free performances at Christmas or Easter to people from the neighborhood.

We wanted workshops, events for children, or the possibility to go out into the community with our improvisations, so that the Bouffes would not turn into a repertory theatre, but remain a Centre. Naturally, all this costs much more than running a theatre night after night with normal prices, and despite the wholehearted support of a new Minister of Culture, Michel Guy, our subsidy from the French government was still not adequate. My stroke of luck was having Micheline as a partner —it was her brilliance and originality of vision that enabled us year after year to cross the tightrope of survival.

THE CONFERENCE OF THE BIRDS
· · ·

In the years before we settled into the Bouffes du Nord, we never believed in corporal expression as an end in itself, even though we worked on the body and its gestures. We studied sounds as a means of expression, yet we never imagined that meant the elimination of our usual forms of language. We worked on free improvisation in front of all sorts of audiences with one simple aim—to understand more fully

the links that exist between the truth of a form and the quality of what an audience receives.

Necessarily, our starting point was ourselves. However, to avoid the danger of going round in narcissistic circles, it is absolutely essential to be jolted from outside, and this comes when we try to work on something which challenges our understanding, forcing us to see beyond our personal universe.

So we soon turned to the Sufi poet Attar, who belongs to a tradition in which the author himself struggles to serve a greater reality than that of his personal imaginings and ideas—he tries to infuse the conceits of his imagination with a universe that stretches far beyond it. *The Conference of the Birds* is a work of limitless facets and levels: it represented for us the ocean we needed. We approached it gingerly, step by step.

We performed short fragments of *The Conference of the Birds* in the African bush, in the suburbs of Paris, with the Chicanos in California, with Indians in Minnesota and on the street corners of Brooklyn: always in different forms—forms dictated by the necessity to communicate—and always discovering with great emotion that its contents were truly universal, that it transcended all cultural and social barriers with ease.

On the last night of our stay in Brooklyn in 1973, we performed three different versions. The version at 8:00 p.m. was rough theatre: vulgar, comic, full of life. The one at midnight was a search for the holy: intimate, whispered, to candlelight. The final version began in darkness at 5:00 a.m. and finished at sunrise—it was in the form of a chorale, everything happened through improvised song. At dawn, before the group separated for several months, we said to ourselves: Next time, we must try to bring all of these different elements together within the same performance.

A number of years passed before it seemed possible for us to return to Attar.

This time we had two aims: to replace improvisation with a production which was not necessarily fixed, but stable enough to be reproduced as often as necessary; and to replace the partial, fragmentary impressions given in the past with an attempt to capture the poem in its entirety, to tell its story more fully.

Now we had a major new element in our work. A writer of great talent and sensibility had gradually become part of our activities: Jean-Claude Carrière took over from Ted Hughes. At first, he sat quietly in a corner watching, then he joined in the exercises and improvisations, suggested themes, wrote fragmentary scenarios. By the time we reached the Bouffes du Nord, it was he who tackled the awesome difficulty of capturing Shakespeare in the language least suited for the purpose, French. When *The Conference of the Birds* became a real project, he was part of us, ready to bring to group creation that unique contribution that can only come from a specialist, a man of words, in the same way that Sally Jacobs, who had been part of our work since the Theatre of Cruelty, brought her own uniqueness as a designer.

In *The Conference of the Birds* as in many other myths and traditions, the visible world is presented as illusion, as shadow thrown upon a surface which is the earth. And of course it's the same in the theatre. The theatre is a world of images, and theatre's glory is the conjuring up of illusions. If the world is illusion, the theatre is illusion within illusion. And from one point of view the theatre can be a very dangerous drug. One of the criticisms that has been levelled for many, many years against what one calls the bourgeois theatre is that by throwing reflections of illusions back toward the audience it reinforces their dreams and consequently reinforces their blindness, their incapacity to see reality.

But like everything this can be seen exactly the other way round. In the theatre the illusions have less body, because they haven't got the ferocious attachment to the very forces that make the illusions in life so impossible to break. The fact that these are imaginary presentations makes it possible for them to take on a double nature, and this double nature is where one approaches the meaning of *The Conference of the Birds.* On the one hand, as it's said in *The Conference of the Birds,* when you turn toward the impressions of life, you see life. But when you turn the other way, you see what is behind these illusions, and both the visible and the invisible worlds appear.

BUTTER AND THE KNIFE
• • •

Something universal in the theatre which lacks specificity is like butter, and something specific devoid of universality is like a closed door. Or one could take the image of butter and a knife instead: the universal element is the butter, the specific is the knife.

In Shakespeare, for instance, one finds both, so one asks: How can one find this outside Shakespeare? Is it possible to have butter and knife by other means? In the Centre we have been exploring many styles, but we have not yet arrived at a point of synthesis.

In *Ubu Roi,* there was great energy, and its form gave it the capacity to attract any spectator and to bring him into contact with this energy. But *Ubu Roi* was never able to touch upon a hidden, inner life—something *The Ik* could do during its best performances. On the other hand, by its very nature *The Ik* as a production was not accessible to everyone: certain spectators reacted to it in a very negative way. The very nature of *The Ik* prevented it from having the kind of energy that draws people irresistibly toward the performance. It is a play that demands something from the spectator, and it could not force attention beyond what the audience wanted to give. Ideally, both would be there, the inner and the outer energies.

The closest we have come to our ideal was when we played the African farce *The Bone (L'Os)* alongside *The Conference of the Birds.* The rough comic vitality of *The Bone* was invaluable as it offered a much more accessible approach to those people who might have been hostile and closed to *The Conference of the Birds.* It warmed them up. In conjunction with each other as a "double bill," these two plays made it possible to start the evening on a very accessible level, then move toward something more profound. But the two plays always remained independent units. Although in *The Conference of the Birds* we tried to combine comic and serious, difficult elements, it could only go just so far, because of the very nature of this play.

In *The Cherry Orchard,* there are two movements: a tempo directed toward the spectators (as in *Ubu Roi*), and another turning inwards (as in *The Ik*). In *Carmen,* the tremendous power of musical expression forces attention and draws the spectator into a secret world.

In *The Mahabharata,* I will start the search again. Perhaps this time we will be able to bring all these elements together in one form.

THE CHERRY ORCHARD

• • •

There are four versions of *The Cherry Orchard* in French, and an even greater number in English. Still, we have to try again. One must reassess existing adaptations regularly—they are always colored by the time in which they were written, just like productions, which are never there to stay.

There was a time when one believed a text had to be recreated freely by a poet so as to capture its mood. Today, fidelity is the central concern: an approach which necessitates weighing every single word and bringing it into sharp focus. This is all the more interesting with Chekhov, as his essential quality is precision. I would compare what is loosely called his poetry with what constitutes the beauty of a film: a succession of natural, true images. Chekhov always looked for what's natural; he wanted performances and productions to be as limpid as life itself. So in order to capture his particular atmosphere, one must resist the temptation to give a "literary" turn to phrases which, in Russian, are simplicity itself. Chekhov's writing is extremely concentrated, employing a minimum of words; in a way, it is similar to Pinter or Beckett. As with them, it is construction that counts, rhythm, the purely theatrical poetry that comes not from beautiful words but from the right word at the right moment. In the theatre, someone can say "yes" in such a way that the "yes" is no longer ordinary—it can become a beautiful word, because it is the perfect expression of what cannot be expressed in any other way.

As soon as we had decided on fidelity, we wanted the French text to adapt itself exactly to the Russian, to be every bit as muscular and realistic. The risk was of lapsing into artificial colloquialisms. Equivalents are possible in literary writing; spoken language, on the other hand, is not exportable. Jean-Claude Carrière used a simple vocabulary, trying to provide the actors, from phrase to phrase, with the movements of thought that Chekhov had conceived, respecting the detail of timing given by the punctuation. Shakespeare did not use punctuation; it was inserted later. His plays are like telegrams: the actors themselves have to compose the groups of words. With Chekhov, on the other hand, periods, commas, points of suspension are all of a fundamental importance, as fundamental as the "pauses" precisely indicated by Beckett. If one fails to observe them, one loses the rhythm and tensions of the play. In Chekhov's work, the punctuation represents a series of coded messages which record characters' relationships and emotions, the moments at which ideas come together or follow their own course. The punctuation enables us to grasp what the words conceal.

Chekhov is a perfect film maker. Instead of cutting from one image to another—perhaps from one place to another—he switches from one emotion to another just before it gets too heavy. At the precise moment when the spectator risks becoming too involved in a character, an unexpected situation cuts across: nothing is stable. Chekhov portrays individuals and a society in a state of perpetual change, he is the dramatist of life's movement, simultaneously smiling and serious, amusing and bitter—completely free from the "music," the Slav "nostalgia" that Paris nightclubs still preserve. He often stated that his plays were comedies—this was the central issue of his conflict with Stanislavsky. He detested the dramatic tone, the leaden slowness imposed by the director.

But it's wrong to conclude that *The Cherry Orchard* should be performed as a vaudeville. Chekhov is an infinitely detailed observer of the human comedy. As a doctor, he knew the meaning of certain kinds of behavior, how to discern what was essential, to expose what he diagnosed. Although he shows tenderness and an attentive sympathy, he never sentimentalizes. One doesn't imagine a doctor shedding tears over the illnesses of his patients. He learns how to balance compassion with distance.

In Chekhov's work, death is omnipresent—he knew it well—but there is nothing negative or unsavory in its presence. The awareness of death is balanced with a desire to live. His characters possess a sense of the present moment, and the need to taste it fully. As in great tragedies, one finds a harmony between life and death.

Chekhov died young, having travelled, written and loved enormously, having taken part in the events of his day, in great schemes of social reform. He died shortly after asking for some champagne, and his coffin was transported in a wagon bearing the inscription "Fresh Oysters." His awareness of death, and of the precious moments that could be lived, endow his work with a sense of the relative: in other words, a viewpoint from which the tragic is always a bit absurd.

In Chekhov's work, each character has its own existence: not one of them resembles another, particularly in *The Cherry Orchard*, which presents a microcosm of the political tendencies of the time. There are those who believe in social transformations, others attached to a disappearing past. None of them can achieve satisfaction or plenitude, and seen from outside, their existences might well appear empty, senseless. But they all burn with intense desires. They are not disillusioned, quite the contrary: in their own ways, they are all searching for a better quality of life, emotionally and socially. Their drama is that

Natasha Parry in *The Cherry Orchard*

society—the outside world—blocks their energy. The complexity of their behavior is not indicated in the words, it emerges from the mosaic construction of an infinite number of details. What is essential is to see that these are not plays about lethargic people. They are hypervital people in a lethargic world, forced to dramatize the minutest happening out of a passionate desire to live. They have not given up.

THE MAHABHARATA

. . .

One of the difficulties we encounter when we see traditional theatre from the East is that we admire without understanding. Unless we possess the keys to the symbols, we remain on the outside, fascinated, perhaps, by the surface, but unable to contact the human realities without which these complex art forms would never have arisen.

The day I first saw a demonstration of Kathakali, I heard a word completely new to me—*"The Mahabharata."* A dancer was presenting a scene from this work and his sudden first appearance from behind a curtain was an unforgettable shock. His costume was red and gold, his face was red and green, his nose was like a white billiard ball, his fingernails were like knives; in place of beard and mustache, two white crescent moons thrust forward from his lips, his eyebrows shot up and down like drumsticks and his fingers spelled out strange coded messages. Through the magnificent ferocity of the movements, I could see that a story was unfolding. But what story? I could only guess at something mythical and remote, from another culture, nothing to do with my life.

Gradually, sadly, I realized that my interest was lessening, the visual shock was wearing off. After the interval, the dancer returned without his makeup, no longer a demigod, just a likable Indian in shirt and jeans. He described the scene he had been playing and repeated the dance. The hieratic gestures passed through the man of today. The superb but impenetrable image had given way to an ordinary, more accessible one and I realized that I preferred it this way.

When I next encountered *The Mahabharata,* it was as a series of stories told to Jean-Claude Carrière and me with passionate enthusiasm by that remarkable Sanskrit scholar, Philippe Lavastine. Through him we began to understand why this was one of the greatest works of humanity, and how, like all great works, it is both far from us and very near. It contains the most profound expressions of Hindu thought, and yet for over two thousand years it has penetrated so intimately into the daily life of India that for many millions of people the characters are eternally alive—as real as members of their own family, with whom they share the quarrels and the questions.

Jean-Claude and I were so fascinated that standing in the rue St. André des Arts at three o'clock in the morning after a long storytelling session, we made a mutual commitment. We would find a way of bringing this material into our world and sharing these stories with an audience in the West.

Once we had taken this decision, the first step was obviously to go to India. Here began a long series of journeys in which gradually all those preparing the project took part—actors, musicians, designers. India ceased to be a dream and became infinitely the richer. I cannot say that we saw all its aspects, but we saw enough to learn that its variety is infinite. Every day brought a new surprise and a new discovery.

We saw that for several thousand years India has lived in a climate of constant creativity. Even if life flows with the majestic slowness of a great river, at the same time, within the current, each atom has its own dynamic energy. Whatever the aspect of human experience, the Indian has indefatigably explored every possibility. If it is that most humble and most amazing of human instruments, a finger, everything that a finger can do has been explored and codified. If it is a word, a breath, a limb, a sound, a note—or a stone or a color or a cloth—all its aspects, practical, artistic and spiritual, have been investigated and linked together. Art means celebrating the most refined possibilities of every element, and art means extracting the essence from every detail so that the detail can reveal itself as a meaningful part of an inseparable whole. The more we saw of Indian classical art forms, especially in the performing arts, the more we realized that they take at least a lifetime to master, and that a foreigner can only admire, not imitate.

The line between performance and ceremony is hard to draw, and we witnessed many events that took us close to Vedic times, or close to the energy that is uniquely Indian. Theyam, Mudiattu, Yakshagana, Chaau, Jatra—every region has its form of drama and almost every form—sung, mimed, narrated—touches or tells a part of *Mahabharata.* Wherever we went, we met sages, scholars, villagers, pleased to find foreigners interested in their great epic and generously happy to share their understanding.

We were touched by the love that Indians bring to *The Mahabharata,* and this filled us both with respect and awe at the task we had assumed.

Yet we knew that theatre must not be solemn and we must not allow ourselves to become crushed into a false reverence. What guided us most in India was the popular tradition. Here we recognized the techniques that all folk art has in common and which we have explored in improvisations over the years. We have always considered a theatre group as a multi-headed storyteller, and one of the most fascinating ways of meeting *The Mahabharata* in India is through the storyteller. He not only plays on his musical instrument, but uses it as a unique scenic device to suggest a bow, a sword, a mace, a river, an army or a monkey's tail.

We returned from India knowing that our work was not to imitate but to suggest.

Jean-Claude then began the vast undertaking of turning all these experiences into a text. There were times when I saw his mind reaching explosion point, because of the multitude of impressions and the innumerable units of information he had stored over the years. On the first day of rehearsal, Jean-Claude said to the actors as he handed them nine hours' worth of text: "Don't take this to be a finished play. Now I'm going to start rewriting each scene as we see it evolve in your hands." In fact, he didn't rewrite every scene, but the material was constantly developing as we worked.

Then we decided to make an English version and I set out to prepare a translation that would be as faithful as possible to Jean-Claude's gigantic achievement.

In the performance, whether in English or French, we are not attempting a reconstruction of Dravidian and Aryan India of three thousand years ago. We are not presuming to present the symbolism of Hindu philosophy. In the music, in the costumes, in the movements, we have tried to suggest the flavor of India without pretending to be what we are not. On the contrary, the many nationalities who have gathered together are trying to reflect *The Mahabharata* by bringing to it something of their own. In this way, we are trying to celebrate a work which only India could have created but which carries echoes for all mankind.

DHARMA

. . .

What is dharma? That is a question no one can answer, except to say that, in a certain sense, it is the essential motor. Since it is the essential motor, everything that is in accord with it magnifies the effect of dharma. Whatever does not agree with it, whatever opposes or is ignorant of it, isn't "evil" in the Christian sense—but negative.

The Mahabharata cuts to shreds all the old, traditional Western concepts, which are founded on an inessential, degenerate Christianity

The Mahabharata

in which good and evil have assumed very primitive forms. It brings
back something immense, powerful and radiant—the idea of an inces-
sant conflict within every person and every group, in every expression
of the universe; a conflict between a possibility, which is called
"dharma," and the negation of that possibility. *The Mahabharata* as a
whole acquires its concrete meaning from the fact that dharma cannot
be defined. What can be said about something that can't be defined, if
one wants to avoid philosophical abstractions? For no one can be
helped in life by abstractions.

The Mahabharata does not attempt to explain the secret of
dharma, but lets it become a living presence. It does this through
dramatic situations which force dharma into the open.

When one enters into the drama of *The Mahabharata,* one is living
with dharma. And when one has passed through the work, one has a
feeling for what dharma is and what is its opposite, adharma. Here lies
the responsibility of the theatre: what a book cannot convey, what no
philosopher can truly explain, can be brought into our understanding
by the theatre. Translating the untranslatable is one of its roles.

THE GODDESS AND THE JEEP
• • •

We were at an enormous ritual drama performance about Kali (the
Indian goddess of destruction), which lasted many hours and which
involved an entire village. Kali appears—she's in a spectacular costume and makeup that's taken hours to put on—and she does a ferocious dance that, theoretically, is supposed to terrify everyone. In the
past, almost all of the people in the village experienced the true feeling
of awe that Kali was actually amongst them. Today, of course, it's play-
acting because everybody in the village, even the kids, has seen Indian
movies and they know what it's all about. But everyone is still playing
along with the idea that it's scary.

At one moment, Kali, carrying a sword and surrounded by attendants throwing firecrackers, set out of the village and started walking
up the main road. About a thousand of us followed her as she led this
procession. We came to a crossroads, and as Kali stood there dominat-
ing everything, a Jeep came down the road.

I thought, What's going to happen? Who's going to give way? And, of course, without even thinking, Kali stepped back, as did her attendants, let the Jeep pass, and then walked forward again and carried on with the ceremony.

Here you have the decline and fall of religious theatre. Because the genuine Kali would have thrown such a look at the Jeep that it would have stopped in its tracks. And a smarter priesthood could have arranged to have had a James Bond Jeep there that would have gone up in smoke just to show the people that Kali is as strong as ever. But faced with a Jeep that wants to hurtle along the highway, the little dancer doesn't for a moment imagine that the goddess who is possessing Kali could actually hold up traffic on an arterial road.

part VII

THE FORTY
YEARS' WAR

. . .

THE ART OF NOISE

. . .

Opera started fifty thousand years ago with people making noises as they came out of their caves. And out of those noises come Verdi and Puccini and Wagner. There was a noise for fear, for love, for happiness and for anger. That was one-note, atonal opera, and that's where it all began. At that point it was a natural human expression, and that turned into song. And, at some later time, that process become codified, constructed, and turned into an art.

So far, so good. But at a certain moment, the art form became frozen; it began to be admired because it was frozen, and operagoers began to express a tremendous admiration for art as artificial.

The disease of the artificial gave very good results for the moment, and so you have beautiful and stylized works by Monteverdi and Gluck. Then you come to Mozart and find a perfect marriage between the artificial and something that's fully alive—here's an example of the rigid pipe and the water flowing through it. But gradually the attention begins to go more and more to the artificial until suddenly you're into sclerosis. Suddenly, that pipe is taking all the attention and less and less water is trickling through it.

Finally you get a fundamentally unwell and crazy society in which people forget that pipes were put into buildings for the purpose of letting the water through, and they now consider them to be works of art. People knock the walls down and admire the piping and totally forget its original purpose and function. This is what has happened in many art forms, and the opera is the clearest example.

I would say the greatest challenge now, at this point in the twentieth century, is to replace—in the minds of performers as well as audiences—the idea that opera is artificial with the idea that opera is natural. That's really the most important thing, and I think it's possible.

SALOMÉ

• • •

When I asked Salvador Dali to design *Salomé* for our 1949 season at Covent Garden, it did not occur to me that this could be seen as a stunt. Quite simply, Dali seemed the best man in the world for the job. Having read the reviews, I feel so strongly that they have missed all the points that this is an attempt to write my own notice.

Critical points of departure: What determines the style of a production of *Salomé?* The music and the libretto. What are their most striking features? They are strange, poetic, unrealistic. Should the visual counterpart, i.e., the set, the props, the costumes, be "straight"? Surely not. Realism must be kept for the works written in a realistic style—most of Puccini's, for example. But to put the fantastic myth of Strauss and Wilde into a document-of-Judea decor is as absurd as playing *King Lear* in a drawing-room set for a West End comedy.

All artistic work must have a tradition. In this case the visual tradition is at hand. Look at Beardsley. How did he approach the problem of illustrating *Salomé?*

By doing snapshots of scenes from the story? On the contrary. He catches the flavor of Wilde by fantasy and distortion. Gustave Moreau's *Salomé* is a masterpiece—in it a head surrounded by golden spikes floats in the air. Odd, outrageous? No, because, as in Dürer, as in Hieronymus Bosch, in fact as in two thousand years of Christian and Oriental painting, religious and mythical subjects have always been treated in a stylized way.

So why Salvador Dali? Because he is the only artist I know in the world whose natural style has both what one might call the erotic degeneracy of Strauss and the imagery of Wilde.

Dali and I studied the score and set out to make a true music drama in the style of the great religious painters. We conceived *Salomé* as a sort of triptych. We made the set symmetrical with a focal point, a stone slab—"Perhaps an altar once"—old, crumbling, buried in the rock far downstage in the acoustic heart of Covent Garden. From the very back of the stage sweeps Salomé's entrance. Traditionally, she comes from the side; we bring her from the centre. Scandalous? Or better theatre? Away from this slab wind the narrow steps into the well. When Jokanaan comes out he stands on the slab, and when Salomé lies in erotic frenzy on the stage she lies across it. When she dances it is as though the whole drum of the set is a vast cistern, under which Jokanaan is imprisoned. When Jokanaan is killed deep underground, the stone bleeds. It is out of it that the head is offered to Salomé. It is on this slab, with fatal logic, that Salomé is crushed to death.

The centre platform is reserved for the protagonists. It is raised to make it better for sound and to help the voices to carry over the impossibly loud orchestra. It is also as small as possible, because we wanted to discourage the singers from movement. We wanted them to take up stylized positions in built-up costumes and express the drama with their most impressive instruments, their voices. We aimed at cramping the dance. No singer is supposed to be a dancer; the more the dance could be *carried* by the orchestra and *indicated* by the singer, the less the embarrassment and the greater the illusion.

Why should we be afraid of fantasy and imagination, even in an opera house? When the curtain rises, strange vulture-like wings beat slowly under the moon; a giant peacock's tail, opening with the opening of the dance, suggests the decadent luxury of Herod's kingdom. A handful of such visual touches over the ninety-six minutes of the opera are designed to lift the audience into the strange Wilde-Strauss world, and to point the essential stages of the tragedy.

I feel I can safely say that wherever this *Salomé* departs from the traditional production, the aim is a musical one. This *Salomé* is designed more for singers than the traditional production. They are all acoustically better off, and by stylizing the scene with the Jews in a formal group downstage on one side, the Nazarenes on the other, and Herod raised in the centre, a far stronger musical effect than usual can be made. The style is an attempt to create a style of opera which is dramatic, visually exciting and yet doesn't pretend that the artists involved are actors, dancers or, in fact, anything but singers.

After any new production one goes through an agonizing process of soul-searching and I have no illusions of how far one is from one's own goal. Criticism, good or bad, is always important and useful, so it seems a pity when the critics miss the very features that might have been worth their consideration. But they all decided that Dali and I were out only to annoy them. There, at least, I might claim that they underestimated us; if that had been our intention, I think that between us we could have done far worse.

FAUST

. . .

I'd had a bad experience of conductors. The true definition of who's in charge is one that few opera houses dare to make, so there is always a latent battle between producer and musician, each of whom believes that he alone should have the last word about what is fitting for the work *as a whole.* I believe that this is the producer's function—naturally, but also objectively—as the nature of the producer's job is to oversee and coordinate activities which he does not practice. He does not need to act, nor to write, nor to dance, nor sing; he has to develop a curious art, a special know-how—in fact, like a conductor's, invisible and essential—by which he prevents the inevitable anarchy of the uncontrolled individual from destroying the whole. He draws from the individual that which completes an idea of the whole, which for better or worse proceeds from a single brain.

In music drama, the producer is in a more objective position than the conductor, who like the actor is limited by his specialty. Of course, the conductor accuses the producer of being unmusical. This is often the case. But were all the unmusical producers stretched end to end they would be just a speck compared with the monstrous army of musicians insensitive to all the atrocities with which the eye is perpetually afflicted in all the opera houses of the world. How is it, I ask myself, that musicians tolerate pictures in a frame forty feet by twenty feet that they wouldn't endure for a moment in a normal frame on the walls of their homes?

I believe that the traditional image presented of Gounod's *Faust* is utterly and completely false to all the pictures that stir in the score, and so consequently the traditional *Faust* production is for us grossly unmusical. Goethe's *Faust* belongs to the heavy, ugly medieval picture we associate with it. But Gounod was not Goethe in any way at all. With lazy thinking, Goethe scenery and costumes have been glued onto Gounod, and equally lazy criticism has assumed that they were right. However, there has always been a loser: Gounod. In the somber realism of this conventional style—with associations via Goethe of serious philosophical intention—his music seems painfully inadequate. Where Goethe is profound, Gounod seems sentimental; his waltzes, marches and ballet divertissements seem inappropriate, incongruous, cheap, banal or silly, depending on our taste. In fact, to like *Faust* is a sign of bad taste.

Rolf Gérard, the designer, and I resolved to create a frame for *Faust* of the right weight; we saw in it not a soul-shaking parable but a lovable early nineteenth-century Romantic work, a kind of tale of Hoffmann—and we felt passionately that in this "lighter" world, the work could take on its true nostalgic, elegant period charm and magic. I remember we spent a long week in Connecticut in the rain, playing the records of the opera over and over again, gazing out of the window at the dripping trees and trying to capture the images as they were thrown up by the music.

But there was one lurking dread. The conductor. We were to stage this opera with the next best thing to Gounod himself—with Pierre Monteux, who had conducted the very first performance of *Faust* at the Met.

As anyone who knew Monteux can guess, we need not have worried. He was delighted at the thought of change and completely agreed with our reasoning. In fact, all went smoothly until our very first rehearsal when Rossi-Lemeni, playing Mephistopheles as a nineteenth-century baron in cape and top hat, asked, "What shall I do with the line describing my appearance which says I wear 'la plume au chapeau'? This will sound absurd with my top hat." "Oh, we'll change it," I said airily and suddenly I caught Monteux's eye. "My dear friend," he said, "I will accept anything you propose, but not a change in the score." In vain I tried to explain that this would be a change in the libretto. He was adamant. Now he was Gounod's representative—and watchdog.

The rehearsal came to a standstill. Rossi-Lemeni, confused, tried to withdraw his objection but it was too late. We discussed variants, compromises, but we had reached an impasse. In the end, I postponed the problem, went on to another scene and said to a very disapproving Monteux, "You're the only person who can find a solution. You're the only Frenchman here."

The next day we did not mention the problem, nor the day after. I began to get seriously worried. Then on the third day Monteux arrived at rehearsal, his eyes twinkling. "I have solved your problem," he said. "Let Mephistopheles change his line to 'le plus haut chapeau.' Then those who are used to hearing 'la plume au chapeau' will undoubtedly continue to hear the same sounds, and to those who write and ask us why we have a line that doesn't correspond with the hat he is wearing, we can quote this line which is—I believe—an exact description."

I would like to pay tribute here to this unique spirit, this great musician and ideal colleague. I can still hear him at the first orchestra rehearsal of *Faust,* after the opening chord, laying down his stick and saying to the orchestra in apparent surprise, "Is it true you gentlemen cannot play louder?" And being rewarded next time with the most exciting attack I had ever heard this orchestra give.

And I can also hear him at the first dress rehearsal, when the curtain rose on Marguerite's garden and he saw for the first time Gérard's set, in which the ghastly traditional cottage was replaced by a Corot-like romantic park. Again he laid down his stick.

"Ah," he said, "Marguérite est donc milliardaire!"

EUGÈNE ONEGIN

• • •

If Faust *was a labor* of love for Gérard and myself, so was *Onegin.* In *Faust* we were dazzled by our collaborator Monteux, and this time we had an equally rewarding experience with Mitropoulos.

Again, we approached the conductor full of trepidation. Again, we had some major changes to propose. Our great love for Tchaikowsky's score did not blind us to its two great weaknesses. The work demands a realistic style of staging. Like *Bohéme,* it is one of those operas where a reconstruction of the period creates the true climate in which the music can breathe. *Onegin* demands those Turgenev-like images of Russian provincial life: a Stanislavsky, Moscow Arts Theatre approach to naturalistic detail. This in turn means solid, believable scenery which takes a long time to change. And Tchaikowsky has written no interludes at all, no time to move a chair or even hoist a backcloth. Is it possible in this day and age to let an audience sit in half darkness many times in an evening, their conversation drying on their lips, while behind a curtain objects squeak, thud and rumble into position? We decided not.

The other theatrical weakness of the work is the last scene. Here the dénouement of the entire story is scrambled into a short unimportant episode in a drawing room, and before the tenor has completed his last tragic gasp the curtain rushes down with hardly enough bars of music to bring it to the ground.

So we went to Mitropoulos to ask him if he would prepare inter-

ludes out of material in the score and extend the last bars to make a
more theatrically satisfying finish. He agreed readily, and we in turn
began to evolve a very different notion for the last scene, one that led
to Gérard's finest set—a frozen park on the banks of the Neva, with the
distant lights of St. Petersburg, a coach, a black iron railing, a street
lamp, urns and a stone bench, falling snow. The two lovers meet for
the last time "dans le vieux parc solitaire et glacé"—an image not from
Onegin but from Pushkin and the Romantic Age. Of course, it scandalized all those who were mesmerized by the printed score which says
"a drawing room." But to me it completely fulfilled the condition I had
set Gérard, which was to end the opera on an image which could have
a resonance appropriate to the climax of the work.

Usually, when a production is finished, almost all emotional ties
to it are cut. But *Onegin,* because of the sets, the whole cast, Mitropoulos, the particular timbre of Tucker's voice and the sheer beauty of the
score, is something I still care for greatly. Perhaps because of the first
night.

We were very proud of what we were offering, and were certain it
would be well received. But I had not reckoned with the odd event
called "the first night of the season." As moment after moment of the
score avoided conventional climaxes, and as aria after aria came to a
quiet close, I realized that the audience was being cheated. They had
come to approve. They wanted big moments, top notes, climaxes, noisy
final chords and the immediate release of applause and cheers. They
expected Tchaikowsky to be vulgar, and were at a loss before this sensitive, lyrical, unspectacular score. When our built-up theatrical end
came, it was too late. They had had a lukewarm evening. Clearly *Onegin*
should never have been chosen for this: it was one of Rudolf Bing's
rare mistakes. But he himself liked it and that was a great satisfaction.

I have always believed that Bing's secret was that he was so easily
bored by bad opera that he took on his nightmarish job so as to get for
himself a few tolerable evenings. Most opera intendants sit smugly in
their boxes enjoying bad performances. What made Bing so remarkable was that he was more impatient and more critical than anyone.
Before you could complain about anything he was already outraged. I
know of no one else from whom I gladly accepted such terrible working
conditions.

CARMEN

• • •

An interview with Philippe Albera after the opening of La Tragédie de Carmen *at the Bouffes du Nord in November 1981.*

ALBERA: With this *Carmen*, you have returned to opera after a very long absence. Why did you stop directing opera?

BROOK: Conditions in opera are bad; it's a constant struggle. The struggle is an almost total waste of time and energy, and that's the time to stop struggling.

Opera is a form of theatre, yet set alongside other forms of theatre, it's encumbered with incredibly unfavorable conditions. So years ago, I abandoned opera. But now it's become possible again because in our theatre we can change the conditions entirely—the nature of rehearsals and performances, ticket prices, and so on. In other words, we can change the relationship with the spectators and the relationship with theatre space. We rehearsed for ten weeks (which is not that much objectively, but is a great deal in terms of the system usually in operation), and we performed about two hundred shows with the same team. In general in music, for major events there is a substantial number of rehearsals, but the rehearsal period is not enough for a development in depth of an ensemble. For this, you need performances.

Rehearsal is a period of preparation, and performance, playing in front of spectators, is the beginning of a new process. Operas are usually performed five or six times, so that at the point when the performers are starting to relax, just when they are beginning to find a real relationship with audiences and with one another, it's over. That's one of the reasons I insisted on a long series of performances of the same piece, and at the same time we continued to rehearse and do exercises during the day. I believe it was very important for singers sometimes to concentrate their energies on one work, and penetrate it fully.

ALBERA: From this point of view, is the choice of *Carmen* unique, or do you feel that this kind of approach could be generalized and applied to other operas? Is your way of reducing a work, of sweeping away the conventions associated with opera only a limited experiment?

BROOK: The experiment was only possible because of our set-up. To have a degree of freedom, one must work in a small group, and it

Carmen

cannot be too expensive. It's exactly the same as with a film: if one wants to make a non-commercial film, one must accept a small budget. If one wants to spend thirty million dollars, one is obliged to make a film that half the world's population will like.

In any case, big opera houses are not going to have to close their doors because of us, they will always have their audience. But there's nothing to prevent small operatic groups from doing experimental work, and it is certainly true that operas can be condensed in a very vital way without harming the work itself. For example, despite the fact that the glory of *Pélléas et Mélisande* results in part from the nature of the orchestral score, one could start afresh with a version for piano and still do a *Pélléas* of great vitality. There are many towns that will never have performances of opera because of costs, but people would be delighted to meet small groups around a piano. I think *One-*

gin would be a very touching and charming opera with a small group and a concert grand.

In England there is a group that has staged performances of *Aïda* in this way. In theatre I have seen versions of Dickens's works or *A Thousand and One Nights* with four or five people playing any number of different roles. One might imagine a few singers taking on both choral and solo roles . . .

ALBERA: Does the working method you adopted for *Carmen,* the fact of having a great number of performances, seem to you unworkable and indeed impossible in opera as it exists?

BROOK: Yes, as it exists . . . But if there are a sufficient number of experiments, I think they could have an influence on institutions. I don't think one gets anywhere through direct assault, because the institution itself doesn't give a damn. You need the collaboration of all those people who refuse to accept the old myths, who can write publicly that it is not necessary for opera to be cumbersome and ossified.

For example, there's no reason for men or women to have grotesque bodies simply because they sing. Today one sees many very beautiful women with beautiful voices and fine bodies. There are thin men who sing as well as fat ones. Ridiculous bodies reflect a certain complacency and even complicity from audiences who accept things as they are. But if the public is more critical, if young, attractive singers are more successful, then these "conventions" will end up by crumbling. What's certain is that within the opera world, the star system must give way to an ensemble principle. For the same people to work together for a considerable period of time is more important than anything else.

ALBERA: Isn't this a Utopian notion in a situation where financial aspects and the star system determine so much?

BROOK: That's why I said earlier on that one cannot launch a head-on assault on these problems; one can only try to create a parallel opera.

ALBERA: In *The Empty Space,* you wrote about the architectural problems of spaces. Do opera houses reflect all the conventions you are challenging, in their very layout?

BROOK: That's why with *Carmen* it was necessary to change all of the conditions at once. In the past there was a small orchestra, only slightly below the stage; almost imperceptibly the orchestra has grown like a giant mushroom and has been driven ever deeper under the stage. In order to make more noise, it had to be enlarged further, to the point where it has become ridiculously inappropriate and out of scale. The resulting competition between the human voice and the immense orchestra can be compared to the history of the dinosaur: after a certain point, it became so top-heavy that it toppled over.

An orchestra which is too big for the human voice creates an artificial demand: the singer is obliged to adopt attitudes which aren't natural. In order to be audible, he must face the auditorium and re-main as near as possible to the front of the stage. As a result, the performer can rarely take up positions and move in a way that corre-sponds to dramatic truth. In general, the form of an opera production is imposed as much (and perhaps more) by the layout of the audito-rium as by the director. Besides, the dignity of a musician is demeaned by putting him in a hole in the ground; this reflects a nineteenth-century attitude, the master above and the servants below the stairs. Part of the beauty of the Javanese theatre is that the musicians are all in full view, they watch and participate in all the action and something happens when all fifty strike their gongs and drums as one man.

ALBERA: If someone asked you, for example, what kind of architectural design to have for the new opera house planned for the Bastille, what would you suggest?

BROOK: Let's use common sense. What do most young couples say to each other when they are in love? "Let's get married. Let's buy a house." They don't start by saying, "I don't know if I want to marry you, but let's design a house, build it, then we'll look after some babies who aren't our own to see if it works. Then we'll think again . . ." You must start with a basic agreement on basic matters before you build a house. But have we this basis on which to construct an opera house?

We are at a moment of great confusion in theatre, a chaotic period of transition to we don't know what. This is not the case in cinema or television; if you want to construct a film studio today, the right form exists. But one cannot create an opera house, because no one can say what resources, production forms, staging the next hundred years will require. What's needed for Stockhausen, for exam-ple, is not at all what's needed for Berio, and the conditions within which their operas could best appear are not necessarily the same as for a new production of *The Marriage of Figaro*. As there is no solu-tion, those who are unfortunate enough to have to build new opera houses have to make a sort of compromise between all available forms. For example, in Sydney there is a wonderful opera house, it's one of the great monuments of modern architecture; but the only success of the Sydney Opera House is its exterior, which has become world famous. Inside this building operas aren't even performed in the space designed for it; they use what was originally intended for legitimaté theatre, and it's a very ugly space indeed.

ÁLBERA: Do you find it much more difficult to work with singers than with actors?

BROOK: A young singer is like a young actor, except that he already has a craft. He has learned something very demanding, the hard way. He's learned music, breathing, vocal technique. He has mastered languages. This actual craft gives him very firm support. Even if he's had only the corniest of acting experience, it's easy to take his bad acting away from him. He doesn't believe in it anyway—he does it because no one's shown him a better way. He's been asked to throw his arms out wide, or he's seen other singers do it. When that kind of false gesture is removed, he doesn't need to conceal himself in any way. He has his real, professional musical craft to sustain him. So I find that a singer with intuition, sensibility and a wish to do a truthful work can actually be truer and simpler than a professional actor. He doesn't need to *do* so much. Sometimes, he can just *be*.

THE TASTE OF STYLE
An After-Luncheon Speech
• • •

Ladies and gentlemen of the Metropolitan Opera House:

I am supposed to speak about style, and yet my difficulty is that I've never seen style. Our work has taken us to all parts of the world. I have seen theatre performances in the most varied conditions, and I think I've looked very intently. I have never seen style. I think that the moment one starts to look for style, talk about style, one goes headfirst into a pit that is almost certain to swallow one up.

I imagine all of us on a desert island where there is nothing to eat. As mealtime comes around, faced with the lack of food—just a few leaves and a few pebbles to eat—what would happen? One would become nostalgic about meals one has once had. And somebody would begin to say, "Do you remember the taste of smoked salmon?" And somebody else would say, "Yes, I remember it, and do you remember the pepper that went with it?" Then somebody else would try to remember what the taste of lemon was. In fact, day after day, these memories would become more and more confused, and after a year of living on leaves and bark and overripe fruit, the person who remembers most vividly the taste of lemon would be beginning in his imagination to muddle it up with the taste of papaya and the taste of leaves. And the conversation, which would become more and more necessary because the real substance was lacking, would go into an endless word game around nothing.

To me, this is what happens most of the time when we are talking about style. We are talking about style—why? Why does this interest arise? I think it is largely because the meal is not there. Because the actual reason for the whole function, the reason everybody is sitting round a table, is to have a certain nourishment because they have a certain hunger. This nourishment having been lost, having been forgotten, the void is filled with dreams and speculations, and I think you will find that in most cases, this is what happens with the search for style.

The search for style becomes more and more prominent when the substance vanishes.

I am particularly struck by the fact that in the theatre in general, and particularly in classical theatre, and most particularly in operatic theatre, there is a strange confusion around whether the word "artificial" is a noble word of praise or a terrible term of criticism. The other night at *Carmen,* a lady came up to me after the show and said, "I want to speak to you about your fires."

We have three real fires in one scene which are very important to us. In every town where we've played it has meant going to see the fire department and explaining to the firemen that we know they don't like real fires, but in this case it's vital. They are usually very understanding, and we get special permission for our fire.

So this lady came up to me and said, "Could you tell me something? Why do you have these real fires when you could have had artificial ones?" I looked at her in amazement and said, "What do you mean?" and she said, "You know, these electric things with blowers and flames."

This isn't a joke, and I thought it was very interesting and a great symbol of our time. Because the way that for us was real, for her was poor. Had there been a marvellous, electronic machine with huge flames perfectly imitating a fire, that for her would have been money well spent.

I haven't invented this as a sort of symbolic anecdote. It actually happened, and seemed to me to be very relevant to the dividing line between two forms of theatre and, you can say, two forms of experience. There can be one direction, which is the direction of looking for what is or seems to be as easy to accept as possible, as being close to us, as being simple, as being real, as being natural. Or there can be another direction, which says everything that is real and natural is pretty odious. This is a disgusting world we're living in, we're close all day to what is real and natural, and heaven help us, let's get away from it as quickly as possible—and we escape. We escape either into dreams, or we escape from the present into the past.

Now, like the people talking about food on the desert island, nobody knows really what the past is, and the farther the past disappears, the less anyone knows about it. One invents imaginary conventions that nobody can sustain, which become the stylistic symbols of a non-existent memory of the past. So you take the eighteenth century, and there are two ways of looking at anything—eighteenth-century music or eighteenth-century words or eighteenth-century behavior. Either these are the expression of something that was once intensely meaningful, alive and real to somebody who is now gone, his period has gone, we have no contact except this work. So this work is of interest to us only if, one way or the other, it can suddenly become alive, real and meaningful to us. If that happens, then it is no longer a work of the past, it doesn't take us to the past, it brings the past right to us here in the present. And I think that when that happens, we have a rich and living human relation with human beings who no longer exist, and this is a miracle of a magical and highly rewarding nature.

Or, there is the opposite direction, which is to say, "That past is gone, but oh, how lovely it would be if we could get into a time machine and go there. How much better than our poor world." And then, with the help of conventions, dubious traditions, documents, paintings, and so on, we build up a completely bogus past in which everybody in the eighteenth century happens to have the handkerchief *there* and there is always some expert to be found who will have spent two years at his university doing a thesis on "The Function of the Handkerchief for the Eighteenth-Century Gentleman." You will find there are other documents that exist, on the expressions that correspond to a man in the nineteenth century, the way his body has to be held, and so on. And this is all false. For instance, somebody in a hundred years' time, making an opera, God forgive them, about our luncheon today, would put me, at this moment, in a tuxedo, because by looking up documents you will see that on all formal occasions everybody, at this point, who addresses somebody in public, particularly an opera gathering, is either in white tie or tuxedo. And that is how a muddled memory of the past survives.

In fact, whether one wants it or not, one cannot reach the *reality* of history through making collections of externals. It can't be done. What one can do is to go in the opposite direction, and return to observation.

The observation that I have had in seeing different theatre styles in different parts of the world has always carried with it the same conclusion: one only thinks about style when one is watching pupils and second-rate masters. The moment that is transcended, even if the form is apparently artificial, what one actually sees is human nature. It is quite extraordinary. If you go to see perhaps one of the most formalized things that exists in the theatre, which is the Japanese Bunraku Puppets, at a really great performance of this highly stylized event, people say, "You would believe they're alive."

Recently in India I met one of the two last masters of one of the oldest dance traditions, and just for a few of us he demonstrated various things in the most theatrically mandarin language of gesture you can imagine, everything formalized, codified to a degree that makes it completely incomprehensible to anybody who hasn't studied all the codes. What came through was a very simple thing, the impression of a man in a very human situation. I saw a great Indian dancer in another style: and what I really saw was a woman's tenderness in relation to a child. In the most simple, extraordinary way that brought it right home. The Indian-ness, the culturalness vanished—it was the simple thing of the woman's way of calling her child toward her that was so direct, and it really happened for those of us who were present. Nothing else. But it was of such quality, of such depth, of such reality, that it was something one couldn't have seen anywhere else.

Now, I asked this very old actor, "I'd like to know, what do you imagine when you are performing?" because he only performs this very formalized dance, and he had only talked about the techniques, the codes of his dancing, and I wanted to know what he was aiming at doing. He said, "It's very simple. I try to bring together all that I have experienced in my life, so as to make what I am doing a witness of what I have felt and what I have understood."

It is obvious that styles exist in the sense that there are thousands of different codes, and not all the codes are the same, and that at first sight, some codes seem more real and some seem more artificial. It is certain that the original Actors Studio naturalism was considered, at the time, to be very close to reality. We now see that it is a code like any other. It is a code that suggests real life, but if you put that side by side with the most artificial form, you find that there is no difference. Every single thing that we do passes through a form. Everything is stylized.

Any image, it doesn't matter what the image is, any note, any sequence of notes, any sequence of words, can be made to look artificial. Artificial in the worst sense of the word. Essentially, it's lifeless. And you can have somebody coming onto a stage in modern clothes, looking at the audience, and reading something about the invasion of Granada, and imitating Ronald Reagan on television, and that doesn't necessarily make it of today. You can still look at it and say, that is artificial, that is lifeless, that is empty of meaning. And somebody can come onto a stage, with words and gestures that no man-in-the-street could ever use, and the impression can be of something immediate, direct and in the present.

All one has to do is rigorously prevent oneself from being seduced by irrelevant artistic questions, and always come back to the central one. Is the word, is the gesture, is the costume, is the scenery, is the lighting, is the total piece, is the choice to do the total piece, are all these decisions coming from the wish to make something come to life now? If one follows this, then one sees that while many things become unimportant, other things become vital. Our practical order of priorities changes.

I think one has to face the fact that there are facts. We are all victims of facts which can't be changed, can't be denied. The opera world has the greatest difficulty in providing for itself the conditions that it needs. The most important thing is to put first things first, and put one's greatest energy where it is most needed. This is to see that the conditions exist in which performers, and all the collaborating artists, can have the time, the tranquility, and eventually the security —economic, psychological, emotional—out of which they can look for that which transcends style.

part VIII

FLICKERS
OF LIFE

. . .

FILMING A PLAY

• • •

I have made several films of plays I had previously produced in the theatre, and each was a different experiment. Sometimes I tried to use the knowledge of the subject that I had acquired in the theatre and recreate it for the cinema by different means. For example, we filmed *King Lear* seven or eight years after staging the play and the fascinating challenge was to make the film without hanging on to any of the images that belonged to the stage version.

The case of *Marat/Sade* was very different. Peter Weiss and I had talked a lot about making a real film of *Marat/Sade,* starting from scratch. We thought of beginning the film with some bored Parisians wondering what to do with their evening and deciding to go to the asylum at Charenton to take a look at the madmen. We began to develop an elaborate and very way-out scenario and then realized that what we were happily inventing would be a film too expensive ever to be made.

One day, the head of United Artists, David Picker, offered a very imaginative English producer, Michael Birkett, and me a low budget—$250,000—to make a film of *Marat/Sade* in complete freedom, any way we chose, provided it came in on time. A rapid calculation showed that this would mean completing the film in fifteen days. This was an exciting challenge, but of course it meant conceiving the picture in a completely different way, keeping as close as possible to the stage version, which was rehearsed and ready. At the same time, I wanted to see if a purely cinematic language could be found that would take us away from the deadliness of the filmed play and capture another, purely cinematic excitement.

So, with three, sometimes four cameras working non-stop and burning up yards of celluloid, we covered the production like a boxing match. The cameras advanced and retreated, twisted and whirled, trying to behave like what goes on in a spectator's head and simulate his experience; attempting to follow the contradictory flashes of thought and stomach blows with which Peter Weiss had filled his madhouse. In the end, I think I managed to capture a highly subjective view of the action and only afterwards did I realize that it was in such subjectivity that the real difference between film and theatre lay.

When I had directed the play for the stage, I had not attempted to impose my own point of view on the work: on the contrary, I tried to make it as many-sided as I could. As a result, the spectators were continually free to choose, in each scene and at every moment, the points which interested them most. Of course, I too had my preferences, and in the film I did what a film director cannot avoid, which is to show what his own eyes see. In the theatre, a thousand spectators see the same thing with a thousand pairs of eyes, but also at the same time they enter into a composite, collective vision. This is what makes the two experiences so different.

In both cinema and theatre, the spectator is usually more or less passive, at the receiving end of impulses and suggestions. In the cinema, this is fundamental, because the power of the image is so great that it engulfs one. It is only possible to reflect on what one is seeing before or after the impression is made, never at the same moment. When the image is there in all its power, at the precise moment when it is being received, one can neither think, nor feel, nor imagine anything else.

In the theatre you are physically placed at a fixed distance. This distance shifts constantly: it only takes a person on the stage to persuade you to believe in him, for the distance to be reduced. You experience that quality know as "presence," a kind of intimacy. Then there's the contrary movement; when the distance increases, something is relaxed, stretched: you find yourself slightly further away. The true theatrical relationship is like most human relationships between two people: the degree of involvement is always varying. This is why theatre permits one to experience something in an incredibly powerful way, and at the same time to retain a certain freedom. This double illusion is the very foundation both of the theatre experience and of dramatic form. The cinema follows this principle with the close-up and the long shot, but the effect is very different.

For instance, in *Marat/Sade* the action on stage constantly evoked additional images, which, in the mind, supplemented what one saw. There was the image of mad actors imitating scenes of the Revolution. They illustrated them only to a limited degree, but what they did was suggestive enough for the imagination to complete the picture. We tried to capture this effect in the cinema, and in certain scenes we succeeded. At one moment Charlotte Corday knocks on Marat's door. In the theatre, we had done this in the simplest, most theatrical manner: someone put his arm out and someone else supplied the noise. She knocked: another person made the noise of a door opening; it was pure theatre. When we were filming, I decided to see if it was possible, despite the merciless literalism of photography, to allow the spectator this double vision or not. This is the sort of problem that arose all the time while we were filming.

Similarly, in the case of *King Lear*. The power of a Shakespeare play on stage stems from the fact that it happens "nowhere." A Shakespeare play has no setting. Every attempt, whether supported by aesthetic or political reasons, to try to build a frame around a Shakespeare play is an imposition which runs the risk of reducing the play: it can only sing, live and breathe in an empty space.

An empty space makes it possible to summon up for the spectator a very complex world containing all the elements of the real world, in which relationships of all kinds—social, political, metaphysical, individual—coexist and interweave. But it is a world created and recreated touch by touch, word by word, gesture by gesture, relationship by relationship, theme by theme, character interaction by character interaction, as the play gradually unfolds. In any Shakespeare play, it is essential both for the actor and the spectator that the spectator's imagination be in a state of constant liberation, because of the need to move through such a complex labyrinth; therefore the value of the empty space takes on all its importance, allowing the spectator every two or three seconds a chance to wipe his mind clean. He is allowed to lose impressions, the better to retain them.

It is strictly analogous to the principle of television. The image and the continuity of the image on television are absolutely inseparable from the electronic principle of the constant return, point by point, to a neutral screen. If the screen were to retain the same image, after a sixtieth of a second you would no longer be able to see anything. And this is exactly what happens in the theatre. Faced with a completely neutral stage, the spectator receives, in the space of a second, an impulse allowing him to situate the image: for example, he hears the word "forest" in *A Midsummer Night's Dream*. The word is enough: the whole scene is evoked, and this process of evocation must remain present and active through the ensuing minutes. Given by a single phrase, the element is perceived all at once, and afterwards everything moves from the foreground of the mind to another level, where it remains discreetly as a reminder to guide our understanding of the scene.

This image can then be almost completely obliterated until the point when, a couple of hundred lines later, you need the image of the forest to reappear. In between times, the image has disappeared, freeing the space within the mind in which impressions of a different order can arise: for example, insights into thoughts and feelings that are hidden behind the surface. With film, it is utterly different. Here you are perpetually struggling with the problem of the excessive importance of an image, which is intrusive and whose details stay in the frame long after their need is over. If we have a ten-minute scene in a forest, we can never get rid of the trees.

Of course, there are filmic "equivalents": there is editing, there is the use of lenses that detach the foreground and throw the rest out of focus, but it's not at all the same thing. The reality of the image gives to film its power and its limitation. In the case of a Shakespeare film, there is a further problem: a link must be established between two rhythms. The rhythm of a Shakespeare play is the rhythm of the words of the play, a rhythm that begins with the play's first sentence and follows through to the end, needing to be varied and sustained constantly. It is very different from the ebb and flow of images that is the basic principle of film. Making these two rhythms coincide is difficult, indeed almost impossible. The same problem emerges from any attempt to film opera. I say it is *almost* impossible because there are moments of grace when one fleetingly touches the ideal.

LORD OF THE FLIES

. . .

Sam Spiegel—one hand covering a sore eye—trod water and a beach ball splashed between us. He had bought the rights to *Lord of the Flies* and had called the first story conference. "What are we going to call the film?" he asked. In a terrible flash the coming year opened up and I saw down a long perspective of frustration. I now knew we would never agree on a single thing.

If Golding's book is a potted history of man, so the story of the making of the film is like a condensed history of the cinema, throwing up all the snares, temptations and heartbreaks of the different levels of production.

Kenneth Tynan first gave me the novel. I laid it down so determined to make it into a film that I could hardly believe the news that Ealing Studios had bought the rights from William Golding for £2,000 and already had a director hard at work. But cynical friends in the Ealing organization reassured me. "There is a pattern in this," they said. "We will never make it. We will discuss it, prepare it, scripts will be written, but in just about a year someone will realize that it's far too risky and that'll be that. You'll see."

I stood by, anxious, doubting, while the process ran its predestined course. I heard disturbing rumors that Nigel Kneale had written a brilliant script, that a location had been found on the Barrier Reef, that casting was under way. Then one day a budget was made and somebody had to decide whether an exciting project about a lot of kids was going to be a sound investment of £200,000. It is hard to blame them for deciding it was not.

The rights to *Lord of the Flies* were now for sale and their price had risen to £18,000. When I heard this, I rushed to Sam Spiegel. Here I made a psychological miscalculation that was going to cost me dear. I proceeded on the assumption that being an old friend, Spiegel would be prepared to take a remote paternal attitude to a small experimental venture. I was going on the theory that if I kept the budget sufficiently low, he would give me a free hand. I misgauged the essence of the Hollywood-formed producer's success.

The big-time producer can only operate by identifying himself totally with anything he is involved in—and so inevitably he has to come to blows with the European-style director, who works on the same principle himself. Orson Welles once said to me when I nearly made a film with Harold Hecht and Burt Lancaster, "Never work with a producer at the top of his success," and I ruefully remembered his words.

All I wanted was a small sum of money, no script; just kids, a camera and a beach. All the producer wanted was a detailed screenplay which would guarantee him that the film had "world values" before any big money was spent. Sam Spiegel's cynical friends soon began to say, "He'll never make it," and to predict a similar pattern to the Ealing one. This time, however, my hopes and feelings were bound up and I believed in disaster only intermittently.

For a year we seemed to go through the motions of production. An art director searched Spain and Africa; I went to the Canary Islands; we interviewed children. Peter Shaffer was engaged to write a script and in a typically Byzantine way, Spiegel secretly commissioned Richard Hughes to write a rival one at the same time.

Shaffer and I lived intensively the lives of conscience-torn Hollywood intellectuals—the whole anatomy of compromise was laid bare. I remember at the start Shaffer asking, "How on earth can we possibly change the title, turn the boys into girls, the English into Americans?" I replied with the rationalization, "Supposing we had never heard of Golding and someone came along with a proposal to make a film about a group of boys and girls of mixed nationality stranded on a desert island. Couldn't we make a new and exciting story out of that?" Of course the argument was convincing because we wanted to convince ourselves.

At the moment when Golding conceived the myth of *Lord of the Flies,* this story, perhaps this alone, crystallized his feelings into one striking form. But it is too much of a coincidence to hope that other writers can find in this exactly the form that their own creative needs are searching for at that moment. This is the basic danger of screen "adaptations."

Shaffer wrote a remarkable six-hour epic. There was a giant trek up a mountain and an extraordinary sequence, lasting nearly an hour, in a cave. I remember three complex rituals playing at once, each of which would have served a whole season of the Theatre of Cruelty. But the mixture of Shaffer and Golding and Spiegel and myself all pulling in opposite directions was too indigestible. The clean silhouette of the novel was lost, and with it the real force of the subject. So reluctantly the six-hour script was put away and Shaffer and I tried to return to the book.

The closer we got, the more we disagreed with the producer. We bartered important positions against unimportant ones and the more we did so, the less we gained: Golding's structure is so complex and so interwoven that any change can undermine it all. So involved did we become and so close to details of the battle that major concessions happened right under our noses.

Our eighth script was a scarred and pitted battlefield, but we were so identified with it that I think we would have gone ahead. However, Spiegel now had a budget made, and when he saw that with his scale of operating it came to £500,000, he did us the true service of abandoning the project. Another year had passed and *Lord of the Flies* was on the shelf again.

A young American called Lewis Allen was in the meantime exploring a new idea in New York. He felt that private backers could be found who would be interested in each putting up a couple of thousand dollars for a film. With this sum they would have no excessive anxiety about losing the lot. He and his partner Dana Hodgdon had just financed the film of *The Connection* this way, and they offered to do the same for *Lord of the Flies.* Of course we now had to negotiate for the rights; the price was cut down to £50,000 plus a third of the producer's profits. Our budget was £80,000, so by the time we had concluded the deal we had spent over half our capital on the rights, which must be some sort of a record.

However, the fact that our useless final script was fat and heavy made it literally worth its weight in gold. In frustration, Shaffer and I had crammed it with long, detailed descriptions of scenery we had never seen and of illusory but most elaborate camera movements. So, on the strength of this weighty document, some two hundred Washington backers felt they were dealing with a reputable proposition. Fortunately, in their remoteness from show business they were not aware of the one key question that any experienced film backer would put—how can you guarantee that the film will ever be completed?

Bitter experience has led once-bitten financiers to develop a self-protective system, and so they insist on approving schedules and checking budgets, and on the strength of these they ensure and guarantee completion. We knew that we could make no budget, as the sum we could raise was clearly not going to be sufficient, and we could make no schedule, as everything to do with children is fraught with uncertainty. We were going into the unknown and we knew that luck and faith were completion's only security.

In France, feature films have been made for $150. The $150 gets you through the first day's shooting. By then, enough wheels are turning to get you through the second day and soon you have enough to show to justify credit for going on a bit longer. Our only question was how to get to the point of no return.

One day an assistant I had in New York named Mike Macdonald came to me, very puzzled. "What's this name Billy Bunter you've told me to quote?"

I explained that he is the eternal Fat Boy in a famous English comic strip, and the perfect model for Piggy. "Ah," said Mike.

"I go to see an English businessman in his office in Manhattan and I tell him we're making a film and looking for English boys on this side of the Atlantic. He's unfriendly, stiff. I'm wasting his time. No, he can't help. Sorry, old chap, not my line. Then I say, 'We're looking for a kind of Billy Bunter.' There's a complete change. He sits back, chuckles, pulls out his pipe. From then on nothing is too much trouble."

We had worked out that we could not possibly afford to bring boys from England, and so we had decided to search for British boys who had already got to the States at their own expense. Macdonald stood on the docks and accosted likely-looking families as they set foot on American soil. He loitered outside the circus, he wrote to the Embassy families in Washington, he found in the New York telephone directory an Old Etonians Club, an Old Harrovians Club and even one of the Old Boys of Mill Hill. We traced an entire Scottish village moved intact by a distillery to New Jersey. I suppose we saw about three thousand children, all anxious to be in the film, with parents ardently keen on the novel and glad to have a quiet summer with the children taken off their hands. There was no pay—only some pocket money and a share one day of hypothetical profits.

Ralph, the leading boy, we found in a swimming pool in an army camp in Jamaica just four days before filming began. And as for Piggy, he arrived by magic through the post—a sticky *Just William* letter on lined paper, "Dear Sir, I am fat and wear spectacles," and a crumpled photograph that made us cry with delight. It was Piggy, come to life in Camberley—the unique boy himself, conceived ten years before at the very moment that Golding was wrestling with the birth of the novel.

We found an island off the coast of Puerto Rico. A jungle paradise; miles of palm-fringed beaches owned by Woolworth's. They lent us the island in exchange for a screen credit. We had resolved to institute rigorous economies everywhere. No one was allowed to fly except on the late-night cut-price fares; no one could phone New York, hire a car, stay at a hotel if buses, writing or sleeping on the floor with friends could do instead. As a result we saved thousands of dollars and were in a position to say that two things would be unrestricted—the care of the children and the wastage of film.

It had always obsessed me that the accountants of the most expensive productions will happily condone all sorts of ludicrous expenses but are strangely horrified by the least waste of the raw material; it is like a writer who is afraid to cross out in case it uses up paper. Being for once in a position to decide, I ruled that no one could ever question the use of film. This was our salvation, because despite bad weather, illnesses, no rushes, no lights, no facilities, we kept on shooting, several cameras turning at once, leaving them to run as we talked to the children, starting again and again.

We ended up with sixty hours of unbroken screening—and a year's editing. Also miles of tapes recorded at all moments of the day, out of which the dialogue was eventually glued onto the film like postage stamps, word by word. This was not an ideal technique, but it was the only technique open to us, and in a sense it was our completion guarantee.

It was heartbreaking after all we had suffered with it to say farewell to Shaffer's script, but there was now no reason not to go back to my first intention and improvise straight from the original novel. All the elements of the story were there in the children. I believed that the reason for translating Golding's very complete masterpiece into another form in the first place was that although the cinema lessens the magic, it introduces evidence.

The book is a beautiful fable—so beautiful that it can be refuted as a trick of compelling poetic style. In the film no one can attribute the looks and gestures to tricks of direction. Of course I had to give the impulse to set a scene in motion, but what the camera records is the result of chords being struck on strings that were already there. The violent gestures, the look of greed and the faces of experience are all real.

It is said that all children can act. This is not really true. It is like the myth that all Negroes have rhythm and big bass voices. Children go to greater extremes. If a child can act, he can often act divinely, but when he is bad, as the nursery rhyme goes, he is horrid. The great advantage of a child is that, being too young to know about schools of acting, he can do things that an adult is too theory-bound to manage. For instance, the director can use mixed methods that would shock a trained actor silly. All children are Method actors to a degree, because they are sensible and logical and want to know what they are doing and why. At the same time, if while he is performing he is given a purely technical direction like "Turn your head, count two, carry on," because he does not know that this is muddling and distracting, he won't be muddled. An adult knowing that this is an inartistic method would be thrown for a loop. Similarly, you can give a child an action that a grown-up might find rationally to be "out of character." The child just does it, and in many cases in the simple act of doing he makes it his own.

The children, before we started, were thrilled at the idea of being "in a film" although none of them knew at all what this meant. I think they imagined they would climb up inside a screen and there they would find life moving at that marvellous tempo where all the dull parts of existence are edited away. It was a truly shocking experience for them to discover that film is just the reverse; long hours of doing nothing, waiting dressed in blazers and woolen socks in the tropical sun—repeating the same thing again and again. It was a sharp confrontation of reality: they had to adjust to a difficult set of facts and find their enjoyment within the very strict and narrow bounds that a hard schedule allowed. I think this was the essential experience for them and it was a maturing one.

Their contact with Golding's harsh material was much less significant. People always ask me whether the children understood, and what effect it had on them. Of course they understood. Golding's thesis is that all possibilities are latent in every child, and they had no difficulty in seeing that this is true. Many of their off-screen relationships completely paralleled the story, and one of our main problems was to encourage them to be uninhibited within the shots but disciplined in between them. We had to cake them with mud and let them be savages by day, and restore prep-school discipline by the shower and the scrubbing at night.

Even the wise and calm Piggy came to me one day close to tears. "They're going to drop a stone on you," the other boys had been telling him. "That scene on the schedule, Piggy's death. It's for real. They don't need you anymore."

My experience showed me that the only falsification in Golding's fable is the length of time the descent to savagery takes. His action takes about three months. I believe that if the cork of continued adult presence were removed from the bottle, the complete catastrophe could occur within a long weekend.

MODERATO CANTABILE

• • •

A year ago I read *Moderato Cantabile* by Marguerite Duras and fell in love with the idea of making it into a film. The story did not depend on a French background, it was the exploration of a singular relationship.

It made no statement, it proved no point. It certainly did not increase one's belief that all men are nice and good and it fell into no accepted category. I realized I would have to make it in France. Marguerite Duras had just become notorious as the author of the much admired and as-much-hated *Hiroshima mon Amour.* Jeanne Moreau, an astonishing actress with whom I had worked in *Cat on a Hot Tin Roof* a couple of years before, was as passionate about the subject as I was, and we were joined by Raoul Lévy, a brilliant and colorful producer who had made a fortune with Brigitte Bardot. ("Il est si inquiet. . ." B.B. once said about him rapturously.) Convinced that this was an intellectually ex-citing project, Raoul Lévy went to his backers and said, "I won't give you a script to read as you won't understand it. I'll just tell you the names of the people involved and you'll have to trust them." The back-ers rose to the challenge. We had our money at once.

I had often wondered how many French films ever get started, how anyone could ever communicate to a man with the purse strings the quality of so many French films. It seems that the only way to sell them is to make them. It is seldom the films that get the backing, it is the individuals, their enthusiasm, their devotion, their excitement. In the entertainment world in France, one endlessly hears the phrase "une belle affiche." Newcomers sometimes make the mistake of think-ing that this means a beautiful poster, a poster that is aesthetically pleasing. Not a bit of it: much as a "belle salle" in a restaurant is not a beautiful room but one full of distinguished people, so a "belle affiche" is a beautiful juxtaposition of unexpected names. The game of affiche-making is obsessional; the blank sheet is the magic surface on which names can be coupled and uncoupled ad infinitum. If in France I proposed to star Picasso opposite Bardot, there would at once be inter-est: if in England I proposed to star Graham Sutherland opposite a member of the Royal Family (with a script by a defrocked archbishop), a financier wouldn't even smile. The more's the pity. For in France this is not just a craze for gimmicks, for stunts. It is a deep longing for yesterday's clichés not to be repeated, a yearning for something new and mysterious, for something to take flight, for the unexpected, the unknown nourished over late suppers—fed by boasts, illusions. Exces-sive, foolish, unjustifiable ambitions soar, followed by malice, anger and disappointment, because in the very nature of things such hopes are doomed to be dashed, dashed and dashed again. Only, very occa-sionally, they are thrillingly fulfilled. We look at the best French films and we wonder why we cannot do the same. We have the talent, the technicians, the means. Only we have too much common sense; a civic virtue, not an artistic one. The foolish mistakes are the price of the splendid achievements.

The experiment which we were tackling was to make a moving picture without action. In fact, the one cry of alarm I ever had from our backers was when I announced to the press that in this film nothing would happen at all. Essentially this was true. Two people meet in a provincial town—and there is no story. Only a week later, they have both invisibly undergone violent and dramatic changes of state. The experiment was to rehearse the actors, and prepare with them an intense inner life. We walked about for days, by the Gironde, in a café, in a deserted house, in a square, on the ferry, reconstructing the lives of the characters before, after and around the film in the way that Rus-

Directing Jeanne Moreau and Jean-Paul Belmondo in *Moderato Cantabile*

sian actors do when they prepare Chekhov. Eventually, when we photographed the simple episodes of the story, the actors were carrying
around with them this elaborate inner structure. Bresson has made
films without actors where the camera is trained on the real gestures
of real people. We, on the contrary, were using that curious being the
actor to create *real* emotions and then photographing their outer form.

Jeanne Moreau is for me the ideal contemporary film actress, because she doesn't characterize. She acts in the way Godard shoots
films, and with her you are as close as you can be to making a document of an emotion. The average trained actor's approach to a part is
based on good Stanislavsky principles: he rationalizes, he prepares, he
composes his characterization. He has some conscious direction of
what he is doing, so that in a way he is like the classic film director
setting up his camera: the actor is setting himself up and directing
himself, beautifully or otherwise.

But Jeanne Moreau works like a medium, through her instincts.
She gets a hunch about the character and then some part of her
watches the improvisation of that and lets it happen, occasionally intervening a bit like a good technician, when, for instance, she wants to
be facing the camera, to be at the right angle. But she is guiding the
flow of improvisation rather than stating ahead of time what hurdle
she wants herself to leap, and the result is that her performance gives
you an endless series of tiny surprises. On each take neither you nor
she knows exactly what is going to happen.

The great criticism of *Moderato Cantabile* was that I didn't move
the camera enough, that I set it up and allowed things to happen in
front of it, and it was assumed I did this because I came from the
theatre and didn't know any better. In fact, there was a lot of conscious
thinking behind it. The narrative we were trying to capture in that
particular film was neither an external one nor entirely an inner one
—you can't say that the characters behave as they do because they live
by a river in a dull town, but you can't ignore the way these things
relate to them either.

So, having found the landscape and these particular actors, my
task seemed to be to set up a camera that didn't comment; to let you
watch, as it were, a documentary record of something so intangible
that you could feel it was really happening. Those long silences, like
that close-up of Jeanne Moreau standing against a white sky, could not
have meaning in the theatre. Shakespeare would have provided powerful words and metaphors to convey what we in a film were trying to
communicate with that weight of silence. And it wasn't actually silence

that one was photographing, or a Japanese composition of an empty white screen, but a look on her face and a tiny movement of her cheek, which to me were valid because she was actually *and at that moment* experiencing something which therefore became interesting to look at as an object.

The particular documentary aspect of filming, the catching of something as it happens, relates in this way to acting: the aim is always to capture that look in someone's eye.

We made the film in seven weeks for about £80,000. This is a liberal budget in France. I could get the best technicians and (despite all that one hears about Latin inefficiency and muddle) the fact must be faced—it is owing to the French being so highly organized, adaptable, resourceful, economical, imaginative and above all flexible in interpreting their union privileges and rules, that one is able to get the same result infinitely quicker and cheaper than in England or in America.

And this matter of a relatively low cost is all-important, as it is the price of freedom. Quite simply, there is a price which makes producers nervous and a price at which they are prepared to take a risk. American films are too expensive to take big risks. Broadway productions are created in an unhealthy climate of panic because the financial gamble is too great. I have spent a whole year preparing a film for an Anglo-American company which proved too expensive to be experimental and too cheap to carry the security of a super production. On the other hand, the breakthrough of the new school of playwrights in England is closely tied to the fact that the money lost in an unsuccessful theatre venture is not cripplingly high; the breakthrough of the Nouvelle Vague in the French cinema is closely tied to the fact that a film can be well made there for sums of money which financiers can invest without losing all their sleep at night.

When the completed picture was shown at Cannes it aroused the most violent controversy. It baffled people, irritated them, even made them wild with anger: equally it has won other people's passionate approval and support. What is important to me is that having passionately wanted to make this film in a particular way, it could be done.

And once made, that it was received, dissected, accepted or rejected with equal passion. In England, the greatest danger that awaits such enterprises is indifference—indifference at the outset, indifference at the completion. Perhaps it is a pity that, artistically speaking, we are not a little more "inquiet."

FILMING KING LEAR

· · ·

In King Lear we have made no effort to reconstitute something that never existed. There was never a king of England called Lear, and the story never happened. Shakespeare wanted to portray several periods of history simultaneously—and it was not the first time he did so, either. Very often he knowingly mixed the Middle Ages and barbaric times, both with the Renaissance and the Elizabethan era. But take a close look at *Lear.* It contains everything. It's a barbaric play, therefore the contents are barbaric. But by its refinement, the dialogue belongs to the sixteenth or even the seventeenth century. Consequently, when we were in the pre-shooting period of *Lear,* the two designers— Georges Wakhevitch, Adele Änggård—and the producer, Michael Birkett, and I concentrated on trying to figure out how we could avoid remaining prisoners of a single historical period.

One after the other we took various historical films and asked ourselves why it was that even the most meticulous reconstruction rang false, why they remained unbelievable. And we came to the conclusion that there is a very simple law which has nothing to do with what the documents relative to the subject impose on you, or even inspire you to. If you want to believe in the setting of any historical period, you have to be able to absorb ninety percent of what you see without really noticing it. Take, for instance, a sixteenth- or a tenth-century dinner. If you reconstruct it with museum-like care, with the utmost concern for the tiniest detail, you end up with a phoney image. The whole thing will be completely unbelievable, no matter how much you tell yourself that twenty highly paid university professors have worked on the film and that everything you are seeing is historically accurate. Whence the paradox: if you reconstitute a historical period for the camera, it means that you ought to try to reconstruct the impression of living at that time, and, consequently, that the camera ought to have the possibility of not retaining certain things, of paying no attention to them.

The upshot of all this is a kind of law that can be formulated thus: the more deeply you plunge into a distant or unknown past, the more you must deliberately simplify and reduce the number of unaccustomed objects that appear at the same moment in your field of vision. If you want any historical period—say the tenth century—to appear absolutely true to the spectator of the twentieth century, you must be aware that such a spectator is incapable of tolerating more than a hundredth or a thousandth of the visual details of the period and still retaining the same impression of reality as though it were a question of his own period. For it is not reality that exists in the film, but only, and solely, the *impression* of reality.

To be sure, the question arises at this point to know how to figure out what should constitute this hundredth, or thousandth. We used as our basis the forms which flow from the living conditions. We decided to start with the idea that the basic element of life in the society in which Lear lived was the contrast between heat and cold. One real element that emerges from the plot is the notion of nature as something hostile, dangerous, against which man has to battle. The play is centered around the storm, but what counts from a psychological point of view is the contrast between the safe, enclosed places and the wild, unprotected places. Which leads you to two denominators of security: fire and fur. Having reached this point, we began to study the life of the Eskimos.

Most of the realistic elements of the film version of *Lear* were taken from the life of the Eskimos and the Lapps, because their life, from the viewpoint that interests us, has undergone very little change over the past thousand years, because it is still controlled by the basic natural conditions, by the contrast between heat and cold. As soon as we realized that we could take the visual aspect of the film from a society whose principal problem and principal function is to manage to survive under the specific climatic conditions in which the action of *Lear* unfolds, we found at the same time a whole series of elements from which our imagination enabled us little by little to deduce others. The coach in which Lear travels does not exist, and never did, but we created it by deduction from what we know. What is more, this coach shows that we introduced into a strictly determined framework a great number of anachronistic elements. Up to the very last moment we meticulously controlled every detail, and any time that we had a choice between what is distant and unusual rather than near and familiar, we chose the latter.

If one is English—and the text of *Lear* is completely English— one will readily admit that the film *Lear* takes place in an England that no longer exists anywhere. Over the past thousand years, the English countryside has transformed itself into an artificial countryside. Try to find today, anywhere in the British Isles, a place that looks like the England of a thousand years ago. It doesn't exist. So what was the solution? There is, obviously, the temptation to follow Eisenstein: to attain the grandeur of an epic historical scene, gamble on the immensity of the countryside. But that's a trap. Shakespeare never lingers very long on the same scene, his style changes constantly, and the author himself, phrase after phrase, oscillates dialectically between the human and the epic.

Thus it is always an error to deal with *Lear* as an epic play. There is nothing in Shakespeare that exists in a pure state; the purity of style does not exist. Each of Shakespeare's plays shows us the coexistence of opposites. In *Lear,* among others, there is specifically the coexistence of grandeur with a kind of completely intimate familiarity. If we were to get ourselves involved with sumptuous scenes à la *Ivan the Terrible,* for example, it might well be magnificent, but it would be neither Shakespeare nor England. Now we wanted something completely English, something noble and large scale, but which would also be human and earthly.

And this is why we were happy to find, as a location for the film, Jutland, which probably very closely resembles what England had been in the far-off time of *Lear.*

We did not use color for a very simple and related reason, which grew out of my experience of *Lear* in the theatre. *Lear* is so complex a work that if you give the slightest bit of added complexity to it, you are completely smothered. The basic principle has to be economy. And black and white film is simpler, it doesn't distract the attention to the same degree. Color is good only if you can put it to some positive use. The purpose of color is to add something and here we have more than enough. Of course, today it's difficult to raise money for a black and white film, and pressures were put on us to shoot it in color. They used the usual arguments on us, maintaining that color can serve one's stylistic intentions just as well as black and white. The only drawback was, it's just not true. Even if you use monochromatic color, you end up with something elegant, pleasant and delicate. And that is precisely what doesn't work for *Lear.*

The same is true for music. All music does in a film is to add something. But in this story silence has an important place, as concrete as music might have in another story.

So the process of preparing *Lear* all the way was elimination—of scenic detail, costume detail, color detail, music detail.

The same principle carried through into the shooting of the film.

No play of Shakespeare is a realistic story. Shakespeare's plays are not slices of life, nor are they poems, nor are they beautiful pieces of ornate writing.

They are very complex, unique inventions, made up of an amazing variety of contradictory pieces cunningly strung together. The impression of great richness that they give is because so many different elements are involved. To capture this mosaic, we tried in the cinema to get away from any fixed film style, so that certain scenes are very realistic—as in the early part of the play, where Shakespeare is setting up the background for us. But soon, the interest becomes more and more focused on the characters and their inner experiences, and Shakespeare's methods become more and more impressionistic, more and more laconic and elliptical.

In a two-hour film it would be absurd to try to include all the elements that make up a five-hour *Lear* in the theatre. So we tried to evolve an impressionistic movie technique, cutting language and incident to the bone, so that the total effect of all the things heard and seen could capture in different terms Shakespeare's rough, uneven, jagged and disconcerting vision.

TELL ME LIES

• • •

Tell Me Lies is a feature film based on the Royal Shakespeare Company production of *US*.

All through the interview I kept asking myself why Barbara looked so tense. This is the fourth time I have been on her television program. She's blond, attractive, she likes my film and I am happy to be in New York talking to her. As soon as the show ends, Barbara is called to the phone. When she comes back her hands are shaking. A torrent of abuse has just reached her long-distance from Pittsburgh: "I thought you were a nice girl. And now I see you taking part in this vicious, disgusting spectacle."

We had been talking about Vietnam. "Why didn't you ask that English guy about Vietcong atrocities? Why didn't you say 'What about the Cong?' " Barbara is very shaken. "Perhaps he's right. Perhaps I did go too far. Perhaps I shouldn't—we're supposed to be objective . . ."

Tell Me Lies (the film of *US*)

We move across a corridor to do a second interview for radio. A green light. We're on the air. I look across the microphone at Barbara. Her face is sealed. Now the first question comes in a voice that is hard and impersonal: "What about the atrocities on the other side?" The next morning on the television show she and her baseball player partner feel compelled to make an apology to viewers, who had been phoning in complaints all day. "You have to hear all sides of the question, but I was against every word he said."

Two nice men, Bob and Lou, gray, experienced journalists with warm hands and soft, strained eyes. As the cameras are lined up, they tell me about the mess in Vietnam. Frustration and days at the UN— this war, they say, is the absolute in nastiness so napalm can't even make it worse. Then the cameras turn and they slip into public roles.

"Mr. Brook, in your film you quote from a book about American torture. Now why in the name of fair play don't you also quote . . . ?"

"What about Vietcong atrocities?"

"What if Nazi Germany . . . ?"

I want to hit back angrily, but something checks me. I'm not looking into hawk faces. The eyes are soft, strained, asking to be understood. Please show us both sides of the question; then it won't be so bad. Please give us a balanced view.

Balance. Day after day we come back to this theme. Of course, two blacks don't make a white, they say, we understand that, and don't think we don't realize what horrible things war can do. But why do you only pick on us? Why do you, the English, only picket our Embassy? Why don't you protest about atrocities on the other side? Why don't you blame Ho Chi Minh?

I explain that America is our concern because she is part of us, her atrocities are committed in both our names. Yet, all the same, they say, your film seems unnecessarily loaded—you don't give our case a fair hearing. What case? I ask, and I'm not being flippant. Once you have heard the words "resisting aggression" and "drawing the line," the arguments for the defense run very thin.

"Dear Mr. Brook, how about when we went over and saved England and France from the Germans?"

"I want to ask you a very simple question. If Great Britain gave up all her army and then one day was attacked . . . ?"

The words stream past, question, answer, both rationalizing, formalizing, until they become formula, incantation.

Day after day, again and again, aggressively and kindly, sharp, tense young men, middle-aged lady columnists, all ask—why did you make the film? Then they add, sometimes with sarcasm, but more often with a kind of desperate hope, do you think it will help to end the war? I ask myself this same question once again. What can we do?

It is said that *The Marriage of Figaro* launched the French Revolution, but I don't believe it. I don't believe that plays and films and works of art operate this way. Goya's *Disasters of War* and Picasso's *Guernica* have always seemed the great models, yet they achieved no practical results. Perhaps we do ourselves a great disservice in pitching the question so falsely. Will this act of protest stop the killing? we ask, knowing that it won't, yet half hoping that in a miraculous way it might. Then it doesn't, and we feel cheated. Is the act, then, worth making? Is there a choice?

In the summer of 1966, a group of actors, writers, directors, a musician and a designer met at the Royal Shakespeare Theatre to start work on what eventually became a show called *US*. This was no action on our part—it was a reaction. A reaction to a Vietnam that was unavoidably there, thrusting itself on us. There was no choice. An image often haunted us, one that still troubles many Americans: Someone is being murdered in the street. At the windows no one moves. I try to put into words that we didn't want to be silent at our windows, and yet our choice of action was perhaps no more than an incoherent cry. I give this explanation and the listener nods, unconvinced. I see, he says, it's just an emotional response.

"Emotion" is the dirtiest word of all, always coupled with the word "just." Just an emotional stand, just an emotional argument. The more intelligent the other person, the more suspicious he becomes—and it is only natural—fascism has made us all wary of emotional traps. So we are trapped instead into denigrating the act of feeling, putting our money on reason.

In *US,* Denis Cannan wrote: "This is a reasonable war. It is run by statisticians, physicists, economists, historians, psychiatrists, mathematicians, experts on everything, theorists from everywhere. The professors are advisers to the President. Even the atrocities can be justified by logic."

I discuss this with Murray Kempton, who is perhaps the sharpest of political journalists, and he points out a simple fact: "Those here who discuss Vietnam have come to believe it's a sort of great American debate. They keep forgetting it's a war." The word "debate" rang true. That was the reassuring music that so many conversations seem to demand.

"Listen to his point of view," "You're entitled to your views"—even those most agonized, made most desperate by the impossibility to be heard, to influence events, still take comfort from the fact that speech is free. Unlike Nazi Germany, they say, a society where all the facts can be told cannot be unhealthy deep down. And yet even this reasoned view does not quite make sense. Everywhere one hears of a growing self-censorship such as I saw on the television shows—a censorship based on nothing other than some nameless fear. And this self-censorship prevents people not so much from saying things as hearing them. The great debate leads nowhere. Persuasion does not persuade. Despite all the newspapers and the paperbacks one is struck by how little wish there is to be informed. The streets of Saigon arrive on television by satellite, but their horrors do not penetrate. "This is more indecent than the concentration camps," Murray Kempton concludes. "Because this time everyone sees it, everyone knows." Everyone. It seems to me he is not only speaking about Americans.

The most suspicious question was the easiest to answer. Where did you get the money? For the money for the film did not come from England, nor from Europe, nor from a Hollywood company, nor from any producer, because they had all turned the project down. Seventy separate Americans came forward, not rich ones but professional people, doctors, businessmen, who felt that this film should be made.

A hawk who was "not afraid of the truth" had invited us to Vietnam at his expense, but this was not where our story lay. One of our possible titles was "Vietnam—A Story of London." We were like someone sampling water, who knows that any one drop of the ocean under a microscope will show the same elements as all the rest.

In the theatre in England the end of the play was silence, a confrontation between the United States and us, Vietnam and London. The actors stopped acting and remained still, switching their attention to a private task in which they evaluated their own personal views in the light of the day's events and the evening's performance. Yet some audiences saw in their immobility nothing but hostility, self-righteousness, accusation. Some took the silence as an insult, others as an evasion. Some took it as rabid Communist propaganda. Sartre thought he saw a red curtain fall and wrote about it. A lady leapt on stage to prevent an actor from burning a butterfly and cried out, "You see, you can do something!" Sometimes, after sitting for ten or fifteen minutes, total strangers began to talk to one another, and would leave the theatre together. Silence became a sheet of white paper on which anyone who wished could watch his prejudice write its name.

In the film a silent monk burns in Saigon, a silent Quaker burns in Washington. In London a man and a girl can't bring themselves to speak. The watchers at the window do not make a sound. Are all silences the same?

"Bad taste amounting to obscenity," writes the *Christian Science Monitor*. "Anti-American." The word stings me each time. Can I accept this label? I do not see myself as anti–this people nor as anti–this country, which I visit and love.

They also call the film "anti-Vietnam," and this at first surprised me until I realized that anti-Vietnam is a telescoped form of "anti-the-war-in-Vietnam." Anti-Vietnam in fact means pro-Vietnam. It is the same with anti-American—it is a telescoped phrase which should read "anti-the-wanton-destruction-of-the-American-ideal." It means pro-America. In North Carolina, this is very clear. We show the film for Duke University (the head of Michigan University had privately requested the exhibitor to withdraw it), and here we are at once plunged into a sympathetic world of warmth, liveliness, knowledge, enthusiasm —and, needless to say, despair.

After a day in this company, you can be convinced that opposition to the war will soon be overwhelming. Indeed, you can take away from America any impression you choose, depending on whom you've talked to last. You can say that Vietnam looms over everything or you can say that life is unaffected by the war, and both are true.

Most disturbing of all, few choose to look beyond Vietnam, to what sort of world "peace" could bring. Sooner or later, it is believed, the Vietnam error must get cleared up and the good times will return. In the story of Bonnie and Clyde the nation has found its image—shooting out of the car window, bang, splash, rattle, smear of corpses, then a moment later on the highway the sun shines and the blood is already in the past, gone, no connection with now, not here, for here's warmth and friendship and being young and attractive and a good future's just ahead. There's no end, no catching up, no death.

Truth is a radical remedy. It has a dangerous snowballing effect. Truth hurts when people or nations have grown accustomed to telling lies. A nation which has been told it can do no wrong when it comes to fighting Communism is likely to react with anguish and terror at the loss of the Battle of Vietnam. The group in my hotel room is silent for a moment, then a publicity man quips, "We'll get a button made. 'Tell Me Lies About Vietnam 'Cos the Truth Makes Me Nervous.' " We all laugh. Fantasy is restored. There is no war in Vietnam.

MEETINGS WITH REMARKABLE MEN
• • •

This film is a story—a not totally truthful story, somewhat Oriental, sometimes accurate, sometimes not, sometimes in and sometimes out of life, like a legend. It is told like a legend in the remote past, for a purpose: which is to follow in a certain order the search of the searcher who is the central character.

The entire film has been constructed around that one essential thread; and this is quite different in structure from George Gurdjieff's book, *Meetings with Remarkable Men.* The searcher begins to search and as he goes on, his search changes color, changes register, changes tone, but it always goes forward until it reaches a certain intensity. So the film is a direct expression, for the person watching it, of a growing search; the sense of the growing search and the changing taste of it is what the film is there to show.

In that sense you have to let the film wash over you to follow the central process. If you ask yourself about logical reasons for transitions, that sets up a difficulty that I don't think is there otherwise.

When preparing the film, many people asked: How is it possible, in a form as documentary as the cinema, to show people in a certain state of inner development, masters, or people on the way to becoming masters, unless you are doing it with the real people? An actor, who has within him the possibilities of being a remarkable man, can't by two or three months of rehearsals turn into one and sustain it for a year or a month; but he can sustain it for the time a given shot may take in a film; and it isn't a lie. It would be a lie if he went off the film set and started an esoteric group! But it can be true for as long as he is in front of a camera recognizing that this moment is between the director saying "Action" and the director saying "Cut," which is often a matter of seconds. Because he's an actor, for a tiny space of time he can become an open way beyond his normal self.

Now Gurdjieff's book *Meetings with Remarkable Men,* when I first encountered it, struck me as being a potentially useful story to tell to a large audience at this moment at the end of the twentieth century. As a book, it can only reach a restricted audience, but I felt that a film could reach a wider audience, where each person could find something very applicable to himself. Here is what I'll call a hero of our time, a man, a young man, with whom we can identify, because his primary situation is a hunger for understanding and a recognition that the answers that the world has given him in no way satisfy his demand.

This is a situation which in different ways can bring us all together. And out of this starting point, his story—in an untheoretical, direct and epic way—gives us ways of feeling what it means to allow that hunger to develop into a real search, what a searcher is, what a searcher has to be, what a search demands so that it isn't abandoned, what quite unexpected obstacles and rewards exist on the way, and what in fact can be found at the end. The end of the story is nothing like what people naively believe: it is not the tale of a man who searches and finds an answer. The end of the story shows us, quite directly, how a man who searches finds the material that enables him to go still further.

There's only one meeting in life that is important, one meeting that changes something. That is when a person meets somebody who has more than he has and is willing to share this with him. What is a remarkable man? Everyone is remarkable in his way, but he doesn't know it. If a film can help give even a taste of these possibilities, then our time will not have been wasted.

part IX

ENTERING
ANOTHER WORLD

. . .

THE MASK—COMING OUT
OF OUR SHELL
• • •

It's obvious that there are masks and masks. There is something very
noble, very mysterious, very extraordinary, which is the mask, and
something disgusting, something really sordid, nauseating (and very
common to the Western art theatre) which is also called a mask. They
are similar because they are both things you put on your face, but they
are as different as health and disease.

There is a mask which is lifegiving, that affects the wearer and the
observer in a very positive way; and there is another thing that can be
put on the face of a distorted human being that makes him even more
distorted, and gives an impression to a distorted observer of a reality
even more distorted than the one he sees ordinarily. And both go
under the same name, "masks," and to the casual observer look very
similar. I think it has now become an almost universally accepted
cliché that we all wear masks all the time. But the moment one accepts
that as being true, and begins to ask oneself questions about it, one
sees that the usual facial expression either conceals that it's not in
tune with what is really going on inside (so it's a mask in that sense),
or it is a decorated account: it presents the inner process in a more
flattering or attractive light; it gives a lying version. A weak person puts
on a strong face, or vice versa. The everyday expression is a mask in
the sense that it's either a concealment or a lie; it is not in harmony
with the inner movement. So if one's face is operating so well as a
mask, what's the purpose of putting on another face?

But in fact, if one takes these two categories, the horrible mask
and the good mask, one sees that they operate in quite different ways.
The horrible mask is the one most continually used in the Western
theatre. What happens here is that an individual, usually a scene designer, is asked to design a mask. He works from one thing only, which
is his own subjective fantasy; what else can he do? So someone sits in
front of a drawing board and draws out of his own subconscious one of

his own million lying or distorted or sentimental masks and then pops it onto another person. So you have something that in a way is even worse than one's own lie—one is lying through the external image of someone else's lie. However, what is worse yet is that because another person's lie comes not from the surface but from the subconscious, it is basically even nastier, because you are lying through another person's fantasy life. And that is where almost all masks that you see, in the ballet and so on, have something morbid about them; because it is an aspect of the subjective subconscious—frozen. So you have this picture impression of something inanimate and basically belonging to the hidden area of personal hang-ups and frustrations.

Now the traditional mask works exactly the other way round. The traditional mask in essence isn't a "mask" at all, because it is an image of the essential nature. In other words, a traditional mask is a portrait of a man without a mask.

For instance, the Balinese masks that we used in *The Conference of the Birds* are realistic masks in the sense that, unlike the African masks, the features are not distorted; they are completely naturalistic. What one sees is that the person who designs them, exactly like the person who sculpts the heads in Bunraku, has behind him thousands of years of tradition in which human types are observed with such precision that you can see that if the craftsman reproducing them, generation after generation, goes one millimeter to the right or to the left, he is no longer reproducing the essential type but a personal value. But if he is absolutely true to this traditional knowledge—which you could call a traditional psychological classification of man, an absolute knowledge of the essential types—you find that what is called a mask should be called an anti-mask.

The traditional mask is an actual portrait, a soul-portrait, a photograph of what you rarely see, only in truly evolved human beings: an outer casing that is a complete and sensitive reflection of the inner life. Because of this, in a mask carved in such a way, whether a Bunraku head or a Balinese realistic mask, the first characteristic is that there is nothing morbid about it. There is no impression, even when you see one hanging on the wall, of a shrunken head—no impression of death. It is not a death mask. On the contrary, these masks, although motionless, seem to be breathing life. Provided the actor goes through certain steps, the moment he wears the mask it becomes alive in an infinite number of ways. A mask of this order has this extraordinary characteristic that the moment it is on a human head, if the human being inside is sensitive to its meaning, it has an absolutely inexhaustible quantity of expressions.

We found this while we were rehearsing with them. When the mask is hanging on the wall, a person could—crudely and falsely—put adjectives to it, saying, "Ah, this is the proud man." You put the mask on, and you can no longer say, "This is the proud man," because it could have looks of humility, it could have humility sliding into gentleness; those vast staring eyes can express aggressivity or they can express fear. It is endlessly, endlessly shifting—but *within* the purity and the intensity of the unmasked man, whose deepest inner nature is constantly revealing itself, while the masked man's inner nature is continuously concealed. So in that way, I think the first basic paradox is that the true mask is the expression of somebody unmasked.

I will speak from my experience with Balinese masks, but I have to go back one step before that. One of the first, knockout exercises that you can do with actors, which is used in lots of theatre schools where they use masks, is putting a plain, blank, white mask on someone. The moment you take someone's face away in that way, it's the most electrifying impression: suddenly to find oneself knowing that that thing one lives with, and which one knows is transmitting something all the time, is no longer there. It's the most extraordinary sense of liberation.

This is one of those great exercises that whoever does it for the first time counts as a great moment: suddenly to find oneself immediately for a certain time liberated from one's own subjectivity. And the awakening of a body awareness is immediately there with it, irresistibly; so that if you want to make an actor aware of his body, instead of explaining it to him and saying, "You have a body and you need to be aware of it," just put a bit of white paper on his face and say, "Now look around." He can't fail to be instantly aware of everything he normally forgets, because all the attention has been released from this great magnet up top.

Now to go back to the Balinese masks. When they arrived, the Balinese actor who was with us laid them out. All the actors, like children, threw themselves on the masks, put them on, started roaring with laughter, looking at one another, looking in the mirror, fooling around—having a ball, like children when you open up the dressing-up hamper. I looked at the Balinese actor. He was appalled; he was standing there shell-shocked—because for him the masks were sacred. He gave me a pleading look, and I stopped everybody short and just said a couple of words to remind everyone that these weren't just things out of a Christmas cracker. And because our group had worked long enough under different forms, the potential respect was there; it was just that in our typical Western way, one forgets. Everybody was too over-enthusiastic and excited, but at the tiniest reminder they came back right away.

But it was quite clear that within a matter of minutes the masks were being completely desacralized—because the masks will play any game you want, and what was interesting was that before I stopped them, when everyone was fooling around with them, the masks themselves appeared to be not much better than what you get out of a Christmas cracker—because that was what was being invested in them. A mask is two-way traffic all the time; it sends a message in and projects a message out. It operates by the laws of echoes: if the echo chamber is perfect, the sound going in and the one going out are reflections; there is a perfect relation between the echo chamber and the sound. But if it isn't, it is like a distorted mirror. Here, when the actors sent back a distorted response, the mask itself took on a distorted face. The minute they started again, with quiet and respect, the masks looked different and the people inside them *felt* different.

The great magic of the mask, which every actor receives from it, is that he can't tell what it looks like on him; he can't tell what impression he is making—and yet he knows. I have worn them a lot myself when we were working on them, for the sake of investigating at first hand this extraordinary impression. You do things and other people tell you afterwards: "It was extraordinary!" *You* don't know: you just wear it and you do certain movements and you don't know if there is any relation or not, and you know that you mustn't try to impose something. You somehow do and don't know, on a rational level; but the sensitivity to the mask exists in another way, and it's something that develops.

One of the techniques they use in Bali which is very interesting is that the Balinese actor starts by looking at a mask, holding it in his hands. He looks at it for a long while, until he and the mask begin to become like a reflection of each other; he begins to feel it partly as his own face—but not totally, because in another way he goes toward *its* independent life. And gradually he begins to move his hand so that the mask takes on a life, and he is watching it—he sort of empathizes with it. And then something may happen which none of our actors could even attempt (and it rarely happens even with the Balinese actor), which is that the breathing begins to modify; he begins to breathe differently with each mask. It's obvious, in a way, that each mask represents a certain type of person, with a certain body and a certain tempo and inner rhythm, and so a certain breathing. As he begins to feel this and as his hand begins to take on a corresponding tension, the breath changes till a certain *weight* of breathing begins to penetrate the actor's whole body; and when that is ready, he puts on the mask. And the whole shape is there.

Our actors can't do it that way—and shouldn't, because that belongs to a whole tradition and training. But in a different way, because they can't play on that sort of highly developed instrument of technique, they can develop something through pure sensitivity, with no knowledge of what are right or wrong forms. The actor takes the mask, studies it, and as he puts it on, his face slightly modifies itself until it goes toward the shape of the mask, and he puts it on his face and in a way he has dropped one of his own masks. So the intervening flesh masks disappear and the actor is in close contact, epidermal contact, with a face that is not his face, but the face of a very strong, essential type of man. And his actor's capacity to be a comedian (without which he couldn't be an actor) makes him realize his potentiality to *be* that person.

So at that moment he is in that role. And that becomes *his* role; and the moment it is assumed, it comes to life, it is no longer hard and fast but something that adapts itself to any circumstance. The actor, having put that mask on, is sufficiently in the character that if someone unexpectedly offers him a cup of tea, whatever response he makes is totally that of that type, not in the schematic sense but in the essential sense. For instance, if he's wearing a proud mask, in the schematic sense he would be forced to say proudly, "Take away your tea!" But in a living sense, the proudest of men can see a cup of tea and say, "Oh, thank you," and take it without betraying his essential nature.

When a Western actor takes up a Balinese mask, he cannot attempt to enter a Balinese tradition and technique which he knows nothing about. He has to approach the mask exactly the way he approaches a new role. A role is a meeting, a meeting between an actor as a mass of potentialities—and a catalyst. Because a role is a form of catalyst, from outside, it makes a demand, and draws into form the unformed potentiality of the actor. That is why the meeting between an actor and a role always produces a different result. Take a great role, like Hamlet: the nature of Hamlet on one hand makes an absolutely specific set of demands; the words are there and don't change from generation to generation. But at the same time, like a mask, although it looks as though it is set in its form, it is exactly the reverse. Its seeming to be a set form is only an outward appearance. In fact, it's something which, because it operates like a catalyst, when it encounters the human material which is the individual actor, creates all the time new specifics.

This meeting between the demand coming from the outside, which is the role that the actor is assuming, and the individuality of the actor, produces always a new series of combinations. So an Oriental actor, a Balinese for example, if he has the basic sensitivity, understanding, openness, wish, etc., can play Hamlet; and a great Balinese actor, bringing the whole of his human understanding to the part of Hamlet, *must* produce, second by second, something totally different

Peter Brook and Jean-Claude Carrière with Maurice Benichou

from John Gielgud approaching the same thing, because it is a different meeting in different circumstances. But in each case, a truth of equal quality and of equal value can appear. In exactly the same way, a great mask put on a Balinese or on an American or on a Frenchman, given the same basic conditions of skill, sensitivity and sincerity, should produce results qualitatively equal, but in terms of form, totally different.

I think it goes through stages. I go back to the concrete experience we had: *The Conference of the Birds,* and why we *had* to use masks. We have always avoided them. I loathe masks in the theatre, and I have never used them before, because every time I have even touched them it has been either Western masks or the idea of getting somebody to make masks, and I have always shied away from the idea of putting subjectivity onto subjectivity, which makes no sense at all. So in place of masks we have done everything with the actor's face—what better instrument do you have? But what we did up to the first time that we used masks was to work so that the actor's individuality appeared through his face; and that work is, by one technique or another, getting rid of his superficial masks.

It would be virtually impossible to take a successful television character, let's say, and get his individuality to appear without a gruelling and perhaps highly dangerous process of smashing his masks, because his identification with certain successful facial expressions is so deeply ingrained, and so much part of his way of life and his stake in the world, that he couldn't let it go. But a young actor, for instance, who wants to develop, can recognize and eliminate his stereotypes—to a degree; and in so doing his face becomes a better mirror—in the way a Sufi would talk about his mirror becoming more polished, a cleaner mirror of what is happening inside his face. You see in many people that their faces reflect more rather than less of what is inside them. The use of the actor undisguised, without makeup, without costume, has been the trend of the experimental theatre for the last twenty years or so; it has been to let the actor's nature appear—and one also sees that in the very best film acting. The actor uses on the surface what he has deep inside him, and he allows the flicker of an eyelid to be a sensitive mirror of what is happening inside him. In that way, through training that doesn't go toward using an actor's *personality,* but on the contrary toward letting his personality make way for his *individuality,* the use of the face in a sensitive way makes the face less a mask and more a reflector of that individuality.

However, we found—which is why we turned to masks—that

there is a point where the actor's individuality comes up against his own natural human limitations. A talented actor can improvise up to the level of his talent. But that doesn't mean that he can improvise King Lear, because his talent doesn't reach beyond his normal range of experience to *that* range. So he can't improvise King Lear, but he can *meet* King Lear if the role is given to him. In the same way, an actor can improvise with his face, and that will reflect anything within his normal circle of emotions, responses and experiences. But for instance, if in *The Conference of the Birds* I ask one of our actors to find the face that corresponds with an old dervish, the leap is too great. He can have the beginning of an intellectual understanding of what it is about, he can have a beginning of respect for what that could mean, but he hasn't got what is needed to be able, unaided, without imagery of any sort, and without a great part like a great Greek or Shakespearean role, just by thinking and feeling to turn his face into the illuminated face of an old dervish.

He can go, let's say, one step in a direction that needs a thousand steps. And it is at that point that you see that the skill of one of our actors (obviously one has to face the reality unpretentiously) can't equal the skill of the carver of the mask fed by a thousand years of tradition. So for our actor to be able to say, "There was once an old dervish . . ." and then extend that image in the public's mind by showing his face as being the face of that old dervish, he can go one step in that direction. But by putting on the traditional mask he leaps a light-year ahead, because he is drawn immediately by the mask to something he can understand when it is given to him, but cannot creatively impose on himself.

To connect with the idea of ritual: in terms of theatre, in *The Conference of the Birds* we used birds when we saw that a big, fat actor flapping his hands doesn't convey flight as well as it can be conveyed, momentarily, by his holding a little object and suggesting flight with it. For a moment what you want is the image of flight, but at another moment you don't want that, you want the humanity of the person, and then you come back to the actor. In the same way we found, having rehearsed with and without masks (which is why we put them on and off), that there were moments when the natural, ordinary reality of the actor is better than the mask because you don't want all the time the exalted impression. It is like using adjectives: there are moments when a good style is naked and uses very simple words, and there is a moment when without a glorious adjective the sentence can't make its point; and the mask is suddenly a glorious adjective that exalts the entire sentence.

Now, we are talking here all the time about masks that in their very nature are so-called realistic, naturalistic masks. And what amazed me when I saw the Balinese masks for the first time was to see that although they come from a very specific, local culture, they don't actually look primarily Oriental. When you look at those masks you see, first and foremost, Old Man—Beautiful Girl—Sad Man—Astonished Man—and then only secondarily, you see: Oh yes, they are Oriental. This is why we could actually do something which in theory is impossible, which is to use a Balinese mask to express a Persian story —which from a purist point of view would be called shocking, scandalous, a total disregard of tradition. In theory, yes; but once one is dealing with certain essential strands, it is like in cooking—things that in theory you can't combine, in practice can be combined very well. In this case, because these masks were expressing certain specific *but universal* human characteristics, put in relation to a certain text that is talking about certain specific human characteristics, the two go together like bread and butter, and there is no mixture of tradition because tradition doesn't come into it.

On the other hand, when you are dealing with non-naturalistic masks, you are dealing with something very delicate. Non-naturalistic masks, I think, again fall into two categories. There are the masks that are so strictly coded that they are like a series of words in a foreign language—so highly ritualized that unless you know the language of the signs, you lose nine tenths of its meaning. All you see is that it is very impressive. Some African or New Guinea masks, for instance, have something very impressive about them, but one can very easily miss the real force of what those masks are saying unless one knows the whole tradition that is behind them and the context in which they are appearing. And I think it is very easy for us to sentimentalize our approach to masks, the way people do who buy one just to hang it on the wall. It is a beautiful wall decoration, but what a degraded use of something whose signs, if read, are infinitely more significant!

But there is another type of mask, where these two categories overlap: one that in a specific way is also reflecting inner experience, but not inner psychological experience. In other words, you can say that there is the type of mask that we have been talking about so far, which shows fundamental psychological types of man through very exact, realistic description of his features. And that is a concealed man that is being shown. But then you can say that there is another concealed inner man, that could be called the essential deity inside each person—in the sense of the traditional societies where you have a thousand gods, each a face of the emotional potential inside each person.

So you have, for instance, a mask that is the expression of maternity—the mask that expresses the fundamental maternal principle. Now, that expression goes beyond the picture of the benign mother, which one sees in paintings of the Virgin and Child which go no farther than the benign mother with a kindly look. You go from that to the icon, for instance, where there is something more essential and more fundamental; the essential quality is present in something that is no longer reflected naturalistically, where the proportions begin to change, until you get into all the range of statues with eyes five times bigger than the nose and so on—and within that, there is a form of mask that is ritualized and is on a knife edge of having a possible theatrical use.

This is just the area where these two categories overlap. There is a mask which doesn't look like a face in the normal sense of the word— like in a Picasso painting with five sets of eyes one on top of the other and three flat noses—yet which, worn by a person sensitive to its nature, still expresses an aspect of the human condition, in a way beyond the capacity of any actor to show, because no actor can exalt himself to that degree. It is just like the difference between straight speech, for an actor, and poetic speech, and some declamation, and chant: these are all steps toward a more powerful, essential, less everyday expression which still can be totally real if it reflects a truth of human nature. And in that way it is possible to use masks—but that is something *so* delicate; it is something I would be very interested in exploring when we get to *The Mahabharata,* knowing how explosive and dangerous it is.

We have one Balinese mask of that sort, a very ferocious sort of demon mask, and we have just used it amongst ourselves in rehearsal, with everybody feeling the incredible forces that are let loose just by putting it on—and there one is going into a big area. For us, for instance, in *The Mahabharata,* we have to find the theatrical version of presenting a god. It is quite clear that an ordinary actor pretending to be a god is ridiculous. One sees that even in productions of *The Tempest* where a lot of girls try to be goddesses; *The Tempest* is usually a disaster. So you have to turn to something that can help you, and the first thing is a mask that contains forces in it and evokes stronger forces than the actor can evoke himself. I have never seen them used in the Western theatre in this way, and I think it is something very dangerous for us to approach without a lot of experiment and understanding. In the East or in Africa, this kind of mask is used more in ritual but in a sense for the same purpose, which is to bring into the open abstract things that otherwise are just called forces, so that they take on flesh and blood.

I think I can put it more simply: the naturalistic mask expresses essential human types, and the non-naturalistic mask embodies forces.

There is something extremely interesting here—which is that the mask is an *apparent* immobilizing of elements that in nature are in movement. It is very curious; the whole question of the life or death of the mask is there. A mask is like a frame of a movie of a running horse. It puts into *apparently* static form something which in fact, viewed in the proper way, is the expression of something in movement. So motherly love is shown as a static expression; but the real-life equivalent is an action, not an expression. To go back to the icon: if we wanted to show a real-life woman with the equivalent of what the icon is reflecting, it would be through the actions over a stretch of time that one would find the equivalent. It would be certain attitudes, movements, relationships in *time;* so that motherly love in life is not a snapshot, but an action or a series of actions in time, within a duration. And there is an apparent denial of time in the compression of that into an *apparently* frozen form, in a mask, or a painting, or a statue. But the glory of it, when it is on a certain level of quality, is that the frozenness is only a delusion, which disappears the moment the mask is put again on a human face, because then one sees this curious characteristic of its having endless movement contained within it.

There are Egyptian statues showing a king taking one step forward, and you actually *see* movement. And you see a million attempts to do the same thing in every town square in the world, a statue of a man who has got one foot forward and there it stays, and he is never going to move the other foot!

But look at the greatest example of all—and heaven help any actor who tries to use it in the theatre—the great Buddha statues, those vast stone Buddhas in the Ajanta and Ellora caves in India. There is a head which is a human head, because it has eyes, and nose and mouth, and cheeks; it sits on a neck; it has all the characteristics of a mask; it is not made out of flesh and blood but other material, it isn't alive, and it's motionless. On the other hand, is it concealing inner nature? Not a bit of it. It is the highest impression one knows of the expression of inner nature. Is it naturalistic? Not quite, because we don't know anybody that looks quite like the Buddha. But is it fantasticated? No. You couldn't even say it is idealized, and yet it is not like any human being one knows. It is a potential—a human being totally fulfilled and realized.

The mask there is in repose, but is not like a dead person; on the contrary, it is the repose of something in which the currents of life are circulating all the time, over thousands of years. And it's quite clear that if you took one of those Buddhas and sliced off the head and hollowed it out and made it into a mask, and put it on an actor, either the actor would pull it down—because of his incapacity to support that head—or he would rise up to it. Therefore it would be an absolutely exact measure of the level of his potential understanding. Each person, even with the help of the mask, can go only so far, and a young acolyte wearing the mask would express something quite different from the great master. So the mask would be pulled down or the person would be pulled up exactly, scientifically, in accordance with what he has and what he brings.

This is very much the way possession takes place among the Yorubas. In their tradition, you have to rise to meet what is inhabiting you, and you serve the god to the level of what you can consciously bring to him. So a beginner inhabited by a god will dance differently, and express something different, from the master. It is exactly the same relation with the mask.

It liberates the person by taking away their habitual forms, as I pointed out earlier; and that's related to an experience I had in Rio. When I was in Brazil, I asked a lot of questions about what possession was among the Macumba and others. Their possession, unlike the Yorubas' but just like in Haiti, seems entirely based on the person losing all consciousness. I asked a very sophisticated young priest in Bahia whether it was possible for them to retain any consciousness at all when they are possessed, and he said, "No, thank God!"

In Rio I went one night to a ceremony—it was a Friday night, when there were about nine thousand little ceremonies in all the little back streets. This was on a *very* little back street—I was taken by a

Conference of the Birds

local girl who knew her way—and here one went into the equivalent of a sort of nonconformist church, in voodoo terms. It was a small room, with rows of chairs laid out rather like a mission hall, and people waiting, and numbers were called out.

When you come in, you ask to have your name put down, you are given a number, and when that number is called by somebody with a loudspeaker, you go to the end of the room where there is something like the altar part of a little chapel, but where in fact nine people stand waiting. They are all local people who do this once a week in a state of possession: each one is possessed regularly by the same god. So you go up to the particular god you want to have a word with and just speak for as long as you want.

The interesting thing is that there are these local people, who have become specialized in it, who are in a state of pure possession; and it's very extraordinary, because they clearly have absolutely no clue as to what's going on. It's totally effaced from their memory. The gods are all smoking cigars (which is a great characteristic of these particular gods —they all like cigars), so men and women are all puffing away, and talking both normally and yet with certain bizarre characteristics that belong to the god—breaking out with strange sounds. So you ask advice, and the person will tell you what to do.

I went and talked to a lady who was possessed, not by a god but by a saint—a man of the parish who died twenty or thirty years ago and became a saint, and returns and inhabits this lady. We had a nice chat; she was very interested in the coat I was wearing and said: "Es impermeable?" So we were having this chat, and she blessed me and blew smoke all over me, and because it was in Portuguese I couldn't get very far, but something suddenly struck me as I looked around at the other people who were having long conversations. I suddenly realized that the fact that one knew that the person was possessed—and so whatever else there was in the eyes looking at you, in a sense quite normally, they couldn't contain subjective judgment—gave you such a freedom. Obviously the Catholic Church provides the same freedom by hiding the face of the person you are confessing to. But here you could look the person straight in the eyes, and because you know that although you would see this little lady, who was maybe your neighbor, in the street the next day, *she*—her subjectivity—was *not* looking at you through those eyes, she had become in that sense a mask, and it freed you to say absolutely anything. I felt that if I had been able to speak Portuguese, I could have told her anything at all, just like that.

The moment the mask absolves you in that way, the fact that it gives you something to hide behind makes it unnecessary for you to hide. This is the fundamental paradox that exists in all acting: that because you are in safety, you can go into danger. It is very strange, but all theatre is based on that. Because there is a greater security, you can take greater risks; and because here it is *not* you, and therefore everything about you is hidden, you can let yourself appear.

And that is what the mask is doing: the thing you are most afraid of losing, you lose right away—your ordinary defenses, your ordinary expressions, your ordinary face that you hide behind. And now you hide a hundred percent, because you know that the person looking at you doesn't think it is *you,* and on account of that you can come right out of your shell. We are so imprisoned, also, in such a narrow repertory that even if part of us wanted to, we actually *can't* open our eyes or furrow our brows or move our mouths and cheeks beyond certain limits. And suddenly we are given the capacity to do it: we open our eyes wider and raise our eyebrows higher than we ever have before.

THE ESSENTIAL RADIANCE

• • •

I have a little figure from Vera Cruz of a goddess with her head thrown back and her hands held up—all so right in conception, in proportion and form that the figure expresses a sort of inner radiance. To create it, the artist must have experienced this radiance. But he did not set out to describe radiance to us through a set of abstract symbols. He told us nothing: he only created an object that makes concrete this very quality. And this to me is the essence of great acting.

If I had a drama school, the work would begin very far from character, situation, thought or behavior. We would not try to conjure up past anecdotes of our lives so as to arrive at incidents, however true. We would search not for the incident but for its quality: the essence of this emotion, beyond words, below incident. Then we would begin to study how to sit, how to stand, how to raise an arm. This would have nothing to do with choreography or aesthetics, nor would we be studying psychology—we would just be studying acting. The classic English definition of theatre, "Two boards and a passion," leaves out the vehi-

cle, the actor. To me what matters is that one actor can stand motionless on the stage and rivet our attention while another does not interest
us at all. What is the difference? Where chemically, physically, psychi-
cally does it lie? Star quality, personality? No. That's too easy and it's
not an answer. I don't know what the answer is. But I do know that it
is here; in this question we can find the starting point of our whole
art.

I have often compared theatre to drugs: two parallel but opposed
experiences. Someone who takes drugs succeeds in transforming his
perceptions. But good theatre can also create this possibility. Everything is there: disturbance, shock, affirmation, surprise, wonder . . .
with none of the tragic consequences of drugs. In the theatre, these
moments that break open the normal limits of awareness are lifegiving and their special value comes from the fact that they are shared.
The experience of a drugtaker may seem to be wider because he is
alone, but the experience in the theatre is truly wider because the
individual is momentarily lifted into a communion with others. Such
moments are climaxes, so there is a process that leads up to them. In
this process, everything has its place: the themes, the techniques and
the talents. What counts for me is the increase of perception, however
short it may be.

Everything in the theatre is an imitation of what is outside the
theatre. An actor is an imitation of a person whom you would find
normally outside the theatre. A real actor is an imitation of a real
person. What do I mean by a "real person"? A real person is someone
who is open in all parts of himself, a person who has developed himself
to the point where he can open himself completely—with his body,
with his intelligence, with his feelings, so that none of these channels
are blocked. All these channels, all these motors, are functioning a
hundred percent. This is the ideal image of a real person. And it is
something that nothing in our world makes possible, except certain
traditional disciplines.

In the theatre there is an imitation of this. The actor has to train
himself by strict, very precise disciplines, and practice to become the
reflection of a unique man. But only for short periods of time. So in a
curious way an actor does something that is not so different from what
a student is looking for in an esoteric tradition. But this is a trap: he
must be pitilessly clear with himself that he is not on a spiritual cloud
and he must keep his feet firmly on the hard earth of his craft. First,
an actor must work on his body, so that the body becomes open, re-

sponsive and unified in all its responses. Then an actor must develop his emotions, so that the emotions are not just emotions on the crudest level—crude emotions are the manifestations of a bad actor. A good actor means that the actor has developed in himself the capacity to feel, appreciate and express a range of emotions from the crudest to the most refined. And an actor has to develop his knowledge, and then his understanding, to the point where his mind has to come into play, at its most alert, so as to appreciate the significance of what he's doing.

There have been different schools; the school of Meyerhold put enormous emphasis onto developing the body, which through Grotowski has led to the present-day interest in body language and body development. On the other hand, Brecht put great accent on the necessity for the actor not to be the naive fool that he was considered in the nineteenth century, but instead a thinking, reasoning man of his time.

Other schools, from Stanislavsky to the Actors Studio, put great emphasis on the emotional participation of the actor—and of course there are no contradictions here. All three are necessary. An actor has to forget "making an impression," he has to forget "showing," he has to forget "fabricating," he has to forget "making effects," he has to get away from the idea that he is there as a showpiece. And in its place he has to put another notion, that of being the servant of an image that will always be greater than himself. Any actor who plays a part and sees the part as being smaller than himself will give a bad performance. An actor must recognize that whatever part he is playing, the character is more intense than himself. So, if he is playing a jealous man, that man's jealousy is beyond his own jealousy. Even if he in life is a jealous man, he is now playing somebody whose jealousy is richer than his own. If he is playing a violent man, he recognizes that the violence he is playing has a greater charge than his own, and if he is playing a man of thought and sensibility, he recognizes that the finesse of that man's feeling is beyond his everyday capacity—with his wife and his friends —to be fine and sensitive. So, whether it's in a contemporary play or a Greek tragedy, he has to open himself up to a range of feelings that are greater than those he finds in himself as a private person.

So it's useless for him to say, "That's how I feel it!" He has to serve the embodiment of a human image that is greater than what he thinks he knows. Therefore he has to put into service highly prepared faculties. And that's why an actor has to train and keep on training. A musician has to do this daily with his hands, his ears and his brain, a dancer has to do it with the whole of his body; but an actor has to put even more of himself into play. This is what makes—or rather, could make—acting the supreme art. Nothing can be left out. The supreme actor is imitating the supreme man. Therefore he has to have available every faculty that can belong to a human being.

This of course is impossible, but if the challenge is recognized, the inspiration and the energy follow.

Our existence can be represented by two circles. The inner circle is that of our impulses, our secret life, which can be neither seen nor followed. The outer circle represents social life: our relationships with others, work, recreation. In general, theatre reflects what happens in the outer circle. I would suggest that theatre research constitutes an intermediary circle. It works like an echo chamber, it tries to capture hints from the formless inner circle. Theatre tends to be an expression of the visible known world—to allow what is invisible and unknown to appear—and special skills are needed. A denser truth is revealed, from moment to moment. It's not a question of permanent truth, since it is constantly in search of itself; it is simply a series of true moments. Sets, costumes or lighting can do little; only the actor is capable of reflecting the subtle currents of human life.

In terms of his function, an actor is entrusted with a three-fold responsibility. The first is in relation to the content of the text (or, in improvisation, of an idea). He must know how to express the content, but if he takes this kind of personal research too far, he risks falling into the trap of failing to meet a second responsibility: his relationship with the other actors. It's very difficult for an actor to be sincere and deeply within himself while at the same time remaining fully in touch with his partners.

When two or more actors perform together, and they experience true intimacy, another obstacle arises: they tend to forget the audience and to behave just as in life. They become private, inaudible, cut off. When this happens, the actors have neglected their third responsibility, which is absolute: the relationship with an audience, which in effect gives theatre its fundamental meaning. An orator or a storyteller, alone in front of his audience, readily accepts as his sole preoccupation his relationship with it. All of his attention is turned toward this audience, he thus becomes very sensitive to its reactions. Actors must also know how to behave in this way, but without ever forgetting to respect at one and the same time the scene and their partners.

Certain great actors, by giving themselves entirely to their own performance, treasure this relation with the audience. Making an audience laugh, establishing a strong, warm relationship with the spectators can act as an extraordinarily intense magnet on an actor, drawing him violently away from himself. He can bask in the pleasure of the spectators' laughter or tears and lose touch both with truth and with his partners. However, if he can find an exceptional degree of concentration, it is possible to maintain a balance between all three responsibilities. If he does so, what the audience gives back will in fact help him to go further.

We live in an age which is very frightened of value judgments; we even flatter ourselves as being somehow superior if we judge less. Yet no society can exist without ideals. The confrontation between an audience and a dramatic action therefore asks each spectator either to agree or disagree with what he sees and hears.

Every person carries within him a hierarchy of values according to which he approves or condemns. The theatre offers the possibility of seeing whether these values have been imposed from the outside or whether they are truly part of one's own convictions.

Art is not necessarily beneficial in itself. A great masterpiece from the past, presented in one way, can send us to sleep; presented in another way, it can be a revelation. Art only becomes useful to man and society if it contains within it an urge to action. And action is a spectrum from bread and politics to being.

Theatre must be reassessed, without losing sight of a few simple, permanent truths. The primary virtue of a performance in the theatre is for it to be alive, and secondly, to be immediately understandable. Explanation and reflection can only come at a later time. In all the other arts, one can always say, "Come back in ten years," when the work is concluded. But the theatre is as primitive and as organic as wine: if it is not good at the precise moment one drinks it, all is lost. It's no use saying it was good the day before or that it will be good the day after. Life only infuses the stage if the actor is convincing. Then one believes what he says and does, and one doesn't judge his gestures. One follows them without hesitation, with an attention fully captivated.

I think that today the theatre must get away from creating another world, beyond the fourth wall into which the spectator can escape. It must attempt to create a more intense perception at the heart of our own world. If one wants the actor to be on a level with the world of the spectator, a performance has to become a meeting, a dynamic relationship between one group that has received special preparation and another group, the audience, that has not been prepared.

Theatre only exists at the precise moment when these two worlds —that of the actors and that of the audience—meet: a society in miniature, a microcosm brought together every evening within a space. Theatre's role is to give this microcosm a burning and fleeting taste of another world, in which our present world is integrated and transformed.

THE CULTURE OF LINKS

. . .

I have asked myself what the word "culture" actually means to me in the light of the different experiences I have lived through, and it gradually becomes clear that this amorphous term in fact covers three broad cultures: one, which is basically the culture of the state; another, which is basically that of the individual; and then there is a "third culture." It seems to me that each of these cultures stems from an act of celebration. We do not only celebrate good things in the popular sense of the term. We celebrate joy, sexual excitement, and all forms of pleasure; but also as an individual or as a member of a community through our cultures, we celebrate violence, despair, anxiety and destruction. The wish to make known, to show others, is always in a sense a celebration.

When a state genuinely celebrates, it celebrates because it has collectively something to affirm: as happened in ancient Egypt whose knowledge of a world order, in which the material and spiritual were united, could not be described or put easily into words, but could be affirmed by acts of cultural celebration.

Whether we like it or not, we must face the fact that such an act of celebration is not possible for any of our societies today. The older societies have, no doubt rightly, lost their self-confidence, and the revolutionary societies are constantly in a false position. They are trying to do after one year—or five years, or ten years—what ancient Egypt took centuries to achieve, and their brave but misguided attempts make them easy targets for scorn.

A society that has not yet truly become a whole cannot express itself culturally as a whole. Its position is no different from that of many individual artists who, though wishing and needing to affirm something positive, can only in truth reflect their own confusion and distress. In fact, the strongest artistic and cultural expressions today are often the opposite of the bland affirmations that politicians, dogmatists and theoreticians would like their culture to be. So we have a phenomenon peculiar to the twentieth century: the truest affirmations are always in opposition to the official line, and the positive statements that the world so obviously needs to hear invariably ring hollow.

However, if official culture is suspect, it is necessary to look equally critically at the culture which, reacting against the inadequate forms of expression of embryonic states, strives to put individualism in its place. The individual can always turn in on himself, and the liberal wish to support that individual action is understandable; and yet one sees, when looking back, that this other culture is equally strictly limited. It is essentially a superb celebration of the ego. The total deference to the right of every ego to celebrate its own mysteries and its own idiosyncrasies presents the same one-sided inadequacy as the total deference to the right of expression of a state. Only if the individual is a completely evolved person does the celebration of this completeness become a very splendid thing. Only when the state reaches a high level of coherence and unity can official art reflect something true. This has happened a few times in the entire history of mankind.

What matters to us today is to be very much on our guard in our attitude toward "culture" and not take the ersatz for the real. Both cultures—that of the state and that of the individual—have their own strength and their achievements, but they also have strict limitations due to the fact that both are only partial. At the same time both survive, because both are expressions of incredibly powerful vested interests. Every large collectivity has a need to sell itself, every large group has to promote itself through its culture, and in the same way, individual artists have a deeply rooted interest in compelling other people to observe and respect the creations of their own inner world.

When I make a division between individual and state cultures, this is not just a political division between East and West. The distinction between official and unofficial, between programmed and not-programmed exists within every society. Both call themselves "culture" and yet neither of them can be taken to represent living culture in the sense of a cultural act that has only one goal: truth.

What can one possibly mean by the pursuit of truth? Perhaps

there is one thing one can see immediately about the word "truth": it cannot be defined. In English one says in a cliché, "You can pin down a lie," and this is so very true that anything less than the truth takes a clear, definable form. That is why in all cultures, the moment a form becomes fixed, it loses its virtue, the life goes out of it; that is why a cultural policy loses its virtue the moment it becomes a program. Likewise, the moment a society wishes to give an official version of itself it becomes a lie, because it can "be pinned down." It no longer has that living, endlessly intangible quality that one calls the truth, which can perhaps be seen in a less hazy way if one uses the phrase "an increased perception of reality."

Our need for this strange, added dimension in human life which we vaguely call "art" or "culture" is always connected with an exercise through which our everyday perception of reality, confined within invisible limits, is momentarily opened. While recognizing that this momentary opening is a source of strength, we recognize also that the moment has to pass. Therefore, what can we do? We can return to it again through a further act of the same order, which once again re-opens us toward a truth that we can never reach.

The moment of reawakening lasts a moment, then it goes, and we need it again, and this is where this mysterious element called "culture" finds its place.

But this place can only be assumed by what to me is the "third culture," not the one that carries a name or a definition, but which is wild, out-of-hand, which, in a way, could be likened to the Third World —something that for the rest of the world is dynamic, unruly, which demands endless adjustments, in a relationship that can never be permanent.

In the field in which I work, the theatre, my personal experience over the last few years was very revealing. The core of our work at the International Centre of Theatre Research was to bring together actors from many different backgrounds and cultures, and help them work together to make theatrical events for other people. First, we found that popular clichés about each person's culture were often shared by the person himself. He came to us believing that he was part of a specific culture, and gradually through work discovered that what he took to be his culture was only the superficial mannerism of that culture, that something very different reflected his deepest culture and his deepest individuality. To become true to himself, he had to shed the superficial traits which in every country are seized upon and cultivated to make national dance groups and propagate national culture. Repeatedly, we saw that a new truth emerges only when certain stereotypes are broken.

Let me be quite specific. In the case of the theatre it meant a concrete line of work that had a clear direction. It involved challenging all the elements that in all countries put the theatre form into a very closed bracket—imprisoning it within a language, within a style, within a social class, within a building, within a certain type of public. It was by making the act of the theatre inseparable from the need to establish new relations with different people that the possibility of finding new cultural links appeared.

For the third culture is the culture of links. It is the force that can counterbalance the fragmentation of our world. It has to do with the discovery of relationships where such relationships have become submerged and lost—between man and society, between one race and another, between the microcosm and the macrocosm, between humanity and machinery, between the visible and the invisible, between categories, languages, genres. What are these relationships? Only cultural acts can explore and reveal these vital truths.

AS THE STORY GOES . . .
. . .

God, seeing how desperately bored everyone was on the seventh day of creation, racked his overstretched imagination to find something more to add to the completeness he had just conceived. Suddenly his inspiration burst even beyond its own limitless bounds and he saw a further aspect of reality: its possibility to imitate itself. So he invented theatre.

He called his angels together and announced this in the following terms, which are still contained in an ancient Sanskrit document. "The theatre will be the field in which people can learn to understand the sacred mysteries of the universe. And at the same time," he added with deceptive casualness, "it will be a comfort to the drunkard and to the lonely."

The angels were very excited and could hardly wait for there to be enough people on earth to put this into practice. The people responded with equal enthusiasm and rapidly there were many groups all trying to imitate reality in their different ways. And yet the results were disappointing. What had sounded so amazing, so generous and so all-embracing seemed to turn to dust in their hands. In particular, the actors, writers, directors, painters and musicians couldn't agree amongst themselves as to who was the most important, and so they spent much of their time quarrelling while their work satisfied them less and less.

One day, they realized they were getting nowhere and they commissioned an angel to go back to God to ask for help.

God pondered for a long time. Then he took a piece of paper, scribbled on it, put it into a box and gave it to the angel, saying, "Everything is here. This is my first and last word."

The return of the angel to the theatre circles was an immense event and the whole profession crowded round him as the box was opened. He took out the paper, unfolded it. It contained one word. Some read it over his shoulder, as he announced it to the others. "The word is 'interest.'"

"Interest?" "Interest!" "Is that all?" "Is that all!"

There was a deep rumble of disappointment.

"Who does he take us for?" "It's childish." "As if we didn't know . . ."

The meeting broke up angrily, the angel left under a cloud, and the word, though never referred to again, became one of the many reasons for the loss of face that God suffered in the eyes of his creatures.

However, a few thousand years later, a very young student of Sanskrit found a reference to this incident in an old text. As he also worked part time as a cleaner in a theatre, he told the theatre company of his discovery. This time, there was no laughter, no scorn. There was a long, grave silence. Then someone spoke.

"Interest. To interest. I must interest. I must interest another. I can't interest another unless I'm interested myself. We need a common interest."

Then another voice:

"To share a common interest, we must exchange elements of interest in a way that's interesting . . ."

". . . to both of us . . ." "To all of us . . ." "In the right rhythm." "Rhythm?" "Yes, like making love. If one's too fast and one's too slow, it's not interesting . . ."

Then they began to discuss, seriously and very respectfully, what is interesting? Or rather, as one of them put it, what is *really* interesting?

And here they disagreed. For some, the divine message was clear —"interest" meant only those aspects of living that were directly related to the essential questions of being and becoming, of God and the divine laws. For some, interest is the common interest of all men to understand more clearly what is just and unjust for mankind. For others, the very ordinariness of the word "interest" was a clear signal from the divine not to waste a moment on profundity and solemnity but just get on with it and entertain.

At this point the student of Sanskrit quoted to them the full text about why God created theatre. "It has to be all those things at the same time," he said. "And in an interesting way," added another. After which, the silence was profound.

They then began to discuss the other side of the coin, the appeal of the "uninteresting," and the strange motivations, social and psychological, that make so many people in the theatre applaud so often and so vigorously what actually is of no interest to them whatsoever. "If only we could really understand this word . . ." said one.

"With this word," said another in a hushed tone, "we could go very far . . ."

index

acknowledgments

Every effort has been made to locate the copyright owners of previously published work. Omissions brought to our attention will be corrected in subsequent editions. Grateful acknowledgment is made to the following individuals and publishers for permission to use adaptations of previously publishd material.

I. A Sense of Direction: "The Formless Hunch," first appeared in *Modern Drama,* September 1980. "Stereoscopic Vision," from Peter Brook's introduction to *Prospero's Staff* by Charles Marowitz, used with permission of Indiana University Press, copyright © 1986. "There Is Only One Stage," from a meeting between Peter Brook and Denis Bablet in *Travail Théâtral,* Lausanne, no. 10, Winter 1973, pp. 3–38. "Misunderstandings," from *Travail Théâtral,* ibid; and from Peter Brook's introduction to *Prospero's Staff* by Charles Marowitz, ibid. "A World in Relief," from *10 Ans du Festival d'Automne,* 1982, published by Temps Actuels. Used with permission of Festival d'Automne à Paris.

II. People on the Way—a Flashback: "Gordon Craig," *Sunday Times,* July 17, 1956, © Times Newspapers Limited, 1956. "The Beck Connection," first appeared in *Encore,* November 1960. "Happy Sam Beckett," first appeared in *Encore,* January 1960. "Grotowski," from Peter Brook's introduction to *Towards a Poor Theatre* by Jerzy Grotowski, © 1968 by Jerzy Grotowski and Odin Teatrets Forlag. "Artaud and the Great Puzzle" and "How Many Trees Make a Forest," from *Travail Théâtral,* ibid. "It Happened in Poland": Peter Brook's preface from *Shakespeare Our Contemporary* by Jan Cott is reproduced here by permission of Methuen London Limited. Copyright © 1964 by Panstwowe Wydawnictwo Naukowe. "Peter Weiss's Kick," Peter Brook's introduction to *Marat/Sade* by Peter Weiss, © 1965 Marion Boyars Limited.

III. Provocations: "Manifesto for the Sixties," first appeared in *Florish,* 1965. Used by kind permission of the Royal Shakespeare Company. "The Theatre of Cruelty," from an article co-authored with Charles Marowitz for the Royal Shakespeare Company Experimental Group, January 1964. "U.S. Means YOU, U.S. Means *US,*" first appeared in *Florish,* 1966, ibid. "A Lost Art," Peter Brook's introduction to *Seneca's Oedipus,* adapted by Ted Hughes, copyright © 1970 by Doubleday & Company, Inc. Used with permission.

IV. What Is a Shakespeare?: "Shakespeare Isn't a Bore," from an interview with Arthur Sutter for *New Theatre,* June 1947. "An Open Letter to William Shakespeare, Or, As I Don't Like It. . . ," *Sunday Times,* September 1, 1957, © Times Newspapers Limited, 1957. "What Is a Shakespeare?" from an interview with Ralph Berry for *On Directing Shakespeare* by Ralph Berry, Croom Helm, 1977. "The Two Ages of Gielgud," from *The Ages of Gielgud,* compiled by Ronald Harwood, published by Hodder & Stoughton Ltd. Reproduced by permission Hodder & Stoughton Ltd. "Shakespearean Realism," from *The Critical Years,* published by Max Reinhardt for the Royal Shakespeare Company, © the Royal Shakespeare Company, 1963. "*Lear*—Can It Be Staged?" from an interview with Sheila More, *The Observer,* April 5, 1964. Reproduced by permission of The Observer Ltd., London. "Points of Radiance," "Dialectics of Respect," and "Shakespeare Is a Piece of Coal," from an interview with Ralph Berry for *On Directing Shakespeare,* ibid. "The Play Is the Message," from *Travail Théâtral,* ibid.

V. The World as a Can Opener: "The International Centre," from *Travail Théâtral,* ibid. "Structures of Sound," first appeared in *Peter Brook,* studies and essays edited by Georges Banu, *Voies de la Création Théâtral* vol. 13, Paris, published by Centre National de la Recherche Scientifique, 1985, pp. 347–349. "Life in a More Concentrated Form," from *Travail Théâtral,* ibid. "Brook's Africa," from an interview with Michael Gibson for *Tulane Drama Review,* vol. 7, no. 3, September 1973. "The World as a Can Opener," *The New York Times,* November 5, 1973. Copyright © 1973 by The New York Times Company. Reprinted by permission. "The Ik," from an interview with John Lahr for *Plays and Players,* March 1975. "An Aborigine, I Presume," *Sunday Times,* August 17, 1980, © Times Newspapers Limited, 1980.

VI. Filling the Empty Space: "The Butter and the Knife," from an interview with Yutaka Wada for *Sogetsu,* no. 142, June 1982. "*The Cherry Orchard,*" from an interview with Colette Godard for the *Comedie Française Review,* no. 96, February 1981. "The Goddess and the Jeep," from an interview with Jonathan Cott in *New Age Journal.* December, 1984, © Jonathan Cott.

VII. The Forty Years' War: "The Art of Noise," from an inteview with Jonathan Cott in *New Age Journal,* ibid. "*Salomé,*" *The Observer,* December 4, 1949. Reproduced by permission of The Observer Ltd., London. "*Faust,*" *The New York Times,* October 27, 1957. Copyright © 1957 by The New York Times Company. Reprinted by permission. "*Carmen,*" from an interview with Philippe Albèra in *Revolution,* no. 136, October 1982.

VIII. Flickers of Life: "Filming a Play," international round table of the Centre National de la Recherche Scientifique directed by Denis Bablet (29 November–1 December, 1977), Ivry, CNRS/Serddav, in *Cahiers Théâtre Louvain,* no. 46, 1981, pp. 16–36. "*Lord of the Flies,*" *The Observer,* July 26, 1964. Reproduced by permission of The Observer Ltd., London. "*Moderato Cantabile,*" as taken from P. Houston & Tom Milne "Interview with Peter Brook," *Films and Filming* Magazine, 1960. "Filming *King Lear,*" from an interview with Antonin Liehm, 1971. "*Tell Me Lies,*" *The New York Times,* February 17, 1968. Copyright © 1968 by The New York Times Company. Reprinted by permission. "*Meetings with Remarkable Men,*" originally titled "Leaning on the Moment," from *Parabola: The Magazine of Myth and Tradition,* vol IV, no. 2.

IX. Entering Another World: "The Mask—Coming Out of Our Shell," originally titled "Lie and Glorious Adjective," from *Parabola: The Magazine of Myth and Tradition,* vol. VI, no. 3. "The Essential Radiance," portions of this chapter were adapted from the following sources: *Encore; Le Fait Culturel* by Gerard Montassier, Editions Fayard, © Gerard Montassier, 1980; *Travail Théâtral,* ibid; and a radio interview with Anton Kenntimich.

photo credits

---

about the author

Peter Brook was born in London and received his M.A. at Oxford, where he founded the Oxford University Film Society. He has been a director of the Royal Shakespeare Company and currently heads the International Centre of Theatre Research in Paris.

A very few of the plays he has directed include *Love's Labour's Lost*, *The Tempest*, and *King Lear* in Stratford-Upon-Avon; *Ring Around the Moon*, *Oedipus*, *A View from the Bridge*, and *Hamlet* in London; *The Visit*, *Marat/Sade*, *A Midsummer Night's Dream*, and *The Tragedy of Carmen* in New York; *Sergeant Musgrave's Dance*, *The Conference of the Birds*, *Timon of Athens*, and *The Cherry Orchard* in Paris. There are over fifty productions in all.

His films include *Lord of the Flies*, *King Lear*, and *Meetings with Remarkable Men*, among others.

And his operas include *The Marriage of Figaro* and *Boris Gudonov* at Covent Garden, and *Faust* and *Eugène Onegin* at the Metropolitan Opera.

He has written many articles, and *The Empty Space*, published in 1968.

He currently lives in Paris.